BULLYING
From
BOTH SIDES

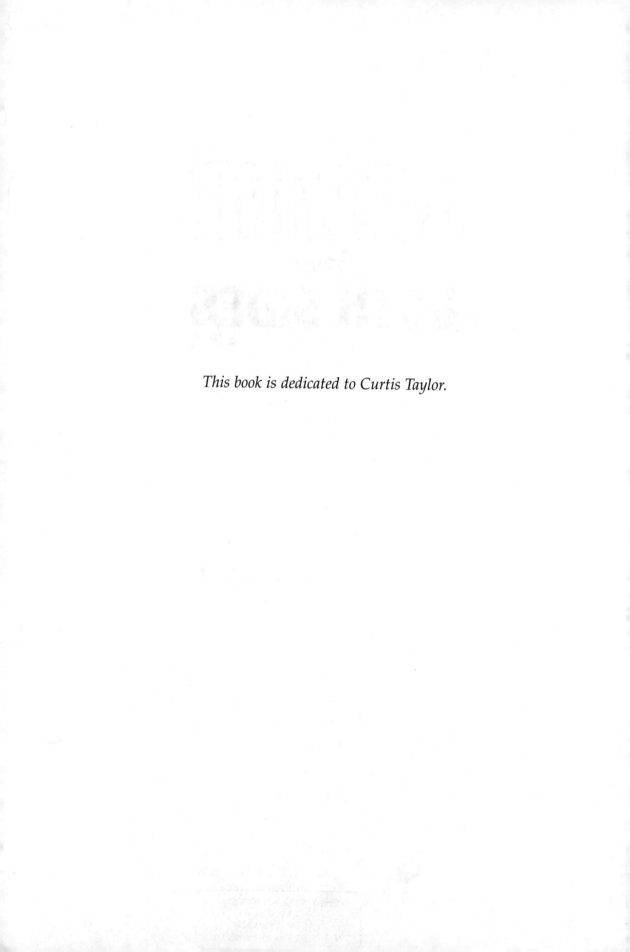

This book is dedicated to Curtis Taylor.

BULLYING
From
BOTH SIDES

Strategic Interventions for Working
With Bullies & Victims

WALTER B. ROBERTS, JR.

Foreword by Rosalind Wiseman
Author of the groundbreaking book
Queen Bees and Wannabes

CORWIN PRESS
A SAGE Publications Company

For information:

Corwin Press
A Sage Publications Company
2455 Teller Road
Thousand Oaks, California 91320
www.corwinpress.com

Sage Publications Ltd.
1 Oliver's Yard
55 City Road
London EC1Y 1SP
United Kingdom

Sage Publications India Pvt. Ltd.
B-42, Panchsheel Enclave
Post Box 4109
New Delhi 110 017 India

Printed in the United States of America

Library of Congress Cataloging-in-Publication Data

Roberts, Walter B.
Bullying from both sides: Strategic interventions for working with bullies & victims / Walter B. Roberts, Jr.; foreword by Rosalind Wiseman.
    p. cm.
Includes bibliographical references and index.
ISBN 1-4129-2579-7 (cloth) — ISBN 1-4129-2580-0 (pbk.)
    1. Bullying in schools—Prevention. 2. Bullying—Prevention. 3. School violence—Prevention. 4. Conflict management. I. Title.
LB3013.3.R63 2006
371.7'82—dc22   2005014947

This book is printed on acid-free paper.

05 06 07 08 09 10 9 8 7 6 5 4 3 2 1

Acquisitions Editor:	Stacy Wagner
Production Editor:	Diane S. Foster
Copy Editor:	Elise Oranges
Typesetter:	C&M Digitals (P) Ltd.
Proofreader:	Cheryl Rivard
Indexer:	Molly Hall
Cover Designer:	Michael Dubowe
Graphic Designer:	Lisa Miller

Contents

Acknowledgments

This book is the culmination of over two decades of research and work with those who bully, their victims, the parents of both, school personnel, and concerned communities. It evolved out of years of practice and scores of workshops I gave during that period dedicated to helping local communities "grow their own" programs for solving their own particular bullying problems.

I am particularly grateful to the people who have enabled me to take time off from the road and finally get this book completed. Toby Ackerman and Amanda Bomstad served tirelessly as graduate assistants in the final stages of manuscript preparation, all the while completing their course requirements and year-long internships to earn their degrees and licensures as professional school counselors. Many times they graciously gave up their personal time (and sleep) to my manic pleas of "Hey, can you do this for me?" on short notice. I am thankful for their patience; and diligence at always completing their requested tasks "by yesterday." I consider them both esteemed professionals and friends.

Karen Wright, of Minnesota State University, Mankato, has provided persistent and incessant support for my work. She has berated me constantly in the right way: "You have got to write this stuff up!" Consider it done, Karen.

Kristin Stinar and her investigative news reports on the maltreatment of children by bullying have helped sensitize the entire nation to the seriousness of the problem. Because she allowed me to be a part of those investigations, I found additional motivation to complete this project.

I had the fantastic editorial assistance of Stacy Wagner and Elise M. Oranges at Corwin Press to guide me through this first-ever book birthing process. Both kept me on task and on time, which is not an easy thing to do, as the people who know me will attest. I hope that all of my future writing projects can be guided by editors as able as Stacy and Elise. All first-ever book authors should be so lucky.

Through the years I have also had the grand fortune of being blessed with the professional assistance and friendship of Dr. Allan Morotti of the University of Alaska, Fairbanks. Allan and I have copresented at national conferences and coauthored professional journal articles on a variety of subjects, including the bully-victim relationship. His gentle demeanor and wise countenance have saved my posterior on more than one occasion (but I don't want him to know, so don't tell him, okay?). As with Toby and Amanda, I am fortunate to have a colleague such as Allan who has been a constant source of encouragement and quiet inspiration through the years.

Both Corwin Press and I gratefully acknowledge the following reviewers for their thoughtful and insightful contributions to the development of this book:

Michael Auer, Professor of Educational Psychology and Counseling, California State University, Northridge

Diana Joyce, Professor of Educational Psychology, University of Florida, Gainesville

Steve Hutton, former elementary school principal, Villa Hills, Kentucky

Mary Ann Sweet, elementary school counselor, Spring, Texas

Their blind reviews and comments in the first draft stages of the book convinced Corwin Press that further drafts were worth everyone's efforts.

About the Author

 **Walter B. Roberts, Jr.**, is a professor of counselor education at Minnesota State University, Mankato. He has over 25 years of experience as a public school teacher, school counselor, licensed professional counselor in private practice, and faculty member in higher education. His primary research has been in the area of violence reduction in school settings. He has consulted across the United States with teachers, administrators, mental health professionals, parents, and communities that are concerned about "growing their own" best strategies for dealing with bullying among children and adolescents.

Dr. Roberts is a frequent source on the topic for media across North America and has been a consultant with investigative news reports revealing the depths of bullying behaviors on unsupervised playgrounds in Midwestern American schools. A tireless advocate for children, he testifies regularly before local, state, and national legislative bodies in support of policies and laws that will increase school safety.

Foreword

The book you hold in your hands, *Bullying From Both Sides,* is a call to understanding and action. It offers a commonsense way of understanding the issues that everyone—students, parents, teachers, and administrators—faces, and a blueprint for creating a culture of safety in your school. This is hard work. Change does not occur with one PTA meeting or by simply instituting an antibullying policy. Change takes place on a larger scale, and it requires significant amounts of time and effort. The good news is, sustained effort *will* work to make your school safe for every person in it.

Every child has the right to be treated with dignity. Every child has the right to go to school, concentrate on their schoolwork, and not fear for their safety. Everyone would agree with me—so why is creating a safe school so hard to achieve? Much of the problem lies in our inability to recognize and acknowledge the tricky nature of our culture. The dictionary defines "culture" as a customary set of beliefs. I define it as everything you know but nobody ever sat down and taught you—what you just know to belong. Our culture tricks us to:

- Define loyalty as backing up your friends by saying nothing, laughing, or joining in, especially when their actions are unethical and cruel.
- Please people who hold more power than you.
- Be silent in the face of cruelty so that the cruelty does not turn to you.
- Believe that those who have power and privilege in a community have the right to do what they want to those who don't. It does not matter if it is a girl sending an "I hate you" e-mail petition around or a boy throwing another boy into the trashcan every day after school. The lesson is the same: People who have power can do what they want to people who don't.

For the past 14 years, I have worked with the Empower Program to change these beliefs and behaviors. The foundation of my message to young people—boys and girls alike—is to (a) understand the ways in which these cultural dynamics form the basis of problems from teasing on the playground to hazing in college fraternities to abusive relationships and (b) learn what actions they can take to change those dynamics.

Most of us do care about the students in our schools and feel that we are doing the best we can. Very few people, however, have the courage to ask themselves, "Can I do better?" You are reading this book, so you have taken the first step—you are committed to doing better. For our own well-being—as well as that of our families, our neighborhoods, and our country—I believe each of us must demand of ourselves that we live according to our values, not only when it is easy but also when it is hard; not when everyone is getting along but when we are so angry that we want to spit nails; when we might be punished for being "disloyal"; when speaking out may turn others' cruelty toward us. If we are serious about stopping our children's suffering, then we must stop thinking that hanging signs around the school about being "a caring community" is the answer. We should not wait to realize this until we see kids humiliating and bullying each other under those very same signs.

We have to challenge ourselves to do better. We have to see these issues as more than just girls gossiping and being catty, and "boys being boys." All communities have a stake in addressing these problems—even if, as many parents in affluent communities assure me, you do not have "those" kinds of issues, like kids physically fighting in the hallways or bringing guns and knives to school. In this book, Walter Roberts gives you the techniques to work with bullies and victims and the tools to reach all the necessary people in your community to create a culture of safety in your school.

Remember, you do not have to march down the street with banners to demand social justice for our children. It is in the small moments on the playground, in the classroom, on athletic fields, and in our homes where children see if adults will empathize when they have been hurt and hold them accountable when they have done wrong. If you do, you are teaching that courage is speaking out when you want to be silent. You are teaching children to admit when they have wronged someone else. You are concretely demonstrating that your actions are consistent with your values. I believe this is our sacred responsibility to our children. It is hard, no matter what your age, yet I believe there is nothing more sacred that you and I will ever do.

—Rosalind Wiseman
President and Cofounder, Empower Program
Author, *Queen Bees and Wannabes:*
Helping Your Daughter Survive Cliques,
Gossip, Boyfriends, and Other Realities of Adolescence

Preface

Going Upstream

Every individual should have the right to be spared oppression and repeated, intentional humiliation, in school as in society at large. No student should be afraid of going to school for fear of being harassed or degraded, and no parent should need to worry about such things happening to his or her child.

—Dan Olweus

Outside my office there was quite a clatter of voices, laughter, and crying. When I got to the window, there were all the telltale signs of a fight. A large group of seventh graders had gathered around several unseen people in the middle and were laughing, pointing, and encouraging someone to do more of whatever they were doing. I shouted out the window for the group to stop whatever the chaos was and raced outside the office as quickly as I could to intervene.

When I arrived at the scene of the commotion, most of the masses had scattered except for the primary participants in the activity, so caught up in what they were doing that they had not heard my call for them to stop. On the ground was the largest seventh grader of them all, covered in dust from head to toe. He was not just a little bit dusty. He looked as if he had been a child laborer in a 19th-century coal mine. Surrounding him were two of the smallest seventh graders—twins—who were still kicking dirt on him, along with the occasional kick to the back or legs. Of those remaining in the gang who had made the mistake of hanging around to see a few more toe loads of dirt go flying across the parking lot were the toadies of the twins.

The seventh grader on the ground was crying, perhaps truly as a result of the blows he had received, but probably more so from the outright humiliation of his circumstances. The seventh-grade twins, the ringleaders of the group (and, in all honesty, two of the meanest children I ever had the chance to meet in my career!), had planned the attack all morning and invited their friends to come and watch. The student they chose to victimize was in special education and, to every teacher's agreement in the school, was a gentle soul, the one most often chosen to be abused by his peers. Teachers often affectionately referred to him as a gentle giant who did not know the full capabilities of his strengths.

I will leave our friends for now because I want to refer back to them as we move through the book as both a point of reference and as a case study for how we might be able to help all the parties involved—the victim, the bullies, and the observers. Your patience will be rewarded.

We have all heard the fable of the people by the river. Great distress was expressed day in and day out as the citizens of the village rescued people who had fallen into the mighty currents upstream. Daily, people were pulled from the river, often at great risk to the rescuers themselves. People of the village would line the banks just to watch for the next person to come floating downstream so as to be better able to save them before they got to the falls below.

One day, while the people lined the banks watching as another rescue was being performed, a man suddenly bolted from watching along the shore and ran upstream. "Wait!" the villagers cried. "Where are you going? You can't leave! We need you here to help us pull these people from the river!"

The man turned and said, "But I am going to help. We will never solve the problem of the people in the river until we find out what it is that is making them fall into it in the first place! The answer lies upstream!"

So it is with the problem of helping our children learn effective methods of stopping the cycles of violence that plague them. Bullying and teasing behaviors, left unchecked, are some of the seeds to our violent society. The research is very clear on this fact: Children imitate what they see and what they believe adults either approve of or give no indication that a particular behavior is incorrect or problematic. Unchecked aggression in childhood becomes a life-long pattern. Aggressive children are more likely to become involved with the criminal justice system as adults. Clearly the seeds of anger and resentment sown in the fields of childhood victimization reap a harvest of sorrow for the bully and victim alike.

Of course, bullying and teasing in childhood and adolescence are not the cause of all the world's evils. However, the fact that such behaviors often occur in our schools offers us a tremendous opportunity to break the early learning pattern where children get the impression that force and intimidation—either physical or psychological—are acceptable means of getting their way and resolving disputes. If we are serious about solving the problem, like the villager rushing upstream, we must start early in breaking both the violent thought and behavioral patterns our children have absorbed from either home or society—and sometimes both. We can continue to pull victims out of the river all day long for many years to come, or we can travel upstream and attempt to solve the problem before it occurs.

The choice is up to us, both as individuals and as a society. While there are no guarantees as to how successful an effort on any task involving human behavior will be, there is one thing that is crystal clear: To do nothing changes nothing. In the case of bullying behaviors among our children and youths, there is every reason to believe that doing nothing will only encourage the problem to expand.

Children look to us for guidance in times of crisis. Let us not let them down. Let us go upstream to see what is causing them to fall into the river.

PART I

The Reality of Bullying, Bullies, and Victims

I t is important for people to know at the outset what this book will and will not do for them. First, this book will not fill the reader's head with jargon. This book is designed to be used by those who have the most to gain by understanding how the vicious cycle of the bully-victim relationship negatively impacts our children. Too often those of us in academia and mental health practice hide behind clinical lingo to discuss problems among ourselves, but we do little to explain important issues to the general public in terms that will enable them to be a part of effective solutions. While we will discuss definitions and terminologies important to helping us understand the bully-victim relationship (or **dyad**), all terms will be explained so that everyone can understand the concepts to increase the likelihood of their willingness to act.

Likewise, this book will not provide feel-good solutions to a problem with many causes and different avenues of intervention. Working effectively to solve teasing and bullying dilemmas is hard work. No *one* solution by any *one* single intervener will accomplish the goal in the long run. There are many paths to the temple of safe harbor. However, effective solutions to stop bullying do come from two general strategies:

1. A unified belief among those who are intervening that bullying and teasing is a problem and that it will not be tolerated without redress and restitution

2. The courage to act

Unless both occur, efforts to address the problem will be haphazard at best.

Parents play a significant role in solving bully-victim interactions. Why? Primarily because the conventional adult wisdom since time immemorial has

1

been that the solution to the problem is to "Ignore it and it will go away." While we will discuss how this faulty premise only contributes to the problem in a later chapter, it is important for us to remind parents of the power and influence they have during times when their children are facing challenges. Advising children to solve a threatening situation by ignoring it sends a dangerous message. Children are likely to interpret those words to mean that adults do not want to be bothered and do not validate the seriousness of the situation.

Those in supervisory and educational capacities carry similar responsibilities. While parents may have the "honest luxury" of truly not knowing what to do to counteract bullying and teasing, educators are supposed to know better. Many do and act responsibly. Many others, however, dispense the traditional "Ignore it . . ." advice or, worse, actually do not believe that working to intervene or prevent bullying and teasing in the school environment is worthy of their time. As with parents, educators and other significant adults in supervisory capacities who do not respond to the requests for assistance from children in need further contribute to the impression that adults would rather not be bothered.

After explaining the dynamics of the bully-victim dyad and profiling the behavioral characteristics of the bully and the victim, we will look at solutions. Those who want a magic wand of chapters or lists of fail-proof ways to stop bullying and teasing will be disappointed. There are no such things, and people who tell you that there are, are deceiving you.

What you will find are suggestions on ways to intervene directly with the bully and the victim, field-proven methodologies that have greatly increased the likelihood of effective intervention with the problem. Particular emphasis is placed on addressing the needs of the bully, who is in as much need of help as the victim. To act on behalf of one party in the dyad—usually the victim—while ignoring the other—the bully—will only create another victim. When one victim reaches a safe harbor, the bully always seeks another unless we "go upstream" and find the reason "why people are falling into the river in the first place."

One last note: In order to create a book that is easy to read and "flows" well, I have chosen to limit direct referencing in the body of the text. For those interested in further study, please see the comprehensive Recommended Resources and References sections at the conclusion of the book.

1

The Prevalence of Bullying

THE MAGNITUDE OF THE PROBLEM

How much of a problem are bullying and teasing in society today? For years evidence has been growing that the problem is far more prevalent than ever imagined. In actuality, the problem may not be larger than what it has always been; we have just not paid attention to it until recently or cared enough to try and measure its dimensions.

Facts and figures abound. Definitions of what is an incident of bullying or teasing and how questions are asked make the numbers say different things. Like the fable of the blind men and the elephant, depending on which part of the elephant one has examined, that becomes the reality. We can rest assured that when it comes to the experience of bullying and teasing, the elephant for our children looks much different to them than to us.

Through the years I have examined many studies on the subject and seen all sorts of estimates on how frequently bullying and teasing occur. Currently there are three studies that may help us the most in conceptualizing the magnitude of the challenge before us.

Hostile Hallways: Bullying, Teasing, and Sexual Harassment in School (2001)

American Association of University Women (AAUW) Educational Foundation

2,064 students, ages 8–11, were surveyed on their experiences with both sexual and generic harassment. The findings:

- 83% of girls and 79% of boys reported having experienced some form of harassment in their schools.
- 76% of all students indicated that this harassment was nonphysical.
- 58% of all students indicated that this harassment was physical.
- 28% of boys and 15% of girls pointed to the gym locker room as a location to receive nonphysical harassment.
- 15% of boys and 9% of girls pointed to the restrooms as a location to receive nonphysical harassment.

And possibly the most alarming numbers from the survey:

- Between 56% and 61% of both physical and nonphysical harassment was reported in the classroom "under the teachers' noses."
- Between 64% and 71% of both physical and nonphysical harassment occurred in school hallways.

Is there little wonder why the AAUW titled its report "Hostile Hallways"?

Talking With Kids About Tough Issues: A National Survey of Parents and Kids (2001)

Kaiser Family Foundation and Nickelodeon Television

A survey of 823 children and adolescents indicated that:

- 55% of 8–11-year-olds and 68% of 12–15-year-olds said that bullying was a "big problem" for people their age.
- 74% of 8–11-year-olds and 86% of 12–15-year-olds indicated that children were bullied or teased in their schools.
- 43% of 8–11-year-olds and 67% of 12–15-year-olds indicated that peers in their schools were treated badly because they were different.
- 38% of 8–11-year-olds and 60% of 12–15-year-olds reported that peers in their schools were threatened with violence.
- 54% of 8–11-year-olds and 40% of 12–15-year-olds said that they would like to know more about ways to stop bullying and teasing.

Bullying Behaviors Among U.S. Youths: Prevalence and Association With Psychological Adjustment (2001)

The Journal of the American Medical Association (JAMA)

JAMA published the most comprehensive study to date on the issue. In a survey of nearly 16,000 sixth through tenth graders in American public and private schools, the findings tell us that:

- Close to 30% of students said that they were somehow involved in the bully-victim relationship either as a bully, a victim, or both.
- Almost 56% reported that they had been hit, slapped, or pushed.

- Nearly 60% indicated that they had been subjected to rumors at one time or another.
- More than 50% had been the victim of comments regarding their sexuality, or of a sexual nature, or had had sexual gestures made toward them.

The *JAMA* report concluded that "The prevalence of bullying among U.S. youths is substantial. Given the concurrent behavioral and emotional difficulties associated with bullying, as well as the potential long-term negative outcomes for these youth, the issue of bullying merits serious attention."

These three reports carry particular weight, primarily because of the large numbers involved in the surveys and the fact that they were obtained from national samples. They indicate that bullying and teasing are indeed substantial problems for our youths, and that our kids are asking for our help in learning how best to deal with them.

VIOLENCE AND THE MEDIA

Children and adolescents are exposed to more images of violence today via the electronic media than at any time in history. Access to vicarious violence is no problem. One example, television wrestling, which infuses both violence and sex to further muddle the developing mind, is clearly not for the eyes of children. Ask any elementary child who their favorite wrestling hero is and you'll get an answer. You might even get more than you bargained for if you ask them what they see when they watch it.

The National Institute on Media and the Family noted in 2000, from a one-year study by Indiana University, the behaviors portrayed on the World Wrestling Federation television broadcasts and identified the following:

- Grabbing one's crotch: 1,658 instances
- Obscene gestures ("the finger"): 157 instances
- Simulated sex: 128 instances
- Simulated use of drugs: 42 instances
- Simulated urination or talking of urinating on others: 21 instances
- Portrayal of prostitution: 20 instances

In 2003, I watched one wrestling broadcast in which the protagonist hosed down his nemesis with the contents from a sewage truck. Whether real or not, the image was stark. Brown sludge of some sort sprayed the hapless victim as he lie on an exit ramp from the coliseum. The audience roared their approval, holding their noses all the while.

Television, computers, and video games all have gore by the bucketful. The American Academy of Pediatrics notes that:

- Over 1,000 studies confirm the link between media violence and aggressive behavior in children.
- Today's 18-year-olds will likely have viewed 200,000 acts of television violence within their lifetimes.

- Saturday morning programming for children has more violent acts per hour than normal prime time—up to 25 acts per hour on Saturday as compared to up to 5 acts per hour during prime time.

The Media Awareness Network in Canada adds:

- 80% of the television violence aired in Canada originated from American programming.
- Nearly 88% of television violence appeared before 9 P.M., and 39% aired before 8 P.M.—clearly at times when even the youngest of children are likely to be watching.
- Between 1993 and 2001, incidents of physical violence on television (excluding cartoons) increased by 378%.
- In 2001, television shows averaged 40 acts of violence per hour.
- Between 1999 and 2001, incidents of psychological violence portrayed on television increased 325%—that's only a two-year period!

The bottom line: Angry children imitate what they see because what they see is, in their minds, the norm. And you know what? It *has* become the norm for them, especially children younger than 8, who often cannot discern or have difficulty discerning the difference between what they see in the media and what actually occurs in real life. Monkey see, monkey do.

As we will see in later chapters, the combination of normal developmental pressures with such societal invitations to violence may well be directed not only from bully to victim or from victim to self but from victim to bully as well.

WHEN BULLYING AND TEASING ARE MOST LIKELY TO OCCUR

Generally, as children age, teasing and bullying become less of a problem. The normal maturation process and life experiences teach children more effective ways of coping with disagreements among peers and with difficult individuals. Additionally, physical maturity tends to correct the earlier growth and size disparities that are more evident in childhood and early adolescence.

The Elementary Years

Teasing is more likely to occur in childhood during the elementary years. Teasing may be as much about exploring the limits of one's personal power, or offered as intentional verbal play, as about inflicting pain on others. When fights occur, and they will, adults are highly likely to step in, end the fight, and redirect the children's behavior. Close adult supervision is a key factor in the limited cases of willful physical intimidation during the elementary years. As a result, teasing is very often the preferred choice of those who actually do intend to inflict distress on their targets.

Teasing does not end, however, in the elementary years and is often combined with its physical counterpart—bullying—beginning in the late elementary years. Both peak during the middle school and junior high years. Children are most likely to be harassed and intimidated in these grades, and, while reports vary on which specific grade level may actually be the worst, it seems clear that the eighth- and ninth-grade years are the biggest challenges for those who are harassed.

The Adolescent Years

Adolescent bullying and teasing are more severe than what is usually manifested during the elementary years. Teasing behaviors at this age take on an additional edge. Words become more cutting. Public embarrassments are often more humiliating and devious in nature and more difficult to forget or forgive.

Incidents of severe bullying become more frequent during the middle school and junior high years. Adolescents are less supervised both in school settings and in the home neighborhood. Lack of adult supervision is always an invitation for predators to attack. Young adolescents, hungry for peer support, move from clique to clique in search of validation. Friendship groups form and dissolve weekly. Last week's best friends are this week's worst enemies. Bullies are quick to seize on such group dynamics and encourage bullying behaviors among those in the outer rings of the vicarious learning circle (see Chapter 3). Teens have the added capability of being more psychologically devious and are more prone to be risk takers, particularly in the area of using physical force as a tool of coercion.

Reported incidents of bullying and teasing begin to decrease in Grade 10 for many of the reasons mentioned at the beginning of this section and continue to decline through Grade 12. However, those who are victimized in these grades are often at greater risk for harm to self or harm to others, because there is the possibility that they have had a long history of being targeted for abuse (**chronically abused**). Few older adolescents suddenly find themselves the target of bullying or teasing overnight. While any child or adolescent is subject to being involved in a short-term bullying or teasing episode, many in the high school years who report being abused for more than one episode will also report that they have been subjected to such abuse in years past.

One should not get the impression, however, that children and adolescents automatically engage in higher levels of teasing and bullying just by virtue of their ages. A high school senior could engage in mild teasing. A first grader could tease and bully other children and threaten physical harm. The emphasis should be on the *specifics* of the behavior, the *context* in which it occurred, and its *frequency* in determining how to categorize a potential incident of bullying or teasing.

BULLYING AS HAZING

We should not become smug in the false belief that bullying behaviors do not occur in the upper secondary grades, because they may well continue under the unofficial sanction of **hazing behaviors**. Traditionally, hazing has been used to initiate newcomers into a particular group of their choice. Hazing activities are frequent among athletic teammates as they—supposedly good-naturedly—"welcome" their younger counterparts onto the team. Have you ever talked to a young man who had his jock strap saturated with hair-removal cream right before he had to hit the field or gym floor, and he had no other option but to wear the thing throughout the entire practice? And how many young women have found any number of sexual items attached to the outside of their lockers for all to see, often with "love letters" supposedly written by the coach or another team-mate? Hazing rituals are historic at the college level for those wishing to enter fraternities and sororities, and they usually involve large quantities of alcohol.

The terrible reality is that the following incidents are not at all welcoming:

New York, 2003

Two boys, ages 13 and 14, hoping to gain placement on the high school foot-ball team, were sodomized with a broomstick, golf balls, toothbrushes, and pinecones during a preseason practice training camp in Pennsylvania. The prin-cipal attackers were three older members of the team. One of the perpetrators had a history of intimidating behaviors and had threatened another student prior to camp, but the coaches still allowed him to attend.

New York, 2001–2003

A high school freshman on the swim team was cornered by an upperclass-man and forced to endure a simulated sex act perpetrated against him; at other times he was forced to watch as the same individual danced naked in front of him in the locker room, pinned down and licked on the chest in full view of his peers, and left bound and gagged once in the band room. The ringleader of the assaults was fined $165 in court after the student pressed charges. The victim transferred to another school district after repeated requests to school officials by his family to intervene yielded no results.

Arizona, 2003

A 17-year-old male who thought he was coming to the track-and-field area for team pictures was thrown to the ground on the athletic field and digitally assaulted through his sweat suit. Later investigation by the sheriff's office dis-covered other such incidents, which led to indictments against the attackers on charges of kidnapping and assault. One of the coaches at the school was also indicted and later fired by the school district.

Ohio, 1999

A freshman on the wrestling team, who also happened to have a learning disability, was held to the ground and sodomized with a broomstick. His team-mates spread rumors at school that the student was gay and that he liked the treatment he received.

An amazing array of degrading hazing incidents has been researched by Hank Nuwer, author of *High School Hazing: When Rites Become Wrongs* and *Wrongs of Passage: Fraternities, Sororities, Hazing, and Binge Drinking,* who has studied the history of hazing and listed many of the incidences on his Web site (http://www.hanknuwer.com). Through the years two phenomena have occurred to change the nature of such hazing behaviors: First, the behaviors inflicted on those being initiated have become more brutal; and second, hazing rituals have moved from the college level to the high school level and are now poised to move into the junior and middle school levels.

Case in Point: Glenbrook North High School, Glenbrook, Illinois, 2003

Americans watched in awe—but not necessarily for the same reasons—at videotapes that documented the beatings and humiliation inflicted on a group of eleventh-grade girls by their twelfth-grade peers (both males and females) as a part of a long-standing and well-known-within-the-community powder puff football game. One girl had a bucket placed on her head while the perpetrators pounded the sides with a baseball bat. Pig entrails were wrapped around some victims, and others were forced to drink paint thinner. Coffee grounds were forced into the ears. Spam, feces, and raw meat were smeared across their faces and shoved into their mouths. And then there were the beatings—kicks and punches hard enough to draw blood and break bones. In truth, the hazing had little to do with girls playing football or building camaraderie but everything to do with wreaking violence on the initiates.

It is no surprise that there was alcohol on the premises, and many speculated that some of the parents of the participants had been the suppliers.

The videotapes played for weeks on national cable and network television and were the topic of conversation on talk radio. The response to Glenbrook was a reflection of the split nature of our attitude toward violence. While many expressed their disgust and outrage over the assault and battery, many others thought that the response of the parents of those assaulted were overblown, "making a big deal out of a little horseplay," and that it was another example of how America has "gotten soft" when "kids can't have a little fun on their own." The widely publicized comment of one of the attackers spoke for many: "It's not that big of a deal. So a girl got her head split open."

Even after America had the opportunity to witness via the media the kinds of humiliation and torment that the students at Glenbrook North experienced, instances just like it still continue with seemingly little outrage. In the summer of 2004, soon-to-be freshman students in a school in Minnesota who had just completed the eighth grade were lured (some might say coerced) into secluded areas and beaten with homemade weapons that included sawed-off hockey sticks, one imbedded with screws. The attacks were a real-life enactment of a scene from the movie *Dazed and Confused,* the story of a group of eighth graders chased and beaten by upperclassmen before their entry into high school. The eight students who were beaten suffered severe bruising. Six upperclassmen were later charged with assault in the attacks. What is equally disturbing, however, is that when the school district and county prosecutor held a meeting to educate parents in the community on the seriousness of what had occurred, relatively few parents attended.

Our culture has become so anesthetized to violence through television, movies, video games, and the Internet that our children are losing the ability to delineate the real pain and suffering experienced among their peers from the very television, movies, video games, and Internet violence they observe every day.

LEGAL RAMIFICATIONS OF BULLYING AND TEASING

Bullying, teasing, harassment, hazing, intimidation, and victimization among children and adolescents may be grounds for legal action. When acts commonly associated with victimization among children and adolescents occur among the adult population, we consider such behaviors to be criminal acts. We call such behaviors exactly what they are—theft, extortion, stalking, terrorist threats, assault and battery. Adults have the means to stop such abuse from other adults being directed toward themselves, their family members, or others important in their lives. So why have we allowed such behaviors to be directed toward our children for so long?

Society has historically assumed that children and adolescents will make mistakes as they explore the world around them. A part of those mistakes is assumed to be contained within the learning curve of interpersonal relationships. A huge part of growing up is learning how to handle the boundaries and power of relationships among peers. Because children and adolescents do not have a depth of experience in these areas, they will make mistakes. Arguments will occur. Fights will break out. Guidance and correction from adults and the larger society, however, particularly in the home and the school environments, are supposed to offset these expected social and behavioral deficits. At least that was the way it used to be in the days of Andy and Opie back in Mayberry. But those days are no more.

Incidents of verbal and physical threats, physical assaults, harassment, and property thefts are extensions of **interpersonal violence.** However, whether these behaviors rise to the level of a "crime" among children and adolescents may be purely dependent on whether a state statute exists defining such behaviors. It is odd to contemplate how a child can suffer a physical assault in one state and have no legal protection or recourse, while a mile away, across an invisible state line, the same incident could result in a prosecutorial offense against the perpetrators.

Most states today have statutes that acknowledge that youths can commit adult-like crimes and suffer the adultlike penalties that accompany such tragedies. Children and adolescents can, indeed, engage in conduct with clear intentions to harm others for personal gain using methods that cross the boundaries of normally acceptable childhood mistakes.

Most states today likewise have statutes or rules that require school districts to develop policies to protect students from peer-on-peer abuses. Unfortunately, those measures have been passed, in most instances, only as a *reaction* to something that has occurred, not as a *preventative* measure. Such school policies typically address behaviors such as sexual or racial harassment, but they may be less clear about other forms of harassment such as nonphysical intimidation. Loopholes may allow bullying and teasing to occur without benefit of policy to specifically address these behaviors. Schools may be reluctant to tackle student misbehaviors that fall into that nebulous realm of the "unidentified infraction." In short, a school may or may not choose to intervene in a behavior not specifically identified as off-limits by school policy. All the statutes and policies in the world, however, will not do anyone any good unless they are (a) realistic, (b) enforceable, and (c) actually enforced.

"What's going on here?!" I shouted.

"Bruce fell down," came an answer from one of the Terrible Two.

"Yeah," said the other one. "We were just trying to help him up."

It was all I could do to maintain some semblance of composure. I wanted to grab both of these kids and physically drag them by the scruffs of their necks to the principal's office, in full view of their toadies and the entire campus. I was angry because I knew that this was just the kind of monkey business that the Terrible Two plotted and pulled off in their spare time.

"You!" I pointed to the twins, "and all of you, too!" I pointed at the remaining inner circle of supporters. "Get to the principal's office immediately!"

As the Terrible Two and their toadies shuffled off to the building laughing, I bent down to see how badly Bruce was injured. Besides being covered in dirt, dust, and pea-sized gravel, there were small scrapes on his face and arms where he had tried to shield himself from the blows and kicks. He was still whimpering.

"Bruce, do you hurt anywhere?" I asked.

He sniffled and opened his eyes for the first time. "No. Not really."

"Can you get up?"

He began to move while still on the ground. When he wiped his nose and tears, the dust became mud across his face and arms. Slowly Bruce rose. He and I began to dust him off as could best be managed.

"I want you to see the nurse, okay?"

He nodded.

"Follow me and we'll get you to my office until I can reach her. Are you sure you feel okay to walk?"

"Yeah," he replied. "I just want to get cleaned up."

We proceeded back into the building, through the remaining crowd, which, by now, had grown to most of the campus. Several of the kids came to Bruce and patted him on the back in empathy, making efforts, as best they could, to try and help.

2

Definitions of Bullying and Teasing

To effectively prevent and intervene in the bully-victim relationship, we must first lay the ground rules to help us define exactly what bullying and teasing are and what they are not. It is critical to understand and accept that both boys and girls can be bullies; the only difference may be in the tactics employed by either group to obtain their goals.

Bullying and teasing are international phenomena. Documented research can be found worldwide on the topic. The Europeans identified bullying as a problem long before we paid attention to it in the United States. Much of today's inspiration for the work in the field of bullying intervention and research came from Norway, under the leadership of Dan Olweus. Olweus and his colleagues responded to a series of high-profile incidents in Norway that resulted in the deaths of adolescents specifically as a result of bullying. The Norwegian response to concerns about the maltreatment of its schoolchildren from peer victimization is considered the foundation of contemporary bullying intervention strategy. This book uses and expands on the Olweus definitions and conceptualizations of bullying, teasing, and victimization.

DEFINING BULLYING AND TEASING

For our purpose, we will conceptualize the terms "bullying," "teasing," "taunting," "victimization," "hazing," and "harassment" as similar incidents or situations that vary only in intensity along a continuum of behaviors. Olweus conceptualized **bullying** as an exposure to long-term, repeated negative actions on the part of one or more persons.

Teasing is considered to be less physical and more verbal than bullying, and occurs more frequently among early elementary-age children. Teasing may not be perceived as intimidating as bullying, either on the part of its victims or of adults in supervisory capacities; however, the seeds of future bullying behaviors are contained in the disrespect and motives behind teasing if it is allowed to go unchallenged. I prefer to delineate between teasing and **taunting**, for reasons we will get to later in this chapter. For now, consider taunting as a severe form of teasing in which the aggressor does not stop when asked or given indications to do so.

Bullying, on the other hand, is often a combination of verbal and physical aggressions and aggravations directed from an **agent** (the bully) toward a **target** (the victim). Bullying often involves direct physical contact between the bully and the victim and should be considered a higher level of concern for interveners. It is important to note, however, that both teasing and bullying carry the potential to inflict long-term damage on the mental health of their victims, particularly if no assistance is provided to offset such harassment.

Negative Action

Let us look closer at these definitions and concepts. What is meant by a "negative action" that bullies direct toward their victims? Olweus considered **negative actions** to be purposeful acts designed and intended to inflict intentional injury or discomfort on a target. Pay particular attention to the italicized key words that we should consider as markers of bullying behaviors:

1. They are *purposeful*.

2. They are *intended* to injure or make the target uncomfortable.

Does an act of bullying or intimidation always have to involve direct physical contact of some kind? No. Bullying involves both **physical** and **psychological components**. The psychological aspects of bullying can be as damaging as the physical. Girls are the divas of psychological intimidation, and we will focus on their bullying prowess in Chapter 5.

Power and Control

Power and control are at play in bullying and teasing interactions. Olweus noted that an **imbalance of power** always exists between the bully and the victim. That imbalance could be very real, such as in the case of an individual overwhelmed by a stronger single aggressor or by multiple individuals, or it could be imagined, such as in the case of an individual who responds to an intimidation out of fear of what might happen.

In many instances, an individual who has observed the bullying and victimization of others may comply with a threat to avoid the unpleasantness they observed happening to others. We will discuss this form of **vicarious victimization** and its ramifications in Chapter 3.

Associated with the imbalance of power is the fact that targets either actually are or believe that they are incapable of defending themselves. The individual who believes he cannot defend himself, even if he may actually be able to, will likely *not* do so. In other instances, individuals may actually be unable to defend themselves. Of particular concern are those individuals with mental or physical differences, who are easy targets for aggressors. It is imperative to emphasize that when we speak of "defending oneself," we are not necessarily implying a physical response. Defending oneself against bullies is far more nonphysical than physical.

THE TEASING-BULLYING CONTINUUM

It will come as no surprise that just as teasing and bullying are separate types of intimidation, they also vary by degrees of severity and frequency. Identifying specific types of behaviors, their frequency, and the targets of such aggression are keys to determining (a) if an aggressive act is indeed an incident of teasing or bullying and (b) how far a child might have progressed toward more severe types of menacing behaviors.

The National School Safety Center published suggestions in its quarterly, *School Safety,* on the prevention of bullying behaviors in 1996. In that issue, Carla Garrity and colleagues proposed a three-tier category of teasing and bullying behaviors. Such behaviors, they hypothesized, occur along a "line" of increasing severity, or a **continuum**. These three categories are classified as **mild**, **moderate**, and **severe** (see Figure 2.1). With each category of teasing and bullying, the discomfort and pain inflicted on the victim increases. While the behaviors listed in Figure 2.1 are certainly not all-inclusive, they represent a few of the most prevalent behaviors and show how they intensify.

The moderate level of the continuum often includes more physical contact between the agent and the target. Sometimes such contact is cleverly disguised so that it can be undertaken in the clear presence of adults, yet it rides that fine borderline between being an obvious violation of rules as opposed to being a true "accident." Incidents of severe bullying are likely violations of criminal law in most states, should parents or the victim choose to press charges.

Physical harm to others, vandalism, terroristic threats, and robbery are hard to explain away as "accidents" by aggressors. They are also clearly indicative of a child or adolescent with a long-term history of aggressive behavior and one whose future may well include more of the same if a successful intervention does not occur. This applies to incidents involving group behavior as well. Remember these words: *Unless misbehavior or "rough play" is redirected or stopped, it will always escalate—always.* And usually it ends only when someone gets hurt. Watch the isolated areas of playgrounds and other areas where kids gather in large numbers. Unsupervised play allows for the escalation of physical activity.

Figure 2.1   The Continuum of Teasing and Bullying Behaviors. Left unchecked, aggressive behaviors escalate to increasing levels of interpersonal friction and potential violence between the agents and targets of bullying

Mild	*Moderate*	*Severe*
Dirty looks	Public exclusion (shunning)	Inflicting total isolation from peer group(s)
Name-calling	Demeaning acts (both public and private)	Regular and routine intimidating behaviors
Taunting	Graffiti (minor and major)	Regular and routine extortion
Gossiping	Vandalism (minor)	Vandalism and destruction of property (major)
Threats to reveal secrets	Intimidating phone calls	Efforts to "mob" or "gang up" on targets
Public embarrassment and humiliation	Ethnic, racial, or religious slurs	Threats with weapons
Graffiti (minor)	Regular, intentional petty thefts	Inflicting bodily harm
Spitting	Verbal or proximity intimidation	
Pushing and shoving (minor)	Threats of harm to or coercion of family or friends	
	Blatant extortion	
	Clearly intentional physical violence	

Source: (Adapted and modified from Garrity et al. [Fall, 1996, p. 21], *School Safety*.

EXAMPLES OF WHAT BULLYING AND TEASING ARE AND ARE NOT

Not every incident of aggression between individuals is bullying or teasing. Sometimes children develop conflicts that end in pushing, shoving, yelling, or fighting, which is considered normal for child and adolescent development. Such conflicts reflect the exploration of boundaries. What is not considered normal is when an agent of aggression engages in such behaviors consistently and fails to stop after sufficient intervention. It might be helpful for us to consider a few scenarios as to what is and what might not be considered bullying and teasing in a general sense. All of these examples are real.

This IS Teasing

- A fourth-grade boy calls a first grader "booger lip baby" every time he sees him as a result of the time the first grader had a swollen lower lip from a bee sting several weeks earlier.

- Several girls surround a new girl at the lunch table who just transferred into their school and ask her embarrassing questions about her clothes, including, "Does all your family get their clothes from the Salvation Army store?" and "I didn't know people from your country knew how to wear pants!"
- A high school senior asks loudly in the hallway of a ninth grader who is developmentally delayed about where he learned his dancing skills following an all-school dance the previous Friday night.

This Is NOT Teasing

- Two elementary students are laughing and calling each other names on the playground while telling "yo' mama" jokes. Both students willingly engage in the exchange.
- A group of adolescent boys greet each other by nicknames that, to the outsider, appear to be derogatory and insulting. No one in the group, however, is upset by the greetings, and all seem to wear their nicknames without embarrassment.

This IS Bullying

- A group of junior high basketball players in a small school, feeling threatened by a new student who transferred into the school and who has great athletic ability, take turns on different days hiding his books, his practice clothes, and his shoes. On game day he finds his jersey in the urinal.
- A sixth-grade girl, who now does not like her onetime friend, spreads rumors among the entire grade that the old friend "sleeps around" with all the sixth-grade boys in the class. Photocopied pictures of a garden hoe with the target's name typed underneath are found taped to the bathroom stalls in several areas of the school.
- At least once a week, outside the school during lunch break, three tenth-grade boys approach a developmentally disabled eleventh grader whom they know is not capable of disagreeing with them and tell him to go to the same girl to ask her for a date.

This is NOT Bullying:

- A group of high school boys duct tapes one of their friends into a bathroom stall during lunchtime. The group constantly pulls pranks on one another and is well known as the campus jesters for the sometimes aggravating, but relatively harmless tricks that they play only on each other.
- Two kindergarteners get into an argument over sharing a toy. The larger of the two ends the argument by shoving the smaller child and running away with the toy. Neither of the two children regularly engages in such behaviors.

It is clear from these examples that certain "rules" are in effect among the players involved in these relationships. Does that mean that there are times when teasing and bullying behaviors are not what they appear to be? Perhaps.

It depends on the circumstances. One of the biggest rules of interpersonal play is how the participants view the interaction. Let us now look at when such behaviors might not be as threatening as they seem to be on the surface.

WHEN TEASING IS CONSIDERED NORMAL

It may come as a surprise that teasing behaviors may well be acceptable and both culturally and developmentally normal under the appropriate circumstances. Researchers indicate that teasing may well be a form of communication between parties that is constructive and encourages playful verbal battle, especially when it is shared between a parent and a child in a loving fashion. Such interactions may well encourage children to develop the skills necessary to withstand the normal day-to-day banter that may occur between children and their siblings or children and their peers in the greater world. The key to such constructive teasing is just that—the purpose of the banter is play and skill building, it is not designed to hurt the target, and it is provided in doses that do not overwhelm the developmental or emotional capabilities of the child.

Playful Teasing and Taunting

Learning the rules of what I refer to as **playful teasing** is an important survival mechanism for all children. Those who are easily provoked by the slightest of life's misfortunes, particularly of the kinds that so easily emerge in childhood and adolescence, are doomed to live a life of misery, because they certainly will become the targets of those who make a living antagonizing the easily provoked victim and may well end up becoming provocative victims, which we will discuss in Chapter 3.

Playful teasing, however, is not to be confused with **taunting**. In truth, taunting is perhaps more descriptive to delineate between the two. Taunting is teasing with malicious intent. It is not playful, and it is not designed as a method for joking with the target. Taunting is intended to create anxiety within its victim and place the target in a "one-down" position of a relationship or interaction.

As mentioned in Chapter 1, most teasing is verbal and is often offered in what the agent considers a humorous fashion, such as making fun of an individual or the calling of humorous names (at least as defined by the agent). Research led by J. P. Shapiro and colleagues also found that other teasing ploys include sarcastic statements, trick questions, fooling the target into believing the unbelievable (or vice versa), exaggerated imitations, and word play with the victim's name. Teasing, they concluded, was along a "continuum of malicious versus benign . . . [and is a] subjective experience" for both the bully and the victim.

Decoding Teasing

It is important to keep in mind that an intended target may not view a tease as abusive. A tease, which in design may be intended to embarrass the target, may be defused entirely by how it is **decoded**, or perceived, by the intended victim. *A tease may work only if the target allows the tease to work.* This is due to two primary factors. First, if the target does not understand that a taunt is intended as ridicule, the response will likely not be what the agent desires. This may or may not encourage additional efforts at teasing on the part of the teaser. Second, if the target is truly not bothered by the tease and, in kind, turns an intimidating situation into a playful one, the interaction may be defused (more on defusing in Chapter 8). Such is the foundation of "yo' mama" jokes and "playing the dozens."

It is not necessarily a good thing if the target does not understand that a taunt is intended as ridicule. Certain individuals may be incapable of understanding the nature of insults thrown their way due to any number of reasons, for example, students with special learning needs, those for whom English is a second language, and younger children teased by older children with taunts they do not understand. These individuals are in need of more assistance than those in the second group—targets who are truly not bothered by a tease and who are capable of defusing the situation on their own.

As mentioned earlier, there are certain rules in effect that can help to decode the teasing interaction. These rules are often complex and do not remain constant. What may be considered allowable one day among an exchange may not be as allowable the next day. What changes the rules? Any number of factors, but primarily it stems from the mood and overall sense of security among those who are playing with each other. For instance, on Tuesday students may trade vicious jokes back and forth about the origins of each other's birth parents. On Wednesday, however, the mood is different and such jokes are not tolerated. What has changed? One member of the in-group (discussed in Chapter 3) has had a rough day and it is clear to all involved that she is not capable of tolerating such verbal assaults today. Same group, different days, different levels of ability to tolerate abusive exchanges.

This is one of the vagaries of the unwritten rules of harmless teasing: Are all the participants on the same wavelength? Is everyone in on the joke? Does everyone understand that "we're just playing around"? Even more complicated is the fact that at any given moment, the limits of what is acceptable may change when a tease crosses some unseen boundary. At some point you really *are* talking about my mama and it is *not* funny anymore! When did the rules change? No one is really sure, but everyone knows now that they cannot continue in that direction because the words are beginning to carry more harmful impact than before.

So, in sum, whether an incident of teasing escalates into a problem is linked to these considerations:

- What is the *context of the behavior* on the part of the agent?
- Is it intended to be hurtful or just an awkward social interaction between the parties?
- What is the *interpretation* by the target of the tease?

Is he bothered by the challenge, does he understand it, or does he seem to take it in stride? In later chapters, we will look at other considerations that help us to determine whether an incident of teasing or bullying was intended as such.

 *I led Bruce to my office, where I contacted the nurse, who was at another building in the district. He sat on the couch while both he and I tried to wash more of the dirt off his arms, neck, and face with wet and warm paper towels.*

"I'm really sorry this happened to you, little buddy," I said. "I can only imagine how you must feel right now."

"I'm okay," he replied. Everything was always okay with Bruce, even when he had just gotten the stuffing kicked out of him.

"Well, it's not okay with me or the school that this happened to you. Do you feel like telling me what happened?"

Bruce began to explain that he had been tricked by the Terrible Two into following them under the guise of playing basketball. Instead, when they got to the spot outside my office, one of the Terrible Two punched him in the stomach. He doubled over and went down on his knees when the other one shoved him to the ground. At that point everyone—there were five in the office with the principal, counting the Terrible Two, and it was unclear how many others had participated in the attack but were gone by the time I arrived—began to kick dirt on him and occasionally land a foot or two in his back, buttocks, and legs. The incident had occurred in an area of the school grounds where no one was on duty. It was just fortunate that it happened outside my office window, because at that time of the day, I was the only staff person along that side of the building who was not eating lunch.

At about the time that Bruce finished his story, the nurse appeared in my doorway and took him to her office.

"Be sure to explain to her where you were hit, okay? We want to make sure that nothing is broken beneath the skin that we can't see on the surface. We'll discuss this later after you and the nurse are finished," I said and left immediately for the principal's office, where the banditos were being summarily interrogated.

When I arrived, the principal was in full glory, bug-eyed and bull-necked. I think he loved this part of his job most of all—at least he seemed to me to enjoy it. He had been after the Terrible Two for the entire year. Their mischief had, for the most part, operated under the radar. The pranks and misdeeds of which they were responsible always left an air of doubt as to who exactly had done what. They were masters at finagling the system, at generating uncertainty among adults as to exactly what had happened. This time, however, they had made a big mistake. They had been directly observed and caught red-handed by a staff member and someone, to boot, whose tendency was to not get involved in disciplinary matters except from a preemptive motive. In truth, I was really angry with this mob and thought that the principal's reaction to them was just what they deserved.

3

Victims

S ometimes it seems that bullies randomly distribute their assaults to whomever gets in their way, and that there may be no deeper reason for their choosing a specific target. At other times, it is more obvious why a particular kid is targeted. While it is our responsibility to come to the aid of all children in our school, knowledge of backgrounds, characteristics, and behaviors that put children at the greatest risk can help us to identify and support victims in our schools as quickly and appropriately as possible.

Early research has told us that, physically, victims of bullying behaviors are typically males between the ages of 12 and 24 who are uncoordinated and younger, smaller, weaker, more lethargic, and prone to exhibit lower pain tolerances than their peers. Males are particularly susceptible to intimidation if they appear outwardly weak. Females are more likely to be targets if their facial appearance or clothing sets them apart from the norm. Puberty is the most likely time for an individual to be bullied.

STUDENTS MOST AT RISK FOR VICTIMIZATION

Three specific categories of students tend to be most vulnerable to abusive peer behaviors at school:

- Students victimized because of their *social status*
- Students victimized because of their *special needs*
- Students victimized because of their *sexual identity*

While these specific categories do not apply to all who are harassed, we know that these three groups rate high on the at-risk rankings for those likely to be targeted for peer abuse. All of those targeted for intimidation have two things in common. First, they are "different" for some reason by "Kid World" standards. Second, they have little or no power to negotiate their status among the group or groups who do have power. As a measure of prevention, then, it is imperative that we pay particular attention to those likely to be the most vulnerable individuals in our schools.

Students Victimized Because of Their Social Status

Along with the advent of successful economic times in the 1990s came the emergence of what I have termed **social status abuse**, which is directly related to the **in-group**, those in power, those who determine the free access of peers to move throughout the many layers of Kid World. It is about money, clothes, cars, fashion, parties, and popularity. I have long advocated that social status abuse is equivalent to a **social caste system** within Kid World wherein the popular in-groups set the standards within the peer environment—both in and out of school—for all others to follow.

Social status abuse was traditionally a phenomenon of wealthy school districts. It was lampooned so painfully, but truthfully, in the 1989 film *Heathers* (a precursor in many ways to the 2004 movie *Mean Girls*), which pitted Veronica and J. D., the two primary outcasts in a wealthy suburban school district, against the entire in-group/out-group mentality. Though a dark, dark comedy—certainly not for children—it foreshadowed the frustrations felt by many adolescents who are shunned by the typical in-group power brokers in school settings. In this instance, the power holders were the athletes and the female socialites. The last 15 minutes of the film have been rendered jarringly real since the shootings at Columbine High School. J. D., in his drive to punish the entire school, plants explosives set to detonate during a pep rally. The movie was one of the earliest in the teenage "revenge fantasy" genre. At one time or another, what kid hasn't dreamed of getting even in a public venue or in another equally painful way? The problem, of course, is when children turn fantasy into reality. Unfortunately, in this day and age, it is not difficult for teens to get access to any number of the items necessary to fulfill most on-screen movie plots.

Markers of Social Status

Social status abuse is painful enough among the economic elite. It is even more devastating when directed from children whose families are economically secure to children who are not. Among elementary children, the three most symbolic forms of social status abuse are shoes, clothing, and video-related equipment. Among adolescents, social status abuse often surrounds the topics of clothing, cars, and peer- and adult-approved in-groups. These groups include the stereotypical athletes, particularly in football and basketball or other major sports within the school (as *Newsweek* in 1993 termed them, the "jock-ocracy"), and the cheerleaders. In some states, those who reach All-Star performance levels are virtually deified.

This is not to imply that successful children should not be properly acknowledged and congratulated. The key word here is *properly*. All children who are successful and make efforts to be so are to be supported and encouraged to continue in their positive directions.

This includes the straight-A student, the beginning cellist, the painter, the debater, and the secretary of the community service club. This includes that kid who does her best to be no one other than who she is, with a shaved head and piercings galore. Children's differences can vary widely, but being different is no cause to label as inferior those who engage in activities that fall outside the mainstream of the in-group, as long as such behaviors are not detrimental to the person or to others.

> *"I'm different. I have more girlfriends than I do guys."*
>
> —15-year-old sophomore, and the lone male on the school color guard, Columbine, Colorado

Unfortunately, our society has chosen— and it has been and continues to be a choice that is willfully made and permitted—to punish those in the out-groups with any number of derogatory names.

We call them "geek," "wimp," "pussy," "faggot," "homo," "gerb," "twerp," "dweeb," "nerd," "dirty," "pizza face," "airhead," "dumb blonde," "the dirties," "brainiac," "egghead," "retardo," "bitch," "whore," "loser," and a litany of other names that could take the rest of this chapter to list. And what are these people's crimes in Kid World? Often they are nothing more than being different from the ruling in-crowd of the moment.

> *"Every day, on a daily basis, I see people getting made fun of for whatever reason—their clothing, their smell, their intelligence level, whether they be extremely intelligent or unintelligent. . . . It can be overwhelming, sometimes, how much bullying goes on."*
>
> —17-year-old peer mediator, Springfield, Missouri

Students Victimized Because of Their Special Needs

The recognition of and response to those with special learning needs has for some time been a highlight in the history of American public education. Millions of adults today live productive lives due directly to the impact of public policy that rehabilitated the way in which we treat those in need of special education services.

In recent years, however, the denigration of those with special needs has reemerged among youths. With the passage of U.S. Public Law 94:142 in the 1970s, to redesign the care and treatment of those with special education needs, and through the 1990s, a certain degree of understanding and respect had begun to be accorded to those with physical and mental challenges. But the turn of the twenty-first century has seen the reemergence of the use of the words "retard" and "retarded" as slang to indicate disapproval of an individual or idea, as in "He's a retard" and "That's retarded."

Representation of Those With Special Needs in the Media

Insensitive jokes mocking physical impairments, complete with imitative body movements, have all made a resurgence in recent years, especially onto the movie screens. The entire premise of the 2003 movie *Dumb and Dumberer: When Harry Met Lloyd* was based on a scam of students with special educational needs. The two main characters throughout the movie are portrayed as adolescents with IQs that (one is supposed to surmise) would in real life qualify them for special education services. The bulk of the jokes center around the misunderstandings and misinterpretations that Harry and Lloyd make in their school setting and the responses they get from their peers.

In the episode "Slow Donnie" of the television series *Just Shoot Me*, which originally aired in 1999 and is now in syndication, we learn that Donnie, the brother of one of the main characters, faked a childhood injury and spent his adult years pretending to be mentally impaired to avoid life's responsibilities. During the episode, Donnie makes efforts to ask an attractive female for a date. His mannerisms are the central focus of the episode's humor.

Such media representations, which are void of all dignity for the sake of cheap laughs, do nothing to generate **empathy**, or an understanding of what it is like to experience another person's circumstances, among viewers for those with mental health and special educational needs. Subsequently, reports of outright bullying and teasing of students with special needs are on the increase.

On the other hand, the 2003 movie *Radio* provides a more true-to-life view of the mistreatment of a young man who was developmentally challenged and whose "adoption" by the football coach and team provided the chance for everyone to learn empathy for those less fortunate than the sanctioned in-groups of a small town. The difference between movies like *Radio* and *Dumb and Dumberer* are like night and day. Students exposed to *Radio* see the true struggles faced by those who are different. Students who watch *Dumb and Dumberer* get the message that those with special learning needs are buffoons whose only value within the school setting is to serve as the butt of jokes. One movie teaches empathy and dignity; the other teaches abuse, ridicule, and scorn.

Students With Special Needs at School

Children and adolescents with special learning or physical needs fall into the category of being higher-risk targets for bullies as they may exhibit many of the characteristics of which predators are likely to notice. They are different; they stand out by virtue of behavioral, vocal, or physical challenges; they may have social skills deficits that are readily noticeable; they may react (or overreact) to the smallest of taunts or intimidations.

A colleague of mine responded to a rural school district's request for assistance in the aftermath of a major school crisis. His role was mainly to make himself available if school personnel deemed a referral necessary beyond their abilities to respond. He spent most of the day in a quiet and isolated part of the building. Occasionally he saw students who were the most emotionally overwhelmed or "overflow students," when too many were sent to the school counselor. At lunchtime, the traffic dwindled to virtually nothing as the students ate lunch in another part of the building.

About 20 minutes into the lunch period, he heard laughter from several adolescent males nearby the room. At first he thought that it was a group coming to see him, but in listening he determined that the voices were focused on another individual. That individual's responses were not in the same tone as the other voices.

Out of concern and curiosity, my colleague rose from his seat and moved to the doorway to see three younger adolescent males harassing an obviously mentally impaired peer. The agents were taunting their victim and would not let him leave the area where, it appeared, they had lured him for the distinct purpose of abuse. My colleague was somewhat perplexed about what to do. Though he had many years of K–12 school experience, he was not an employee of this particular district. Was he entitled to say something to the group of bullies? There were no other school faculty in his part of the building, both by the design of the day's events and because it was lunchtime. He figured that by standing in the doorway and being seen, the boys would stop their misbehavior and disperse. He waited for what seemed like an eternity until one of the gang spotted him and alerted the two others that an adult was watching them.

To his amazement and consternation, after the others had been notified of his presence and after all three had made direct eye contact with him, they continued to harass the target. He was dumbfounded by their brazen disregard of the presence of an adult—any adult. He surmised that the tormentors had determined that he was not a member of the school staff and they put him in the "He doesn't work here, he can't do nothing!" category of Kid World logic. And it was just that rationale that backfired on the group.

My colleague rightly decided that he had no option other than to intervene, faculty member or not. He slowly walked toward the pestering group until their notice of him gave them pause for concern. They stopped their activities. "I think it best that you boys move along now," he said in a calm voice. They stared at him in disbelief for a few seconds, giving that "Who *is* this guy?" look that precedes the "Maybe he's somebody we need to worry about" thought.

"Yeah," one of the group said. "We're leaving now." They turned and put their arms around the target's shoulders to take him with them.

"I think he stays here," my colleague said. "He and I have some things to talk about."

"Sure, whatever you say." The group walked hastily down the hallway and around the corner out of sight.

At that point, my colleague went to the boy who had been the subject of the abuse, asked him if he was all right, and walked with him back to the commons area of the building. Along the way, he asked the student's name and some details about exactly what had happened. As expected, the gang of three had more or less "walked" the student into that part of the building solely for the purpose of taunting him until the end of lunch period. My colleague shared the information with the school counselor at the close of the day, suggesting that they follow up on the deeper concerns after the immediate chaos of dealing with the current crisis.

This example illustrates the depravity of those intent on intimidating others. Even in the midst of the pain generated throughout an entire school by they death of a student, there were those who would still use it to their advantage to victimize others. A staff distracted and an unsupervised area of a building complex were the key ingredients to these bullies' modus operandi. My colleague's response was right on target: the presence of an adult and an "I mean business" yet calm tone; the willingness to follow through with the intervention as much as he could under the circumstances. How many adults in his circumstances would have walked away under the rationale "Hey, I don't work here. I don't know what I'm supposed to do"?

Particular attention must be afforded to addressing interventions with those whom we know are at higher risk for intimidation as a result of special learning needs. While the bullying of anyone must be addressed, such inexcusable taunting of those with special needs must receive heightened emphasis.

Students Victimized Because of Their Sexual Identity

There are several things that we do not contend with very well in this country. One of those is the topic of sex. More specifically, we do an awful job dealing effectively with the sexual behavior and curiosities of our children and adolescents. We send them conflicting messages through the media: Women are supposed to be thin, tight-bodied, and show lots of leg. This is made ever so clear in the fashion magazines and clothing catalogs. And the message begins very early. Have you browsed through the clothing options for young girls lately? If not, you should. Children are offered miniature versions of the same style of clothing available to adults, complete with peek-a-boo tops and bikini swimsuit bottoms.

It is no better for adolescent males. They are supposed to be muscular hunks with rippling abs, bulging pecs, and a healthy head of hair. The message is very clear: Sissies need not apply. Real men have lots of women clinging to them, too. They are desired by women and women exist for the pleasure and entertainment of men.

Am I exaggerating? Maybe, maybe not. But one thing is certain: Woe be unto children who exhibit behaviors that are not socially accepted as specific to their gender. In Kid World, one of the two categories of ultimate slams is to be branded a "homo," "faggot," "queer," "dyke," or "gay." A 2003 survey and Web fact sheet compiled by the National Mental Health Association found some unsettling statistics when it comes to attitudes among teens related to nontraditional sexual orientations:

- While 78% indicated distaste for antigay slurs and bias, only 5% of them indicated their willingness to intervene on behalf of those targeted by such behaviors.

- Another 78% of the same respondents indicated that peers who are openly gay, or thought to be gay, are bullied both within their schools and the larger community.
- For every single student who is harassed for being gay and actually is, another four nongay students are harassed under the suspicion of their peers as being gay.
- Those teens who identify themselves as nontraditionally sexually oriented hear derogatory sexual insults about their orientation an average of 26 times each day. That equates to one slur every 14 minutes within the school setting.
- At least 31% of gay youth indicated that they had been threatened or actually injured at school within the previous 12 months.
- Up to 22% of the teens who identified themselves as nontraditionally sexually oriented reported that they had skipped school at least once within the past month because of safety concerns.
- The dropout rate for gay students is 28%. This is three times the national average for heterosexual students.

Who wears the moniker of gayness in Kid World? Today, everybody, from time to time. The phrases "That's gay" and "Don't be so gay" are dished out in Kid World as insults. To be slammed as gay is to be wrong, different, and out of sync at the present moment. In truth, to be slammed in this manner has little to do with a legitimate discussion of sexual identity and everything to do with the association of "wrongness" attached to those whose sexual identity is different from the mainstream.

Kids and Sexuality

Children and adolescents go through sexual exploratory stages as they grow. In fact, throughout early childhood and prepubescence, children are rather sexually ambiguous in their treatment of one another. To a child, another child is just that—"someone like me." They are not concerned about genitalia or their gender-specific role in society. Adults are the ones who teach children about role identity and the "difference" between boys and girls.

Childhood sexual ambivalence is normally maintained (unless subverted by exposure to improper sexualization through either sexual abuse or exposure to sexual images) until the emergence of puberty and adolescence. This is most clearly exemplified by the behaviors of a fifth-grade boy and girl who have been best friends throughout their first 11 years, who have played tackle football and never twice given a thought about the sexual differences between them. This behavior may well carry over into the early years of the seventh grade, at which time social pressures and puberty normally begin to force a more segregated view of their interaction on the two. Up until this period boys may well exhibit many behavioral characteristics that can be stereotyped as "effeminate." Likewise, girls may well be called "tomboys" and be able to equal or outplay their counterparts in physical activities. As young adolescents struggle with the changes of puberty and a new social order, sexual behavior becomes one of the major social keys into the palace of Kid World. Suddenly, some of those conversations about the difference between boys and girls become important (especially the ones about that genitalia stuff!). As they age, many adolescents personally struggle with real issues related to sexuality.

Rumors, Stereotypes, and Mislabeling

Rumors about the "gayness" of a peer's behavior are directly linked to efforts to ostracize, embarrass, and shun the target. They carry exceptional weight during the years of young adolescence as children attempt to model the behaviors they think they are supposed to grow into. Of course, these efforts to normalize childhood's ambiguous sexuality into stereotypes of masculinity and femininity are fraught with trial and error. One day a young boy's voice shows signs of depth and he swaggers up and down the hallway showing off his muscles; the next day his voice cracks and squeaks and he cries in the principal's office after having been called on some kind of school infraction. One day a young girl wears the same type of shirt that she has always worn, yet the signs of emerging breasts cannot be ignored by her classmates; the next day she wrestles with a boy and rubs his face in the dirt because he called her a derogatory name.

The worst thing in Kid World that can happen to a middle schooler is to be pegged by peers as a "real" homosexual because of behaviors that are peculiar to that individual but are entirely unrelated to sexual identity. This occurs among two primary groups of kids:

- Boys who show sensitivity and behave with mannerisms not deemed as stereotypically male
- Girls who may be physically strong, athletic, and seemingly uninterested in boys

Though these kids may be sure of their sexual identity, the fact that they behave differently from the mainstream makes them easy targets for ridicule.

Real Sexual Identity Issues

The reality is that there are adolescents in our schools, especially in the younger age bracket, who do truly struggle with issues of sexual identity and who, for the sake of staying in the in-group or out of fear of rejection from peers, parents, and/or other significant adults in their lives, feel as if they cannot speak to anyone about their feelings. A few brave souls choose to proclaim publicly their not-of-the-in-group sexual preferences. This is more common in later adolescence and within urban environments, where a wider band of community tolerance is present. Rarely are adolescents in rural areas allowed the luxury of a safe environment in which to discuss their nonheterosexual curiosity.

Suicide Among Those Dealing With Gender Issues

The suicide rate among adolescents dealing with sexual identity issues is huge. Research studies have shown that perhaps 30% or more of adolescents dealing with sexual identity issues may attempt suicide, a rate two to three times higher than their heterosexual peers. That figure refers to studies in which those adolescents who had attempted suicide and who self-identified themselves as gay, lesbian, bisexual, or transgendered. Please take a moment for this figure to sink in: 3 or more of every 10 adolescents dealing with concerns about their sexual identity may resort to a suicide attempt in an effort to deal with their pain and isolation. The numbers could be even higher if one takes into consideration the likelihood that not every adolescent who attempts suicide will likely be willing to identify sexual identity struggles as a precipitating factor. They may even refuse to accept or not recognize what is driving such behavior. How many adolescents with sexual identity issues actually complete suicide is unknown. Not every adolescent who commits suicide leaves a note or indicates a reason for the act.

Adult Accountability

No matter what the actual numbers are, it is clear that to wear the mantle of gayness, particularly among males, is a big scarlet letter within Kid World. Whether the label is correct or incorrect, the outcome is largely the same—automatic rejection and shunning by the in-groups and into target status for bullies. That includes physical and sodomy assaults under the guise of hazing. Adults within the school environment who are supposed to know better often do little or nothing to create a safer place for these adolescents. Following are some examples that demonstrate increasing accountability for schools and communities.

Wisconsin, 1996 Three school administrators were held personally liable in U.S. District Court for their consistent failure to intervene on behalf of an openly gay student. The courts ruled that the student suffered as a result of the negligence and awarded him $900,000.

California, 1997 The mother of a 12-year-old boy filed suit against a school district over the homophobic bullying her child received. School officials, it was claimed, failed to respond to repeated requests for intervention. The case was settled out of court for $160,000, and the district agreed to offer sensitivity training for its staff.

Arkansas, 1998 The Office of Civil Rights forced a school district to enter into a "commitment to resolve" agreement that would enforce Title IX protection for gay and lesbian students. The case was filed on behalf of an openly gay student who received harassment from the eighth through tenth grades. At one juncture, the gay-bashing resulted in a broken nose and bruised kidney. Three students were convicted in the attack, but they received probation. The agreement was the first time that the courts ruled that Title IX protection extended to the sexual harassment of gay students.

Pennsylvania, 2000 The mother of an 18-year-old son who committed suicide two months before his graduation in 1997 won the right to sue police officers in her small community over their threat to expose her son's homosexual identity to his grandfather. Six years later, the case was settled out of court for $100,000.

Nevada, 2002 A gay high school student, who was forced to transfer to three different high schools as a result of gay-bashing, won a $451,000 prejudgment settlement against the school district. The student had been spit on, called derogatory names, and lassoed with the threat of being dragged behind a truck. His suit documented instances of school personnel observing violent acts against him and failing to intervene. The case also forced changes in the school district's policy toward the open expression of student sexuality and increased its training of staff regarding the proper responses to intimidation of students.

California, 2003 The father of an artistically talented 12-year-old boy sought damages of $100,000 in response to 120 instances of documented abuse by peers. Claims were made that contacts with school administrators over a dozen times yielded no response. The same school was sued in 1997 for similar homophobic attacks against another 12-year-old boy.

There is no excuse for adults who tolerate these kinds of behaviors against students who are either openly declarative or questioning of their sexual orientation. These individuals need protection. Alert supervisors must be aware of the potential for harassment that exists for these individuals.

Recognizing Students at Risk for Victimization

Now that we have familiarized ourselves with students who are especially vulnerable to victimization, it is important to be able to recognize all students at risk for victimization. In general, these individuals tend to fall into six types. In general, victims:

1. Are *social isolates* and *outcasts*

2. Have a *transient school history*

3. Exhibit *poor social skills*

4. *Desire to fit in* "at any cost"

5. Are defenseless

6. Are viewed by their peers as "different"

Students Who Are Social Isolates and Outcasts

Children who are social isolates are always at greater risk for any variety of developmental issues, but particularly so for being singled out for abuse. As social outcasts—for any number of reasons, some identified previously—they have no support network of peers to help them sort out the typical challenges of growing up. Subsequently, they stand out by virtue of the very thing that makes them unnoticeable among their peers—their lack of peer support. Such isolation sends a message to predators that "this one is weak" or "no one will help this one" if attacked.

The ultimate insult among children is to be rejected by one's peers. Adult rejection is considered routine by children and adolescents. Adults do not understand the world of the child, particularly the teenager, so the routine thinking goes. The inability of adults to understand their children is a large part of what teenage rebellion is all about. But to be outcast from peers—those who supposedly understand them, support them, and relate to them—well, that kind of rejection is the kiss of death in Kid World.

No matter how cutting an adult's comment might be, the same words yielded by a peer cut deeper and heal slower. Peer rejection in the form of verbal taunts and ridicule is the equivalent of a public stoning.

Students With Transient School Histories

This second factor can certainly be a contributor to the first. Students with a transient school history typically have no support network for that very reason—they frequent different schools, never having the opportunity to form peer networks. Many who are used to moving often know that they will not be attending their current school for any different length of time and choose not to make many, if any, friendships out of what they perceive is the uselessness of doing so and the pain of losing what friendships may form. In their minds, it is easier to enter a school and remain invisible. These students may be shy or quiet—again a signal to the agents of intimidation that the students will not defend themselves if confronted.

Students Who Exhibit Poor Social Skills

Children with poor social skills are yet another group at higher risk for bullying than others. These children may be awkward in their abilities to interact with others or may lack the abilities to play well within the peer group. At the other end of the spectrum are those children who get along better with adults than with the peer group and are labeled "teacher's pets" by the group. Students with special learning needs may fall into this third group.

Provocative Victims

Within the group of children with poor social skills is a subgroup of individuals whose behaviors seem to attract the attention of bullies more than the average child. These individuals may be oversensitive to teasing, may cry easily, or stand out in a peer group by their evident visible and vocal frustrations. Others in this subgroup may tend to seek attention by seeming to "pester" peers, inclusive of those whom they know are likely to respond by bullying them. These individuals are called **provocative victims**. They create a special challenge in understanding the bully-victim relationship because their behaviors draw attention to their vulnerabilities. Clearly these individuals are in need of special attention in the intervention process and may require special assistance to acquire the social skills necessary to lessen their attention-seeking mannerisms. These individuals also may be acting out of a desire to force themselves into *any* group that will acknowledge their presence, so great is their need for validation of some kind at any level.

Students Who Desire to Fit In "At Any Cost"

While provocative victims may lack the social skills to know how to successfully interact with peers, others tend to be willing to put up with any kind of abuse to be a member of the group. These individuals often subject themselves to becoming the "dog" or "gopher" or "bitch" of a group, fetching and running errands for the group's more dominant members—which may well be the entire group. They receive little (if any) praise, but all of the group's scorn. Typically those who engage in such behaviors are children in the upper elementary age group and beyond. Their reward is clearly the chance to belong to a group that, in their minds, brings some kind of recognition to their otherwise empty self-esteem. At least they are recognized as being alive in the eyes of this set of peers; to them they are not invisible. As you may recognize, such needy characteristics and behaviors make one ripe for inclusion in gang-type activities later in life.

Students Who Are Defenseless

The fifth characteristic marking children as more vulnerable for potential bullying or teasing is that of not having learned to defend themselves, do not try to defend themselves, or simply do not defend themselves well. Defending oneself is not only a physical response to intimidation, it can also be done through simple nonverbal or behavioral messages, such as walking away from a confrontation, not responding to verbal insults, or grouping with safe peers in the presence of bullies. Those who are incapable of any sort of defense place themselves at great disadvantage when confronted with intimidation.

Similarly, there are some students who do nothing in the face of a challenge. Such a response may be the direct result of fear. They freeze. Typically, animals take one of three defensive actions in the face of danger: fight, flight, or freeze. Humans have the luxury of responding with more sophisticated and disguised behaviors in the first two categories. But freezing usually cannot be faked.

Students Who Are Viewed by Their Peers as "Different"

The sixth characteristic is one that may well be all-encompassing for the other five factors. Children who are "different" are always at risk for abuse by bullies. Different is used in this sense as "different" from the norms of the community. What does that mean? Without intending to complicate the uncomplicated, it means different things in different communities. However, it is always the prerogative of the dominant culture within a community (the previously mentioned **in-group**) to determine what "different" is. This is not an endorsement that the dominant culture is "correct" or that the way a dominant culture within a community treats its nonmajority members (the **out-group**) is always acceptable.

For example, students who belong to a specific racial, ethnic, or religious group impoverished students attending an otherwise wealthy suburban school district; or students who live in a particular section of town (the trailer park) are groups who may become targets by predators for abuse. Such predominant social status abuse is often directed at the misfortunate over such petty social delineators as not wearing the right brand of clothing or shoes. Who has made such a determination of what is "cool"? The in-group, of course.

Any child or adolescent with any one of these characteristics is at a greater risk for being selected as a target by an abusive peer. Obviously, many who may exhibit any one of these characteristics usually exhibit more than one. For instance, most children who exhibit poor social skills automatically are classified as "different" by their peers. Pity the poor child who has moved to nine schools in seven years, whose self-esteem is so low that he is willing to eat dirt in order to tag along with a group who treats him pitifully, and who cannot defend himself in the face of the humiliation that comes his way.

THE VICARIOUS VICTIM

One does not have to be directly involved in an activity to learn of its consequences. This is the basic concept behind "vicarious learning." **Vicarious learning** occurs when an individual observes an event at a level of personal significance so as to impress the incident into the permanent memory. We learn vicariously all the time. Observation through modeling is a common technique used to teach. Most vicarious learning, however, is not structured and occurs as a result of simply participating in everyday life and observing what happens to one's peers, both positive and negative.

Learning is always more likely to occur in direct participation. The farther away one is from the center of a learning activity—farther away in terms of distance or emotion—the less impact the learning event will have. Vicarious learning is similar to ripples of a rock thrown into a pond. The waves are larger at the point where the rock enters the water. We will refer to Figure 3.1 as we provide an example of how **vicarious learning circles** can create additional victims of an incident of bullying that occurs to others.

A bully corners an intended victim in the boys' bathroom at lunchtime at the beginning of the school year in a fourth- to sixth-grade building. The bully is in the sixth grade, the target is a fourth grader and substantially smaller than the aggressor. Another fourth grader with no connection to the bully or the target is also in the bathroom. He hides in one of the stalls as the bully approaches the intended victim and watches through the crack between the door and the stall wall.

The bully proceeds to yell at the fourth grader, shoving him against the urinal. He slaps the younger child twice and knees him in the stomach. By this

Figure 3.1   The Geometry of Vicarious Learning. Responses to an activity are like ripples in water. The closer an individual happens to be to the action, the greater the impact. Both bullies and victims learn about their "roles" by watching bullying behaviors. Bystanders in the outer rings are either unconcerned or least affected. Bystanders, observers, and indirect participants in the inner rings are more likely to be impacted by the behavior and make a personal decision as to what their role should be in the future

time, the victim is crying and begging the older student to stop. As the bully leaves the bathroom, he threatens his target, "If you tell anybody what happened today, you'll get more of it every day until I decide to stop!" The victim composes himself and quickly leaves the bathroom. It is unclear if the bully or the victim knew about the observer in the bathroom stall or if, in the fury of the moment, they both forgot about his presence.

The fourth grader in the bathroom stall is terribly frightened by what he just observed. He is nauseous and shaking and feels as if what he just watched unfold had happened to him. Additionally, he feels as if it *could* happen to him in the future. This is a new school building for all fourth graders, and rumors traditionally abound about how fourth graders are "initiated" by the sixth graders in the opening weeks of school.

The innocent observer to the attack is a **vicarious victim**. Though not in Ground Zero/Circle 1 of the vicarious learning circles—that is where the bully and the victim interacted—his observation in Circle 2 placed him as close to the direct bully-victim interaction as he could possibly be and still not be the target. The impact of observing the attack was traumatizing for this individual, so much so that he gets "sick" the next day and stays home. He is afraid to return to school and feels as if he cannot tell anyone—not his parents, not his teachers, not his friends—what he observed for fear that he will be the next victim of the bully.

Those in Circle 2 of the vicarious learning circles are not always traumatized by their observations of a bully-victim interaction, but the probability is high that if a vicarious victim is created, he or she will be in Circle 2 and less likely to have as strong a reaction in Circles 3 and beyond.

Vicarious learning circles do not apply only to vicarious victims. These learning principles also apply to those who have a curiosity or penchant for wanting to be a bully. We will explore how this occurs in Chapter 5.

While the principal performed his typical routine of trying to scare the willies out of the gang who had attacked Bruce, I came into his office and sat in the back listening. None of the five in the office claimed responsibility for what had happened—no surprise there—no knowledge of exactly what had happened. They were clueless, stumped, just as puzzled as everybody else about what had happened to Bruce. As best as I could determine from the stories they told, the five had managed to concoct the same story to stick to and had most likely done so during the length of time it took for them to get to his office from my commands to leave Bruce at the scene of the crime.

"Honestly, we just found him that way," explained one of the Two.

"All we were doing was trying to help him get up," said the other one. "He was already down when we got there."

The other three participants offered nothing unless asked directly, and when they responded, it was always corroborating the story line of the moment.

The principal told the mob to go outside and wait in the outer office. "I'm tired of this!" he shouted. "You are all going to pay for this, this time." He was exasperated and angry, frustrated by the audacity of the boys' bald-faced lies and his distaste for what they had done to Bruce.

When the boys had left his office, he reviewed with me all the details that he had already gleaned from others prior to my arrival with Bruce back into the building. "Honestly," he said, "I don't know what I'm going to do with those boys, especially the Terrible Two. I'm about ready to kick them out of here for good. Of course, I'm sure you wouldn't want me to do that." He and I worked very closely together with students in trouble—a sort of Good Cop, Bad Cop approach—and although we did not always agree with one another on what avenue might best be pursued with those who ran afoul of the rules—especially repeatedly—we respected each other's viewpoints.

"Don't be so sure," I replied. "I'm glad you didn't see Bruce all covered in dirt and with the tears making mud across his face. You would have really lost it then."

We discussed the situation for several minutes and came to the conclusion, under the circumstances and because of the Terrible Two's track record, that he would send the Two home immediately with a parent and put the other three on in-school suspension until the next day. The following day, each parent and each of the five attackers would have to meet with him to discuss the seriousness of what had happened and determine how best to proceed from there. In all honesty, it was probably the best plan, because neither he nor I were in any mood to do anything constructive with the bullies at the moment.

"One last thing," he said as I exited the door to go back to check on Bruce. "You know how you always tell me that inside every kid are other ones trying to get out and that it's our job to make sure that the ones who do are the positive ones?"

"Yeah," I replied. It was true. It was my template for my Good Cop argument with him to try and to make sure that any decision he might make before suspending a kid was one that always had some semblance of learning attached to it. I had seen too many quick and intemperate decisions with too many principals through the years that convinced me that sometimes some effective educational moments were missed in the heat of a fracas.

"Well, with the Terrible Two, I don't think there are any other kids in there except the spawns of Satan!"

Ouch. Not a high moment of educational inspiration. The problem was, I was not so sure I did not agree with him. I snorted a small chuckle and left to check on Bruce back in the nurse's office.

4

Victimization and Retaliation

To fully appreciate the impact of bullying and teasing, it is important to look at what we have learned about the effect of bullying behaviors on their victims. Intimidation seems to be a universal tactic, and research worldwide documents similar negative impacts of such abuse.

Individuals who experience direct intimidation are impacted at three levels:

- **Cognitively** (the way they think)
- **Affectively** (the way they feel emotionally)
- **Behaviorally** (what they do)

As a result of bullying, victims think, feel, and behave differently from their peers. Their negative thoughts and feelings as a result of the abuse lead to a downward spiral of additional woes. Bullying and teasing, then, impact the *whole being* of the developing child or adolescent in ways that may have a life-long, detrimental impact.

COGNITIVE, AFFECTIVE, AND BEHAVIORAL EFFECTS

Targets of bullying behaviors attribute cause and effect to powers outside their ability to control (an **external locus of control**). They are given labels that denigrate their humanness and increase their attractiveness to other bullies. Victims often blame themselves for the bad treatment they receive from others. As a result, they are prime candidates for developing **learned helplessness**—the belief that no matter what they do, it will make no difference in improving their situation.

Negative thinking patterns clearly have negative effects on the ways victims feel and treat themselves and others. Often, they become depressed, experience low self-esteem, and try to hide their failures. Additionally, they report feeling vulnerable to any number of actual or perceived threats.

Victims tend to exhibit very passive, or passive-aggressive, behaviors. Some other characteristics include self-punishment and self-destructive behavior, such as cutting or suicide attempts. They may also exhibit anger and obsess about revenge, not only toward their tormentors but also to others less powerful than themselves.

Targets often have poor communication skills and do not know how to effectively interact socially. As a result, they are often isolated by the combination of these social skill deficiencies and peer rejection. Shyness, nongregariousness, and a noninterest in others may be present. On the other hand, their awkward behaviors from the lack of social skills are cited as reasons for provocation by assailants. Hypersensitivity, too, is considered grounds for attacks by bullies. Peers report that targets are generally less popular than other students.

SCHOOL PERFORMANCE AND HOME LIFE

School is a mixed bag for targets. They may have a positive attitude toward schoolwork and do well academically. However, they fear school because of the bullying they endure. They cite their high grades as a reason for why they are bullied. A positive change in academic status increases an individual's risk of being bullied.

Others who are bullied often cannot concentrate on their schoolwork. They are distracted from educational goals, largely because they are preoccupied with (a) how miserable they feel as a result of their victimization and (b) thoughts about when and where the next abusive incident may occur, and how they might be able to avoid it. As a result, academic performance is likely to be below expectation. There is a direct correlation between the level of their fear and their grades: The higher the level of fear within the school setting, the lower a target's overall grade point average. It is quite clear that when a child's mental energies are spent generating escape routes from tormentors, there is little time left for concentration on schoolwork.

As with bullies, the home life of targets is not necessarily stable. A variety of problems may be present in the home: Inconsistent discipline, financial worries, social concerns, marital difficulties, and abuse have all been reported. Family members may overprotect the victim through overinvolvement in the individual's daily life. More likely, parents ignore or do not know how to respond to their child's request for assistance in the face of bullying.

AVOIDING BULLIES, AVOIDING SCHOOL

Needless to say, school life for the harassed is unbelievably difficult. Younger students often have little ability to escape bullies. As previously noted, misbehavior among children is most likely to occur in the absence of direct adult supervision.

The most likely place to be unsupervised in the entire school environment is the bathroom. Younger students who feel unsafe in bathrooms simply avoid taking care of their basic biological needs. They just do not go to the bathroom if at all possible. Many, unbelievably and incredibly, may not go to the bathroom until they get home. If they have attempted to go to the bathroom during the school day, they may have only had partial success before being interrupted or frightened away. Needless to say, this creates additional distractions for such students in the classroom. In addition to being worried about avoiding the next confrontation with the bully, they may also be in great physical discomfort because of the need to go to the restroom.

Older students, however, can be more creative in their avoidance activities of unpleasant situations. They simply avoid school altogether. This may appear in one of two ways. Many who are bullied create excuses and illnesses to not go to school. Others just do not go at all on the days that their stress levels are unbearable. While this is far more likely to occur with adolescents, severely harassed elementary children have also been known to resort to such direct avoidance as a means of circumventing victimization. Truancy then becomes an issue. In essence, victims further victimize themselves to avoid bullies. Some may choose to drop out of school altogether. This may be related to the combination of truancy and its direct impact on poor school performance. There are many downward spirals in the life of the harried and harassed; poor school academics is just one of them.

THE PSYCHOLOGY OF VICTIMIZATION

The psychological harm done to children and adolescents who are continually harassed is incalculable. Their torment manifests itself both physically and mentally.

Children who do not reach out for assistance to others may develop somatic complaints and feel as if they are ill—real or imagined. Studies have found that victims of bullying are particularly susceptible to feeling as if they are not in good health, anxiety, or not enjoying daily activities. Girls seemed to report more physical complaints than boys.

Of particular concern is the likelihood that peer victimization will result in the development of longer-term mental health issues, specifically:

- Generalized anxiety
- Depression

- Self-injurious behaviors
- Suicidal ideations

Those who are constantly hounded live in fear of what will happen next. They get little respite even at home, where, while safe, their minds continue to dwell on the abusive behaviors they receive at school and blame themselves for what happens. In short, their nervous systems are always "on." Then self-esteem plummets. The more desperate the situation, the deeper the pain and self-blame. Isolation grows, particularly if significant adults in their lives do little to intervene or listen to their concerns.

Helpless and Hopeless

Desperate, isolated individuals are clearly at great risk. We know that children and adolescents can react negatively under such pressures. A few lash outwardly (**explode**) at their tormentors; more turn inward (**implode**) against themselves. Children who view themselves as failures among their peers and who feel as if adults are unconcerned about their lives are trapped. Those who feel the most **helpless** and **hopeless** are at the greatest risk to develop depression and harbor suicidal ideations. While we are no longer surprised by adolescent suicide anymore, it is important to remember that elementary-age children, too, do act on depressive feelings and are capable of committing suicide.

Two of the most important intervening questions we can ask of individuals who we think are at risk for self-harmful behaviors are

- What do you think can be done to improve the situation?
- What does the future look like for you?

Of course these questions must be asked in an age-appropriate fashion and with a vocabulary to match. While a high schooler might be able to answer these questions in the exact way they are posed here, the elementary counterpart to these questions might be phrased as "What do you think would make things better?" and "How do you think things will be for you tomorrow or next week?"

Responses that indicate a sense of helplessness to the template question "What do you think can be done . . . ?" are such answers that contain variations on themes of "Nothing," "It won't make any difference," and "Nobody cares." Responses that indicate a sense of hopelessness to the template question "What does the future look like?" may contain such generic replies as "I don't know," "It doesn't matter," and "I don't see anything out there for me."

Children and adolescents who express such visions of their predicament are in great emotional despair. Children who feel a sense of helplessness cease to strive. When their efforts to do something—in this instance, *anything*—seem to make little difference, a self-perpetuating downward spiral begins. When a child believes that it will do little good to take any action to improve a predicament, the situation will likely stay the same, or possibly even grow worse.

People are less likely to feel helpless when there is a sense of hope to drive them forward. If there is nothing else that youths should have throughout their developing years, a sense of hope should permeate all that they do. Hope is the rocket fuel that makes us reach for the stars. It is not natural for youths to feel empty of the promise of things better. Without hope, as with helplessness, children are less likely to make the efforts necessary to improve their condition.

Children and youths who respond in either a helpless or hopeless fashion fall into a high-risk category for intervention. It must be determined if the origin of the sense of despair is immediately identifiable and remedied, or if its nexus is rooted in a much deeper field of woe. Early-elementary–age children in particular are truly sending a message that we must not fail to hear when they express little or no sense of enthusiasm about life. It is strongly recommended that adults take direct action and seek additional advice and counsel from helping professionals, such as the school counselor, if and when our youths express or behave in such a desperate manner. It is far better to err on the side of caution and be wrong than to discover years later that such behaviors were markers of developing long-term depression caused by the trauma of abuse at the hands of bullies.

HIGH-TECH VICTIMIZATION

Bullies have gone high-tech. There are more ways than direct physical contact or face-to-face insults to harass others these days. As schools become more savvy in their abilities to interrupt traditional bullying and teasing behaviors, the bullies have gone deeper underground, off-campus, and into cyberspace to keep the intimidation going 24 hours of the day.

Cyberbullying

Employing electronic media to harass and intimidate is known as **cyberbullying**. In my workshops, I add an additional category of less severe cyberbullying that I refer to as **cybertaunting**. Like teasing's older cousin, cybertaunting refers to harassment and intimidation that falls "right below the line" of being able to be classified as outright bullying. Victims of cyberbullying, however, have been subjected to horrible instances of embarrassing slander and libel through the aggressors' creation of demeaning Web sites, the sending of e-mail, instant messaging, and the use of cell phones. In some instances, such behaviors are subject to school discipline or even criminal liability—provided that such penalties are enforced. Indeed, those who have studied Columbine are aware of the threatening Web page constructed by one of the murderers in the weeks preceding the attack and the fact that the parents of one of the intended targets complained to local law enforcement, but that little was done.

The technological sophistication of our kids has not been lost on those who would choose to use it as a tool of intimidation. Reports have been made citing that children as young as age 7 have received harassing text messages via cell phones. The text messaging was supported with additional calls to the target's cell phone, upwards of 20 per day from multiple aggressors. Many of the bullies would hand the phone to nearby supporters and have them leave additional messages for the victim.

Cyberbullying at the secondary grade levels is more pronounced. As might be expected, it is also more viciously creative. Girls tend to be more adept at using cyberspace as a vehicle of intimidation. Such behavior fits the pattern of female aggression being more covert and less visible to the supervising eye. Girls are particularly abusive in the spreading of gossip and rumors about the sexual behaviors of other female targets, complete with all the negative terminologies that go along with it. Boys are more likely to create Web sites in which they spew antiauthority messages about school and school personnel, as well as proclaiming threatened harm to those they do not like. There exist some commercial Web sites specifically designed to share rumors on others in the school or peer group setting. So sophisticated was one that contributors could add their school to the Web site along with whatever rumors they wanted to spread. It is not uncommon for those who can build their own Web sites to configure the electronic channels to make it appear as if another student has written it.

There are dangers in the creation of such Web sites. When a Web page designer posts information about the sexual attributes of peers, it may be accessible for all to see, particularly if the key terminology gets picked up by powerful search engines such as Google. Cyberbullies often post the picture, name, phone number, and address of their target. This creates the possibility that sexual predators could enter into the picture. With the advent of picture cell phones, compromising photos can be taken in school locker rooms and downloaded as-is or "morphed" (the imaged altered by computer) into more embarrassing creations via the Web and e-mail attachments. Videotaped incidents of beatings and bullying also can be downloaded on computers for distribution (or, as in the case of Glenbrook North High School, with its powder-puff game gone awry, end up on national television!). Rumors spread in chatrooms and by instant messaging—the modern-day equivalent of kids spending hours on the phone—and are passed on to others, often in repetitive cycles. E-mails are forwarded to the peer network and entire listservs. Cyberbullying has been attributed to the suicide of a 12-year-old target whose cyberbullies tormented her about being overweight. Other suicide attempts have been documented as directly linked to the abuse heaped on them by cyberbullying.

Detecting and Dealing With Cyberbullies

Of course, the use of electronics to harass others may also be exactly the thing that exposes those responsible. Text messaging and cell phone calls can provide the identification numbers of the originators of the threats, and Web sites have server addresses. Unless sophisticated and disguised, most cybertaunting can be traced, so saving the evidence for the proper authorities is of great importance. The best method of dealing with cyberbullies is to report the incident as soon as it occurs and especially if a long-standing pattern of abuse is present. Saving copies of the offensive messages or materials is useful in helping to document exactly the extent of the problem.

School officials may or may not be able to assist in the stopping of cyber-bullying. If the offensive behaviors originate on school property and with school equipment, then they can act decisively. If it originates outside of the school's authority, the school may not have the ability to legally respond. Under these conditions, reporting the harassment to law enforcement may not be out of the question. But federal court rulings in 1996 determined that electronic communication is a protected free-speech zone. Unless a message is explicitly threatening, there may be barriers to legal recourse under this interpretation.

This does not negate the possibility of civil action against an offending party for slander or libel, and in the case of children and adolescents, an argument might well be made by a sharp attorney that the repetitive posting of negative rumors is more damaging to their psychological and developmental well-being than singular verbal incidents. Under this same argument, the courts might likely rule that children and adolescents make errors and should not be held liable for childish mistakes in judgment. Perhaps an even better approach would be to file civil actions against the parents of those responsible for reprehensible electronic mayhem. If parents are ultimately responsible for the actions of their minor children, could not an argument be made that parents are accountable for the misbehavior of their children's cybermischief?

THE VOICES OF VICTIMS

As a professor of counselor education, I have the opportunity to keep updated on the lives of K–12 schoolchildren via the reports from our interns, as well as making on-site visits with school counseling practitioners. Their reports of the tales of both victims and bullies are both sad and compelling.

Our interns are required to record multiple examples of their on-site work for review of their clinical skills by staff at the university. Over the years, many interns have chosen to construct separate counseling groups with victims or bullies. The sadness and torment spoken by these children and adolescents— both bullies and their victims—are palpable.

Several memorable comments from victims:

- "That happened to you, too? I thought I was the only one they did that to."
- "All I wanted to do was disappear. I was so embarrassed that they did that to me in the cafeteria. Everybody saw it."

- "I don't want to come here anymore. Nobody cares what happens to me."
- "Sometimes I wish I was invisible so nobody would see me and just leave me alone."
- "This stuff has happened to me all my life. I sometimes think that the only time it will end is when I'm dead."

These children and adolescents are speaking of their experiences in both public and private school settings, places where they are supposed to be safe and treated with dignity. These are the voices not of healthy or happy children, but of victims in every sense of the word. They are defeated, feel abandoned, and, worse, are convinced that no one—adult or peer—values them enough to help them find a way out of their predicament.

Our professional school counseling interns report that their interactions with the victims of bullying and teasing provided the first important steps toward healing—listening and validation of their experiences. Those who have been bullied and teased say consistently—right or wrong, as kids sometimes have that tendency to exaggerate—that the interaction with our interns was the first time that anyone had ever listened to them, the first time that they had shared their pain and frustration about victimization with an adult. Without counseling interventions, victims are at serious risk for long-term scarring, both emotional and physical. While they may go on to lead seemingly normal lives on the outside, many never overcome the mental anguish they endured as children or adolescents. Early intervention helps bullied children to understand that they are not at fault, they are not alone, and that their stories are important. When we do not recognize their pain and help them to overcome it, isolated victims are capable of hurting not only themselves, but others as well.

WHEN VICTIMS STRIKE BACK

Those who are victimized by bullies often harbor a well-understood dose of resentment and may hold the smoldering coals of burning hatred toward their tormentors for years. While some turn inward with their pain, others may be less able to hold their mistreatments privately in a peaceful fashion. Much to the surprise of many, when someone is seriously or fatally injured in a bully-victim interaction, it is often the bully who has received the explosion of rage from a frustrated and frightened victim. Many of the young adult and juvenile fiction dealing with the issue of bullying, in fact, plays out this very revenge fantasy. While such teen novels may be an excellent source for adults to understand the torment of the victims of harassment through their fictionalized (or maybe not?) descriptions, one cannot help but wonder if such "get even" scenarios endorse many of the same fantasies displayed on television and in movies.

In the summer of 2003, police in New Jersey stopped a plot by three teenagers, ages 18, 15, and 14, who intended to settle old scores with, among others, those who had bullied them by going on a shooting rampage in their community. The 18-year-old leader of the group had recently graduated from high school and was known to have kept a list of all who had slighted him since elementary school. Of particular concern to the leader was the fact that kids in school mistreated his 14-year-old brother, who spoke with an impediment. To offset the teasing from his peers, the older brother tried to look and act as intimidating as possible, dressing in black and often carrying a baseball bat.

The 18-year-old carried all the classic earmarks of the victim. He was ostracized by his peers. His younger brother's speech impediment made his family situation different by peer standards. His father noted that "The younger one was verbally and physically abused by the neighborhood children. . . . [his older brother] had to fend the people off, and after a while, they didn't even want to go out anymore." He isolated himself with dark fantasy games and envisioned himself as the real-life character Neo from *The Matrix* films. One of his classmates noted that "He wouldn't even talk. He was just by himself." As if a reward for his silence, but just as much in all likelihood another swipe from, his classmates voted him "Most Bashful."

When arrested, the three teenagers had rifles, a shotgun, multiple handguns, swords, and 2,000 rounds of ammunition. Their targets, for starters, were three specific individuals who had made fun of them. The would-be perpetrators also indicated that the initial killings would be followed by a random killing spree throughout the community.

Not every such revenge fantasy by victims is interrupted or discovered. There are ample cases in which those who have been bullied have resorted to deadly violence in their misguided and painful efforts to even the score.

The *Chicago Sun-Times* reported that as of 2001, in the 37 highest-profile school shootings and violent eruptions in this country, two-thirds of the aggressors cited persecution, bullying, or feeling threatened as a reason for their actions. By my count, clearly 11 of those 37 incidents are directly attributable to victims of bullying and teasing retaliating against their actual or perceived aggressors. A handful of examples include the following:

1985: A 14-year-old junior high school student in Kansas killed the principal and wounded three others. He identified as his motive the fact that he was bullied and beaten by other students for years.

1988: A 16-year-old in Virginia took a pistol and firebombs to school in retribution for being called racist names. One teacher was wounded and one was killed.

1995: A 16-year-old from South Carolina, who indicated that he was teased, wounded a teacher, killed another, and then killed himself.

1996: A 14-year-old in Washington killed a peer who had teased him, another student, and a teacher.

1997: A 16-year-old in remote Alaska killed his principal, another student, and wounded two more students. He had repeatedly reported to school staff about being teased.

1997: A 16-year-old in Mississippi, with a long history of family disruption and instability, killed his mother and two classmates and wounded seven other students. He remembered being harassed all the way back to the third grade.

And then of course there was Columbine, Colorado. The total body count came to 38: 12 students and 1 teacher were killed; 23 classmates were wounded; and the 2 teenage gunmen committed suicide. The butchers at Columbine shared many of the same traits as the gang in New Jersey in 2003 whose plot was foiled. They were alienated from their peer group and allowed their fantasies of revenge to become reality. Cited specifically by parents in testimony to the Colorado state investigation of the massacre was their belief that school administrators had failed to respond to the intimidation, assaults, bullying, and taunts by student athletes toward specific groups of students. Such incidents were directed toward those who were considered out of the main in-group and included reports of religious intimidation between one athlete and a Jewish student.

A quick overview of just the bare essentials of these cases reveals certain threads:

All of the perpetrators of retaliatory violence in these instances were male.

Although there have been incidences of female retaliatory fatalities, they are rare. Virtually all incidents of victims using deadly force against their tormentors are among males.

All of the perpetrators had previously asked for help from adults and, failing to get it, made known their plans to retaliate.

When a review of these cases was conducted by law enforcement agencies, in almost all instances the victims reported that they did two things before their retaliation—they first asked adults for assistance (and felt as if they were either ignored or that the intervention was superficial, and more an effort to "go through the motions" rather than respond with an effective strategy), and before they struck back, they told or otherwise indicated their intentions to others.

The ages of 14–16 were the peak years for the carrying out of retaliatory acts.

Research and surveys tell us repeatedly that the middle school and junior high school years are the peak years for bullying and teasing to occur. Recent evidence suggest that the ages of 12–13 are becoming the peak years of those who are bullied attempting to harm or succeeding in harming themselves. It may well be that targets may first turn their frustration inward, before exploding. With the advent of age comes bravado. Combine this with a boiling frustration and greater access to weapons and the chemistry is ripe for someone to light the fuse.

Someone other than the intended targets were often injured or killed.

When the fuse is lit on blind rage, the explosion harms all those within the blast zone. In high-profile incidences of school violence, no one is safe. Typically the target looking for revenge has a specific tormentor in mind. That innocent victims get in the way may not register with a revenge attack until after it is over. It is not called "blind rage" for nothing.

Were bullying and teasing the sole contributing factors to these tragedies? No. But the frustration and sense of hopelessness and helplessness combined with the victims' belief that they had no alternatives, no escape mechanisms, and no one to turn to whom they trusted to intervene effectively, mixed with the "mythology of manhood" that "real men" retaliate with force, formed a volatile fuel that ultimately was ignited by the availability of deadly weapons and homicidal revenge fantasies.

No written word of mine can convey the victims' experiences as acutely as their own voices and, in some cases, their violent actions. Their stories speak of deep hurt and anguish, the kind of agony that afflicts the heart and soul and is not easily forgotten, if ever. It is a pain that resonates to the bone.

But victims are not alone in their pain. Surprisingly, bullies often have their own stories of sadness, chronicles that explain much of the reasoning behind their behaviors. We will learn more of their situations in Chapter 5.

The day following the attack on Bruce was a long one. One by one, each set of parents came in to meet with the principal to discuss what had happened and to listen to his decrees. I was not a part of that meeting. The Terrible Two were going on out-of-school suspension for a school week. The other three would be on in-school suspension for three days. There was not much argument to it—at least not with the principal. I, on the other hand, had managed to get myself into quite a mess during the principal's and my Good Cop, Bad Cop discussion after school the day of the original beating.

Bruce was medically sound. The nurse reported that he had a few bruises and scrapes and had dust and dirt in every possible pocket or opening on his clothing, but that most of the blows were only going to leave him sore. He and I met for another short time after he left the nurse's office to see what he wanted to do the rest of the day.

"I really don't want to go to class," he said quietly. "But I guess it's the best thing to do to show everybody that this stuff doesn't bother me." He wasn't very convincing.

I studied his countenance. He was so large, not obese by any means, but of the size that would have made a high school football coach drool over the prospects of Bruce playing the line. He was also so mild and gentle in spirit. At that moment I wanted to take him home with me and adopt him.

"Let's get together tomorrow and talk about everything, okay?" I offered. "It will probably be a busy day for all of us because of all the meetings that will be going on with the principal and the parents of those who attacked you, but we'll do it to start making things better around here for you. You're worth it, kid!" My last statement was a weak effort at trying to make Bruce feel better. I should have known better.

He was quick to pick up on my mistake. He sighed, then said, "Well, I don't feel like I'm worth much of anything right now. In fact, I don't feel worth much of anything any time, these days."

Bruce's comment echoed in me the remainder of the day. It also made me angrier with the Terrible Two and their toadies. By the time I went down for the pre-arranged meeting with the principal after school to discuss the day's events and help design a plan for meeting with the parents—well, actually, do my Good Cop part, because I knew pretty well what he intended to do with the lot, anyway—I had managed to work up a pretty good head of steam about the whole mess. I was angry at what had happened, and I was angry that all that would happen would be that the aggressors would be punished and life would go on as it had before. I was angry at my inability to do more to make the situation better and I was angry at Bruce's words, which had rumbled through my head the rest of the day: "Well, I don't feel like I'm worth much of anything right now. In fact, I don't feel worth much of anything any time, these days." I marched to the principal's office, angry but still unsure of what I would say.

5

Bullies

As with those who are the targets of bullying and teasing, the agents of such behaviors may also display certain general behavioral characteristics.

A summary of the research tells us that the bully has a need to be in control. The use of physical and psychological power is the primary weapon. By being in control and using power to control the situation, the bully avoids the self-determined appearance of failure. Avoiding the appearance of failure compensates for an underlying fear of inadequacy (the **insecure bully**). In other instances, bullies intentionally use their power and control to be abusive (the **power bully**).

BULLIES AND AGGRESSION

In the world of the insecure bully, the best means to solve dilemmas is through aggression. Aggressive actions preserve the dignity and self-image of these bullies. This is ironic, because in truth, the insecure bully is caught in a cycle of fear and uncertainty and has difficulty reaching out to others for help. Their feelings of being unloved, unimportant, and inferior are projected onto others. Victims become scapegoats for the bully's own sense of these emotions. Physically, bullies are usually greater than average in strength, are more energetic, and generally older than their victims.

To power bullies, physical image and projecting the persona of invincibility are important. Because power bullies act from a base of superiority, they make conscious efforts to dominate all they can. Society often supports the creation and maintenance of the power bully, particularly if the individual is one of the "sanctified" in-groups "officially endorsed" by adults within the school setting, such as an athlete or cheerleader.

The targets of victimization are selected carefully. Aggression is learned through modeling, often from the home environment, the media, or the larger society. One of the central markers of determining if an act of aggression from an individual classifies the perpetrator as a bully is the *chronic nature* of the behavior. Repeated aggressive acts directed toward others in efforts to dominate and control may be classified as bullying behaviors. **Chronic bullies** end up having more violence- and crime-related problems as adults.

Bullies may have difficulty with their verbal and relationship skills. Girls bully more through verbal intimidation and social actions, particularly shunning or excluding a target. In general, both male and female bullies tend to see hostile intent in the actions of others, particularly in those whom they target for aggressive actions. They are quicker to anger and use force sooner than their peers. They often have selective recall of events leading up to an incident of bullying, teasing, or intimidation. In spite of stereotypes to the contrary, bullies are not intellectually inferior. They often do not, however, have a positive attitude toward school or schoolwork, particularly the insecure bully. Academic requirements may be one of the contributing factors to that insecurity.

BULLIES AND HOME LIFE

The home life for the bully may not be a happy one. They report three times more family problems than their nonbullying peers. Violence in the home may be a frequent occurrence. Their parents often do not keep up with their whereabouts. Family interactions are often disengaged. Positive role models are scarce for the bully. No one has shown them how to get along with others or how to solve problems in lieu of aggressive and intimidating acts. Home discipline may be inconsistent and arbitrary. Punishment is often harsh and meted out according to parental mood. Little empathy is present. The transmission of aggression through the child is often intergenerational.

While not an ironclad profile, these characteristics are gleaned from what researchers have found through the years. Perhaps more important than what this information tells us about what we see in the life and behavior of those who bully and tease is the process that gets us to this point in the first place. Following are some key ingredients.

Recipe for a Bully

Want to know what makes a bully? Bullies usually learn their behavior from adults, such as parents or other caregivers. The following recipe of adult behaviors sheds light on what most bullies have experienced prior to bullying others.

• *Harsh and capricious punishment.* Punishment seems to occur totally at the whim of the adult. It is usually extreme, either physically or through long-term removal of privileges.

• *Physical punishment.* Abusive adults believe that punishment works only if it is physical, and it usually involves hitting. Spanking is the common way of dealing with all missteps; slaps are even easier to administer.

• *Blowup after minor infractions.* Exaggerated responses help instill fear into a child. They also teach children who is the boss and who has the power. More significantly, they show how power is to be used.

• *Violent and emotional outbursts.* These keep the element of surprise in the adult's favor. Emotional extremes are always effective tools for making certain that children remember a point for the rest of their lives. If one can inflict emotional pain at the same time as a violent memory, the likelihood of a long-term effect is increased.

• *Ignoring the child for long stretches of time.* Being an adult with the power is something that comes with the privilege of paying attention to children only when desired. Besides, if adults allow children to be unsupervised, they are more likely to place themselves in a position where they can be punished.

• *Disinterest in the child's welfare.* This works well with the ingredients of ignoring for long stretches of time. Children are noticed only if they are bad. They learn that adults are not interested in their health and well-being.

• *No praise, no encouragement, no humor.* Humor is used only if it is a part of punishment, but sarcasm is more common, especially if it is belittling (see the next step for further suggestions). Praise and encouragement are used only when children behave aggressively.

• *Put-downs, sarcasm, and criticism.* These negatives are used to keep children in their place. Adults who speak to their children in this way believe that acknowledging the success of children will only spoil them and make them less likely to develop the traits they want.

• *Making certain that the child feels insecure and rejected.* Overreactions to infractions increase the child's sense of insecurity, along with the use of heavy criticism. Rejection naturally occurs with the proper amounts of put-downs and criticism.

• *Making no effort to counteract aggression with more appropriate behaviors.* Aggression is viewed as good. It makes children strong. The belief exists that no one should abuse your child and that teaching children to be aggressive increases the likelihood that they will grow up tough and be able to take care of themselves. Watching violent and aggressive movies and playing or participating in the same types of games also help with this ingredient.

• *In general, bombarding children with negativisms as often as positives.* This is probably one of the key ingredients to making an effective bully. All aspects of life are typically as difficult as possible. Bullies must feel as if life is all about yielding power over others. The iron fist rules, both physically and emotionally. The more anger that is fostered within, the greater the likelihood of making a "successful" bully.

All of these ingredients are, by the way, essential learning tools for helping the child, in turn, inflict such behaviors on others. Any singular item, in and of itself, may do the trick if intense enough, but the "best" bullies are made when several or all of the ingredients are combined and mixed thoroughly in the home. Children learn that it is important to bring the anger to a boil often and never let it simmer long. But they also recognize that their explosions must always be directed elsewhere—particularly not toward adults—and such behaviors are not to be tolerated in the home. After all, we are the adults. We have the power. They are to have none. Let them sort out all their frustrations among their peers. That is what kids do. It is, after all, only kid stuff.

WHEN A BULLY IS A BULLY: THE FOUR MARKERS

Allan Morotti, a colleague and professor of counselor education at the University of Alaska-Fairbanks, and I identified four central questions, with subparts, to help determine if aggressive interactions on the part of an agent should be considered outside the realm of an age-appropriate normal developmental dispute.

1. What Is the Nature of the Behavior in Question?

Is it age-appropriate? To whom is it directed? Is it specific to only one sex or to both? Is it directed toward vicinity-aged peers or those younger or older in age? What is the content of the behavior?

Examples of problematic behaviors include the following:

- A 10-year-old uses derogatory names to embarrass a 5-year-old on the way to school.
- In the lunchroom, a 13-year-old boy loudly accuses a same-age girl of sexual misbehavior with his friends.

2. What Is the Level of the Intensity of the Behavior?

How severe is the behavior in question? Is the behavior verbal, physical, or psychological? Is the behavior seemingly done in a humorous fashion or with anger, harshness, or malicious intent by the agent?

Examples of problematic behaviors include the following:

- A group of 8-year-old girls go to all their friends over the course of a week and ask them to not ever ask a former same-age girl in their group to spend the night at their house because "she's a bed-wetter."
- A seventh-grade boy places photocopied notices on school lockers, outside the school, and on neighborhood utility poles showing an embarrassing picture of another seventh grader with the caption "Retardo Supreme!" typed underneath.

3. At What Rate Does the Behavior Occur?

Is this a frequent occurrence or an isolated incident? Are there times when the behavior occurs more often than others?

Examples of problematic behaviors include the following:

- A fourth-grade girl has scratched with her fingers and pulled at the hair of those she does not like for the past month.
- A tenth-grade male has left crude drawings and graffiti on the locker of a tenth-grade girl he has not liked since the beginning of school in September; it is now December.

4. How Does the Target of the Agent's Behavior Respond?

Is the target upset or offended by the behavior? Does the target understand the behavior? Does the target reciprocate in kind to the agent? How does the agent respond to the target's attempts at self-defense against the behavior?

Examples of problematic behaviors include the following:

- A group of junior high school boys wait for a mentally challenged boy to leave the lunchroom so that they can ask him questions about his sex life. The student does not totally comprehend the questions, but he laughs with them because he thinks they are talking about sex with girls in general and he is trying to fit in with the group.
- An elementary-age girl, who is new to the school, is teased about her clothing, which is reflective of her family's religious beliefs. She does not know to whom to turn and cries alone in the hallway as the group continues to ask her questions about "why she dresses so funny."

An agent does not have to "hit" in all four of the question areas. Clearly it is possible to intimidate by behaviors listed under only a single marker question. However, those who intimidate most likely will engage in behaviors found in all four question areas. The ability to answer with some degree of accuracy and certainty these four markers is key to identifying if an aggressor's behavior warrants a higher degree of scrutiny than normal. Documentation and examples are helpful and will assist us in developing remedies for intervention in our later chapters.

BULLIES AS VICTIMS

A major premise of this book's approach to understanding the bully-victim relationship is that bullies, particularly insecure bullies, may well be as much victims of life's training as the choices they make to engage in intimidating behaviors. It is my experience that one of the major failings of the intervention process has been that while we are generally quick to respond to those who have been aggrieved, especially those whose mental and physical injuries are inescapably evident, we have tended to write off the aggressor as a "worthless kid" and one who is not worthy of the time and effort to see what is behind his or her actions. Victims naturally elicit our empathetic and sympathetic responses from our tendencies to be caregivers. Bullies provoke our defense mechanisms, compelling us to want to drive away the offenders, as if it is some kind of innate survival mechanism. The most common method of dealing with those who bully and tease is through punishment, not a concerned effort to invest the time to "go upstream" and discover the reasons why bullies act the way they do in the first place.

As those of us who have had the opportunity to engage the parents or guardians of bullies know well, it is often easy to come to an immediate understanding as to why some children who tease and bully do so and do it so well. While parents are not necessarily responsible for the misbehavior of their children, many aggressive children do indeed come from homes and family situations wherein aggression may not be encouraged, but neither is it frowned on or discouraged. These children are particularly at risk and at decreased chances for successful interventions, as any suggestions to incorporate alternatives to their aggressive behaviors are likely to be ignored, if not outright rejected, by their parents.

BULLIES AND THE MEDIA

While children and adolescents may indeed be a product of aggressiveness learned in the home, others are not so easily explained. Many children are aggressive because of vicarious learning, which operates on the same principles we discussed in Chapter 3. These children are modeling behaviors they have observed within general society, particularly the electronic media such as television, movies, Web sites, and video games. I refer to these indirect influences as **nonpoint** or **floating** sources. In sum, nonpoint sources of vicarious learning "float" everywhere throughout Kid World. They are not formally "taught," but rather are absorbed, akin to osmosis, through everyday life.

We have known about vicarious learning and its impacts—both positive and negative—since the days of Albert Bandura's studies in the 1960s with children and television. Children who watched television shows with aggressive content subsequently played aggressively, more so than those children who watched television shows with nonaggressive themes. The exposure opportunities of children to violence today via the electronic media are nothing like they were during the time of Bandura's studies of over 40 years ago: three channels (ABC, NBC, CBS—well, four if one could also get PBS in its infancy) and no remote! Children's access to television and portrayals of violence in the 1960s could not hold a candle to a child's access to the mayhem of the twenty-first century.

The observation of violence expands from its point of origin outward to the peer group. It has a particularly strong impact on the ages preceding the age in which such violence is role-modeled. The 5-year-old is much more impressed and impressionable by violent behavior modeled by an 8-year-old than is the 11-year-old. This is what I have termed the **reverse ripple effect**. It refers to the chances of a specific action occurring among one particular age group having more impact on the ages *below* rather than *above*. Vulnerability, then, works with *both* groups. Victims are certainly vulnerable to attacks by those who prey on the weak, but bullies are susceptible to absorbing and living out the violent fantasy world they believe to be reality.

For many children, reality is filtered through the lens of unsupervised media. And there is no such thing today as a "children's hour" safety zone on cable access television. Flip through the cable today at any hour of the day or night and you will find something with a violent image occurring within a 5-minute scan. For children and adolescents raised on high standards and expectations of visual stimulation, such fast-moving scenes of mayhem provide the type of eye candy they seek. *Captain Kangaroo* and *Mister Roger's Neighborhood* it ain't! Shades of *Silence of the Lambs*, *CSI: (Fill in the Name of Your Town Here!)*, and body bags are more of the typical fare that catches our kids' eyes these days.

BULLIES WHO MAY HAVE DIAGNOSTIC DISORDERS

Still other children and adolescents behave aggressively toward their peers for different reasons. Some of these children who bully may—and the emphasis here is on the word *may*—be exhibiting characteristics of deeper-seated mental health problems, or behavioral disorders. It is important that the reader understand two basic ground rules before we proceed.

1. An Aggressive Act Is Not Always an Act of Bullying

As previously noted, children and adolescents have disputes that may end in verbal or physical confrontations as a matter of normal human development. Because two children exchange words or fisticuffs does not necessarily mean that a bully-victim interaction has occurred.

2. An Aggressive Child Is Not Necessarily Behaviorally Disordered

Truly only a few individuals meet the criteria described in the following discussion. Some children are aggressive because that is the way they learned to obtain their goals, and they do what they do because it works. In truth, we all engage in a sort of **behavioral inertia** that propels us to keep doing what we have always done until we have a reason to change. Such change often occurs only by way of a greater force being imposed on us—perhaps because we were caught—to make us change. At other times, we continue to do what we have always done because no one has shown us a different way—an alternative—to accomplish the same goal. It is important to remember these two basic ground rules and not "see" bullying where it does not exist.

Recognizing and Responding to Conduct Disorders

Occasionally a situation arises in which a bully exhibits behavior that may indicate a behavioral disorder. The proper course of action is first to recognize the behavior, and then administer appropriate corrective action. When these students, after intervention, remain unable to self-monitor and self-correct their behaviors during unsupervised or unmonitored situations, they are telling us something. Just what, however, is unclear, and it is left to us to interpret the meaning. Some children fail to self-correct because they willfully intend to continue their behavior no matter how many interventions are applied and at what level they occur. Such individuals may be exhibiting characteristics of what is referred to as *conduct disorder.*

Conduct disorder as identified by the *Diagnostic and Statistical Manual, 4th edition* (DSM-IV), a manual used in the mental health professions to describe and classify categories of behaviors that create problems in daily living, delineates specific characteristics that may be indicative of the disorder. Conduct disorder may be present in "children or adolescents . . . [who] often initiate aggressive behavior and react aggressively to others. . . . They may display bullying, threatening, or intimidating behavior . . . initiate frequent physical fights . . . use a weapon that can cause physical harm . . . [and] be physically cruel to people . . . or animals."

The DSM-IV indicates that children who might be conduct-disordered engage in a "repetitive and persistent pattern of behavior . . . [in which] the basic rights of others or major age-appropriate societal norms or rules are violated." Such behavior patterns are "usually present in a variety of settings." Frequency of behavior is important in a diagnosis of conduct disorder. A child displaying three or more such characteristics during the past 12 months, with at least one such behavior evident during the past 6 months, *may be* (my emphasis) a candidate for a diagnosis of conduct disorder.

Children and adolescents who are eligible for a DSM-IV diagnosis are certainly in need of more intensive therapeutic assistance than what can normally be provided in the school or home setting. Consultation with one's family physician or a qualified counseling therapist is in order.

A Precautionary Note: The Fallibility of Diagnoses

I cannot emphasize enough my distaste for diagnosing and labeling children unnecessarily or, worse, for the sake of making a child reimbursable. The correct identification and diagnostic labeling of a behavior may well be the first step toward designing an effective therapeutic treatment intervention. Unfortunately, all too often society tends to manufacture and "see" diagnostic problems where none may well exist. We are often too quick to diagnose, prescribe, and medicate problems today when what is actually needed is longer-term intervention designed to reach the root causes of a behavior. Medication may reduce symptoms, particularly with behavioral issues, and is often extremely effective with problems of a biochemical nature. However, there is no substitute for the longer-term face-to-face interactions that may be most effective for children and adolescents who need to talk about their concerns and behaviors. Children and adolescents may be very aware of the reasons they behave the way they do. Sometimes we just simply need to ask them. We might be very surprised to learn how intelligent our children really are when we take the time to treat them with respect and give them the most important thing that they need—our time.

BULLIES AND LONG-TERM IMPLICATIONS

Bullies and Gangs

Before aggressive children become aggressive adults, if such is to be the case, there is another stage they must pass through—adolescence. As we know, the adolescent years are most likely to produce bully-victim relationships, particularly in the middle and junior high school grades. It is during these years that another aggressive diversion takes place for some: exploration into **ganging** or **mobbing** behaviors, wherein groups of individuals band together for a common purpose—in this instance, not for the common good.

We must not confuse ganging and mobbing behaviors with the various cliques and ever-changing social groups that preteens and teens join during this same period. Cliques form and disband as often as the wind changes. They are often the result of short-term friendships or idolizations or are centered around similar-activity interests. Cliques can direct bullying and teasing behaviors toward nonmembers, particularly under the direction of a strong and charismatic leader. Though problematic to the intervener, they are not to be equated as the breeding grounds for eventual movement into gangs.

Teens emulate what they believe is the standard for their generation. Clothing and hair style are the most common examples of copycat behaviors among youths. Behavioral norms, as modeled today via cable and satellite television, have gone coast to coast and worldwide in their influence on children and adolescents. A recent phenomenon of the music and video industry is the mainstreaming of ganglike behaviors and the glorification of a "gansta" lifestyle. No longer are the rural hinterlands immune from the entanglements of big-city life. If anything, farm kids in Iowa are just as likely to be the "posers" and the "wannabes" of what they see on MTV (and its more "mature" cousin, VH1) as are the adults who are the real things in real life.

Bonds of Peer Affiliation

Peer affiliation is essential for the establishment of positive self-esteem and a sense of belonging. Children will obtain the peer affiliation they need, unless the most extenuating of circumstances exist, irregardless of whether such alliances are healthy. Contact with a peer group, any peer group, is that powerful a force in the life of adolescents. The strongest relationships are formed when a connection of worth and value is transmitted between the two parties. This is called **bonding**. Bonding, remember, does not have to be based on positive events or activities. Where and from whom children obtain their sense of self-worth and are told that they are valuable is where and with whom one bonds.

A gang or a mob can be considered a group of individuals who have bonded for certain negative purposes. In the case of bully-victim interactions, gangs become agents of terror seeking targets to mob. Their strength is both real and imagined to their victims. They have the advantage of numbers and strength, with a reputation of intimidation that leads others to be fearful of their collective or individual presence. To insult one member of the gang is to insult them all. Gangs are forces that must be broken apart. No good comes from a gang that makes life miserable for others.

Aggressive individuals, particularly those with no positive role models and who are looking for someone or something to provide them with meaning and value, are ripe for being noticed by negative gangs. While there is no direct linkage, prediction, or certainty that today's bullies will become tomorrow's gang members, several behavioral characteristics of bullies, particularly the adolescent bully, show similarities with violent gang members. For example, both the bully and the violent gang member do the following:

- Show strong capacities to deal with fearful situations
- Are not easily intimidated
- Show little interest in responsible performance
- Do what is necessary to be in charge of a situation
- Rationalize their aggressive behaviors as justifiable under the circumstances

These are factors of enormous concern. As with the studies that show a direct linkage between the likelihood of aggressive children becoming aggressive adults, more study is needed to determine the strength of the correlation of adolescent bullying and those who eventually join violent gangs.

Bullies at Age 30

Research is clear that children who consistently engage in aggressive behaviors are more likely to continue such behaviors as adults unless they are provided reasons to change. Landmark studies on hundreds of children as they matured into adulthood provide us with information that cannot be ignored.

L. Rowel Huesmann and his colleagues followed a group of third graders through the 1960s into the 1980s. They found that among those children who engaged in aggressive behaviors at age 8, such behaviors were remarkably stable over time. Some of their findings included the following:

- Aggressive 8-year-olds were more likely to have juvenile records
- Aggressive 8-year-olds were more likely to have done poorly in school.

By age 30, aggressive 8-year-olds were more likely to have been:

- Convicted of a crime
- Convicted of a crime of a more serious nature
- Charged with more moving traffic violations
- Convicted of a traffic violation involving chemical intoxication
- More abusive of their spouses

Overall, aggressive 8-year-olds in the study were found to have achieved less than their nonaggressive peers in the areas of academics, in their professions, and socially. A clear, direct correlation existed between aggression as a child and criminal involvement as an adult. But the most important finding is one that validates other research in this field and has strong implications for parents: Aggressive 8-year-olds who grew into aggressive adults were more likely as well to have children who were also aggressive.

We must be clear on the implications of the studies by Huesmann and his colleagues. Children who exhibit consistent aggressive behaviors as early as the third grade may be establishing a behavioral pattern that will last the rest of their lives and be passed along to their children. This is a profound piece of the puzzle in our efforts to understand the importance and implications of the bully-victim relationship. Failure to act early in countering the aggressive behaviors of children may well be a life sentence for those individuals to (a) continue a lifetime of aggression, and (b) pass those aggressive tendencies on to their children, hence setting the stage for the next generation of potential bullies.

GIRLS JUST WANNA HAVE FUN—OH, REALLY?

As previously noted, aggressive behaviors are not limited to only the male side of the human species. Girls can be just as vicious in the use of intimidation. While girls do become physically aggressive, particularly when involved in gang activities, most female harassment is nonverbal. It attacks the most sacred item within Girl World—the relationship.

Relational Aggression

Bullying among females has been termed **relational aggression** and has been viewed with much the same foolish neglect as with boys. While "boys will be boys," with girls and relational aggression it is "well, that's just how girls solve their problems."

Intimidation among girls relies heavily on psychological prowess. Because of the way girls are raised in Western society, with an emphasis on relating to and communicating with others, it only follows that girls will use the tools with which they are most knowledgeable during disputes. While boys are raised to be more physical and outwardly expressive of aggression—hence they are more likely to hit—girls are encouraged to suppress their aggression and to express frustrations in more "socially acceptable" ways. The expression of aggression, then, is manifested in attacking other females at the sources of their power—social skills and relationships.

Rumors and Misinformation

Girls use rumors and misinformation as a primary mode of attack. Rumors often focus on the sexual reputation of a target, particularly among adolescents: "She's such a ho" or "slut," along with whomever the target is supposed to have been having sex with (usually multiple partners), and the number and names of sexually transmitted infections the target is supposed to be carrying are common themes among heterosexual rumors. Of course, labeling one a lesbian is always a favorite. Misinformation is designed to create more havoc in the life of a target. Its most common form comes under the ruse of "Did you hear what she said about you?" or in the exaggeration of incidents to make them appear more ominous than they really were. Both rumors and misinformation are designed to chip away at the status or reputation of the target. The basic goal of intimidation is the same, be it practiced among boys or girls—either take power *away* from a target or exert power *over* the target.

Shunning

Shunning is another form of nonphysical aggression practiced to an art form among females. This is especially true in the formation of cliques during the middle school and junior high school years and is especially painful. Shunning is the equivalent of the kiss of death among teens, especially girls, because it involves denying to the target that which is most valuable within Girl World—social interaction. Shunning may result in a target's forming new friendships, which is often the case wherein students bounce from clique to clique and sometimes back again over the course of a school day. In the worst-case scenario, the agents manage to convince all within the social realm of the target to avoid having anything to do with her, making the target a social pariah within her peer group. Shunning of this magnitude is "deadly," because it is designed to totally isolate a target from any peer contact. No one talks to the target, sits by her at lunch, agrees to willingly partner with her in school day assignments, or invites her to informal afterschool social activities—all peer interaction is eliminated. This type of shunning is usually instigated by a strong in-group leader who exerts tremendous power over her domain. She is truly, as Rosaland Wiseman penned in 2002, the *queen bee.* The target becomes, in Rachel Simmons's words, the *odd girl out.*

I highly recommend the writings of Rosalind Wiseman (*Queen Bees and Wannabes: Helping Your Daughter Survive Cliques, Gossip, Boyfriends and Other Realities of Adolescence*) and Rachel Simmons (*Odd Girl Out: The Hidden Culture of Aggression in Girls*). Both of these books examine the phenomenon of female aggression through the eyes of female writers with an insight that only females can provide. The books are different in their approach. Wiseman's book is more informal, conversational, and perhaps even a little humorous; Simmons's book is more studious, yet easy to read. Both books are filled with examples of Girl World reality, which both educators and parents need to be keyed in to. Wiseman's book ultimately became the basis for the 2004 teen flick *Mean Girls*, a movie I wholeheartedly recommend for both its insight into relational aggression and the view it gives into the lives of kids who are incessantly hammered to fit in. It is quite well done, too.

Female Intimidation and Consequences

It is important to recognize the power of intimidation among females and its potential to do just as much long-term psychological damage as intimidation among boys. In addition to all the other silly stereotypical messages we send females in society about appearance, demeanor, and behavior, a chronic dose of put-downs from their peer groups will likely cement low self-esteem for those girls who are less resilient. Words can and do hurt in ways not marked by physical bruises. Words can become either the inspiration to overcome the challenges one faces or the nails in the coffin of self-loathing. Put-downs drill themselves deep into the psyche of a child and fester during times alone, especially if that solitude is the result of shunning. And if relational aggression at school is combined with negative messages from home, how do children in these circumstances learn anything positive about the self or their futures? The world does not appear to be such a nice place to live under these conditions.

That was the conclusion of a 15-year-old girl subjected to many of the textbook examples of relational aggression. She had been targeted by two girls since the elementary grades. The harassment only got worse with each year's progression into high school. She had threatening messages written to and about her in school bathrooms and at bus stops. The agents started rumors that she had been raped. They made intimidating phone calls to her home phone and did the same via text messaging on her cell phone. Her grades plummeted. As a last resort, her parents tried to have her transferred to another school, but she could not gain admission because it was filled to capacity and was taking no more students.

"I was sick of it all," she said. "I just wanted it all to stop. I did try to kill myself—I just couldn't take it anymore."

Fortunately, in this instance, her suicide attempt was unsuccessful. But many others do not have the same outcome. A 12-year-old middle school girl chose to end her life after years of taunting. She was the odd girl out of the in-group. She was quiet and shy. She dressed in dark clothes and identified with the Goth community. She read about Wicca, a religion identified with witchcraft. In retaliation, her peers would sing Christian hymns to embarrass her. Her private journal revealed much of the pain she felt during her time at school: "Everyone is against me. Still death will come sooner or later for me. Will I ever have friends again?" She hanged herself in her bedroom closet.

Over 100 classmates went to her funeral. "I'm sorry if I said mean things to you. I didn't mean them. It was the easiest way for me to hide what was wrong with me," wrote one of her classmates. "I am sorry that it led to this," wrote another. "None of it should have happened. If only they had understood, then you would still be alive."

But she did not believe that anyone understood. The actions of her tormentors supported that belief. She made a decision to stop the suffering.

BULLIES AND SUPPORT

As I have conducted my workshops across the nation, I am probably one of the few (and maybe the first) who have taken the controversial stance of publicly advocating *for* bullies. That's right—I advocate for bullies as well as their victims. Clearly a full explanation is in order, and you will have to wait until the final chapters to understand exactly what I mean. But in the short run, let me make it crystal clear: Those who act aggressively must be held accountable for their actions. I have no sympathy for the actions of those who harm others—but I also have much empathy and understanding for what encourages their actions. Bullies are accountable for their behaviors, but we often do not hold them to it under the quick-fix guise of punishment. In the next section of the book, we will dig deeper into the stories that bullies tell and the ways in which we can help them to stop their destructive ways.

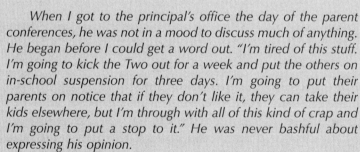

When I got to the principal's office the day of the parent conferences, he was not in a mood to discuss much of anything. He began before I could get a word out. "I'm tired of this stuff. I'm going to kick the Two out for a week and put the others on in-school suspension for three days. I'm going to put their parents on notice that if they don't like it, they can take their kids elsewhere, but I'm through with all of this kind of crap and I'm going to put a stop to it." He was never bashful about expressing his opinion.

I just listened. I honestly could not disagree with his sentiments about wanting to solve the problem by making it go away through punishment, but there was something grinding inside me that I could not exactly put to words—at least not at that moment. He continued to talk about his frustrations with the Two, about how unruly the whole school had seemed to be of late, and other things of which I lost track. I had managed to put myself into a self-absorbed trance as he talked, thinking about what I had seen outside my office that day and Bruce's words.

"Except it won't," I blurted out. The words just came out before I realized what I had said. It interrupted the principal's rant in midstream.

"What?" he asked. "Excuse me?" He actually meant, "Excuse you!"

"Nothing will change if we just boot the boys out and go on with business as usual." This was not my Good Cop role speaking; it was the result of my mulling over Bruce's words for two days.

The principal looked at me with both curiosity and vinegar. "What?"

"Nothing will change if all we do is kick out the Two and the others and then leave them alone until they get caught doing the same thing again to somebody else. Those boys are trouble, there's no argument there. But maybe the reason they do what they do is because we haven't looked at them from any other angle except only the one we want to see."

The principal was not amused. "What are you talking about? Have you lost your mind? These kids are the ones who poison the well for all the others! The sooner we're shed of them, the better."

"No!" I shot back. "It won't get better. They'll just go somewhere else and do it again to somebody else's kid."

We were truly at loggerheads. This was no Good Cop, Bad Cop routine now. We were legitimately butting heads with each other, both philosophically and professionally.

"Well, as long as it's not in this school, let somebody else deal with it. I've made up my mind. The Two are out of here for five days and the others are on in-school, and that's that. And when the Two come back, I'm going to watch them like a hawk and do everything in my power to get them out of here for good. And we're through for today, Walt." He shuffled his hands my way to shoo me out of the office. I got the impression he was hinting that I should leave. Hey, I can read nonverbal communication with the best of them!

I turned to walk out the door, still frustrated over the previous two days. And that's when he said it.

"Unless . . . ," he smirked. I stopped in the doorway. He didn't say anything else. When I turned, he had an impish look on his face, that small grin he so often shared with me when we wrangled over kid issues. He was going to make me beg.

"Unless what?" I asked.

"Unless you think you can do something better."

Something better? Something better. Hmm. Something better . . .

PART II

Effective Intervention Strategies for Bullies and Victims

Parents and Schools as Partners

It is important to note the name and focus of the second half of the book. Intervention points are provided, but not solely for teachers, administrators, or school-based helping professionals in the "eduspeak" that so often excludes parents. The chapters that follow are intended to bring a common ground of understanding to help school personnel work with parents so that a partnership can develop on behalf of both those victimized by bullies and the bullies themselves. Remember, unless we are willing to include the bully in the problem-solving process, the problem behavior will continue somewhere else.

Schools achieve success in large part due to high levels of **positive parental involvement**. Notice that I said *positive*. There is nothing more unfair to an educational system and those who work in it than parents who carp about the problems within the schools but do little or nothing to improve the situation.

Schools are not responsible for raising our children. That is Parent Priority Numero Uno, and it is hard work. School personnel *do* have a responsibility to take all the positive attributes that we parents impart to our children and enhance them. One of those opportunities to enhance the positives that come from home is to teach additional skills of personal and social problem-solving and how to resolve disagreements with their minds instead of their fists. Children must understand that it is acceptable to have differences of opinions and that it is not necessary for someone to always be the winner in a dispute. School personnel must provide the role modeling of these behaviors. They must be able to show that it is okay to live in a world wherein we can learn to disagree agreeably.

THE ROLE OF THE TEACHER IN ADDRESSING THE BULLY-VICTIM RELATIONSHIP

The first and foremost interactive adults in the lives of our children outside of parents are the teachers in our schools. Society owes them a great debt for the nourishing intangibles that they bring with them for our kids. Teachers inspire us. They motivate us. They excite the passions of seeing new things in the world. Theirs is an awesome responsibility—they truly *do* teach the future—and it is one that, thankfully, so many of them take seriously and give straight from their hearts as well as their minds.

There are few things in life better for kids than a great teacher. There is also, unfortunately, nothing worse than an ineffective one or one who, while an expert in subject matter, knows little about or has forgotten the enthusiasms, pratfalls, and pains of growing up and how those personal foibles affect the overall well-being of a child and the ability to learn. One of the most disrespectful things that any teacher—good or not so—can do to students is to ignore the impact of harassment and how such behaviors poison the entire atmosphere of the school environment.

I know that of which I speak. I have heard comments and observed it firsthand too many times, as a teacher, as a school counselor, and even today when I visit as a supervisor of my interns and overhear conversations among teachers in the hallways of the schools in which they are training. Although I do think that schools do a better job than they did just five years ago, kids have told us these things for years, and they still claim it to be a factor in why they do not come to us today for help. My interns share some of the saddest stories of how bullying and teasing behaviors negatively impact the psyche of both young children and adolescents. I even hear excuses offered by some school personnel in the workshops I do across the nation. The following are exact quotes:

"My job is to teach. It's not my responsibility to take care of their petty squabbles."

"I wasn't taught in my teacher education program how to deal with their personal needs. For that matter, I'm not sure I want to."

"Kids just do that stuff to one another. It happened to me and I survived without too much wear and tear."

"With all the other responsibilities dumped on me, I simply don't have the inclination to pay attention to the fights between kids unless it gets physical right in front of me."

"They say that stuff to every kid these days. They're so used to it, they don't pay any attention to it, anymore."

These kinds of excuses do not dignify the profession of teaching. And if there is truth to any or part or all of the sentiments behind them, what does it say about how we are not responding to the needs of our kids since bullying and teasing behaviors are an *intergenerational* phenomenon?

Because teachers are such important role models and have the most contact with children second only to parents, teachers must recognize the powerful influential roles they play in every aspect of their responses to the lives and dilemmas of their students. Students are like sponges. They absorb every waking minute of what they see in their environment—even when they are not necessarily paying attention. In the elementary years, they are extraordinarily responsive to adults who generate fun and creativity in the classroom. In adolescence, as they individuate and try to become less dependent on adults for guidance, they become incredibly sensitive to the issues of fair play and equal treatment for their peers. Teens live by a mantra of "That's not fair!" and "You're not treating everybody the same!" As such, what teachers do and do not do on behalf of children and adolescents when bullying or teasing rears its ugly head are some of the most important teachable moments. It is at these moments that adults are judged by students as true to their words or hypocrites when it comes to providing a safe atmosphere for all children.

THE ROLE OF THE ADMINISTRATOR IN ADDRESSING THE BULLY-VICTIM RELATIONSHIP

Superintendents, principals, and vice principals have enough work to do without having to deal with all the complications of students who are bullied or teased. But they are in large part responsible for creating and maintaining a safe and inviting atmosphere for students, teachers, and parents alike. Administrators have a vested interest in addressing the issue of intimidation within the school setting. And, as has been evidenced, they may ultimately end up being held accountable in court decisions claiming that state or federal policies were not followed correctly. In the end, all roads lead to the administrator's office.

Through the years, administrators have been accused—in some cases rightly and in others wrongly—of neglecting the issue of bullying and teasing. Effective administrators accept the responsibility to oversee the proper implementation of bullying and prevention programs, and to ensure that all of the necessary measures are taken, such as:

- Meeting individually with parents of both victims and aggressors
- Disciplining aggressors appropriately
- Notifying all school staff to watch for specific behaviors directed toward victims, and providing them with materials to help them address issues of intimidation within the school
- Insisting that the school counselor (or related school-based helping professional) intervene extensively with all of the students involved, both targets and agents

School administrators do not have to be the ones to select which bullying prevention and intervention program is best for their schools. Their job is to lead and delegate. Certainly, they have a responsibility to be a part of the decision-making process and will, in all likelihood, end up in the accountability measures taken against the perpetrators of school disruption. An effective leader finds those within the school structure who can help to determine the type of approach best utilized for such a program. In doing so, they end up doing themselves a great favor. The more effective the prevention and intervention program is for a school, the less time that the administrator will have to deal with the fallout from when bullies act out. And some of the most helpful people that an administrator will be able to turn to within their school are those trained in the school-based helping professionals.

THE ROLE OF SCHOOL-BASED HELPING PROFESSIONALS IN ADDRESSING THE BULLY-VICTIM RELATIONSHIP

What do we mean by **school-based helping professionals**? They typically are those employed to assist the classroom teacher by attending to the mental and physical health of the child. The most common of such individuals in every school are the *school counselor*, the *school social worker*, the *school psychologist*, and the *school nurse*. It may also include helping professionals from the same backgrounds as those who are in private practice or who work with county governments who are hired by the schools or placed there by grants to provide similar services. It is important to note that the designation of "school" before each of these professions is not simply because of their placement. For example, a school counselor has a different expertise and focus of study from that of the private therapeutic counselor. School counselors have taken coursework specific for working with school populations and understanding the culture of the school environment. Many have backgrounds as former teachers. They are likely to be more aware of the networks of referral and assistance available in school settings than the counselor in private practice. Most importantly, because of their selection of the school in which to ply their skills, they may have a greater communication ability and desire to work with children and adolescents in these settings rather than the clientele selection of the private therapist.

Most school nurses are not involved directly in working with bullies, but they may well see their handiwork through the injuries sustained by the victims. School psychologists are primarily employed as assessment specialists and consultation experts to work with those in need of special education. While many prefer to work solely in the area of tests and assessment, others may have had additional interpersonal skills training so as to increase their communication quotient with kids. Most states, but not all, employ school counselors at both the elementary and secondary levels. They are the helping professionals most likely to be familiar to parents who desire to speak with someone who deals with "kid problems." School counselors have extensive training in interpersonal communication skills designed to increase the effectiveness of their abilities to understand the surface and subsurface communications of the children with whom they work. The vast majority of states require a minimum of a master's degree for licensure or certification to work in schools. School social workers are typically employed to work with the children of families in need of home intervention. Many schools choose to use outside social service agencies and county government social workers in lieu of hiring their own. School social workers may or may not have had the training in interpersonal communication skills as that required of school counselors. School social workers in many states require only a bachelor's degree to be eligible to work in school settings.

Regardless of which helping professionals are employed within a particular setting, they are likely the primary professionals who should be employed to help design a violence prevention program within that school. Because helping professionals focus on those aspects of student life that most commonly fall outside direct classroom instruction, the nature of the kinds of interaction that they have with those students is also much different. When administrators and teachers are not able to communicate with a child, school counselors often can because of the nonbiased way that they are viewed by that child. When no one can understand why a student is falling asleep in classes, a visit to the home of the student by the school social worker may reveal that nine people are sharing a one-bedroom home. When the school psychologist determines that there is no functional reason for a student to perform so poorly in school, a few minutes spent with that student beyond the tests may reveal that the student has had his homework destroyed by bullies for the past 6 months. And when a female student habitually complains of stomach pains on the way to school and wants to avoid coming altogether, the school nurse discovers the bruises inflicted on her body by her aggressors on the playground every day at lunchtime.

Helping professionals in schools, when left unimpeded to do their jobs, are a great boon to teachers and administrators. They can head off discipline problems before they occur. They can share necessary information with teachers to help them better understand the conditions under which a child functions. Operating with ethical and legal obligations of confidentiality, students can share information with them about their personal lives that they do not feel comfortable sharing with anyone else. When students will not tell other adults about their mistreatment at the hands of bullies, they may well tell the school helping professional because of the sense of privacy that they know they will receive from them.

If possible, it is strongly suggested that any committee or team effort to design a school's violence prevention program include all of these individuals. The helping professionals within the school best skilled in the art of interpersonal communication can usually facilitate team meetings most effectively. *Under no circumstance should these groups of professionals be left out of the planning loop.* They know far too much about the secret life of Kid World to be excluded from such planning.

A FOUR-POINT STRATEGIC INTERVENTION FOR SCHOOL PERSONNEL TO STOP BULLY-VICTIM BEHAVIORS

There are a multitude of suggestions that profess success in breaking the cycle of the bully-victim relationship. Some work and some do not. Some work in some situations but fail to work in others. Finding the right solutions for a particular school environment or to reach an individual personality type requires hard work and persistence.

No one solution will work for every aggressor or victim, nor will one curricular approach be able to solve all aggressive behaviors in a school setting. Do not buy into the mind-set that one size fits all. Such a belief is doomed to failure.

So much of what works in bullying prevention and intervention efforts are the *people* who can make a connection with a kid in need. If I were to advocate for one factor that is more effective than others in an intervention approach, that would be the magic key.

The four points that you are about to read do work. I know because not only did they work for me as a practicing school counselor in a seventh- through twelfth-grade setting, but those who implement these steps today report back to me that they still work. The level of success varies for different schools and different school personnel. There seem to be two constants when a school reports that these four points worked:

1. A sincere commitment exists among a majority of the participants to make their school a safe place for all kids.

2. School staff are effective in matching kids in need of assistance with the right school personnel who have high levels of trust between student and adult.

To what degree a school chooses to tackle the problem of peer-on-peer abuse is up to its staff. Likewise, the kind of curricula it chooses to use is a matter of budget and recommendation (for more information on curricular considerations, see the last chapter of the book). While I identify some curricular options available to schools, the school must ultimately determine what is best for its particular setting and students. The approaches needed to be effective on the prairies of South Dakota may not—and probably would not!—be the same as what would eventually be found to be useful in urban Atlanta. School personnel are likely to find that the effort is even more effective when it enlists the support and advice of parents and members of the community.

6

Strategic Intervention Point 1

The Best Intervention Is Prevention

W hy wait until an ugly or high-profile incident occurs within a school setting? It is always better to be *proactive* rather than *reactive* to any problem. Because we know that bullying and teasing behaviors do occur among all segments of children and adolescents in school environments, it is safe to make the assumption that these behaviors are occurring in every school within the nation. But to what degree and under what conditions do they exist in your particular school or throughout the school district? If this information is not known, school personnel have a need to know, because knowing the frequency and dynamics of a misbehavior is the first step toward designing a plan to deal with it.

SURVEYING THE STUDENT BODY

Surveying the student body of a school does not have to be a complicated task. It should, however, focus on the major types of information that are needed. Examples of survey instruments can be found in many bullying prevention books and curricula such as those highlighted at the end of this book, but it is not necessary to have a particular survey in hand or administer a specific one. Any school can design its own data-gathering instrument, and every school should modify any survey model it uses to be most relevant for its situation. For instance, if a question on a template survey that an elementary school is using asks students to identify different locations where intimidation occurs and one of the options is "student parking lot," but there are no such things on the campus, then why should that item be included on the survey? By the same token, if there are options that need to be added for a specific school situation that are not included in the survey model being consulted, why should they not be added? Common sense dictates that all data-gathering instrumentation used in a school setting should gather the *right* kinds of information, not just *more* information that is useless and clutters the problem-solving process.

DESIGNING THE SURVEY

There are certain basic sets of information and conditions that are necessary for any survey related to examining the frequency of bullying and teasing in a school setting. This section explores six basic considerations.

1. Safeguard the Anonymity of Those Who Take the Survey

Children are far more likely to tell us the truth when they know that their answers will not be traced directly back to them, especially if they are afraid of being persecuted for revealing the truth. As such, only generic descriptive information is needed for each survey inclusive of sex and grade. Always remember, the more identification that is requested on a survey, the more likely it is that the child who responds to it can be identified and may feel unsafe or insecure in responding. Additionally, children should be afforded the opportunity to provide their answers in as private a fashion as possible. Cover sheets can help in this endeavor, as can adequate seating space between each student so as to reduce the possibility of anyone seeing another student's replies. One helpful way to increase privacy is to remind everyone about how important privacy is to each other and how it is respectful to honor privacy among friends and peers.

2. The "Language" of the Survey Must Be Appropriate and Comprehensible for the Group That Will Be Reading It

While this certainly refers to age and grade levels, it may well also refer to the primary spoken language of the respondents. That decision must be made at the local level. If translations to other languages are necessary, it is imperative that the wording remain as true to course as possible so as to avoid misinterpretations within different cultures. The most important element in the reference to "language" refers to the wording used within the age and grade levels to which a survey is given. It is my recommendation that serious consideration be given to four distinct groups of students and how the wording may be understood within each group: early elementary grades, upper elementary grades, middle or junior high grades, and high school grades. Each of these groups may require different types of surveys, especially between the elementary and secondary levels. Clearly, the ways in which a survey is administered to students will change. First and second graders cannot read independently well enough to respond and will have to have their surveys read to them. Likewise, the ways in which students answer the surveys will differ. Younger children are more likely to be able to answer with happy faces for "Yes" and frowny faces for "No." Older children and adolescents can determine degrees of an answer: "On a scale of 1 to 5, with 1 being 'least' and 5 being 'most,' how do you feel about the following statements?"

3. Always KISS the Survey: Keep It Short and Simple

Perhaps one of the hardest tasks for designers of a survey is determining the *most relevant* issues for which they are seeking answers. There is always the tendency to ask too many questions. While in-depth information is better, a survey that is too long will likely become less accurate toward the end as the students tire. Adolescents can answer more questions than early elementary–age children. The format must lend itself to the time requirements of the instrument. While multiple-choice options to questions will provide a broad-based spectrum of behaviors in a shorter time span, short-answer questions will provide deeper explanations but require more time. A solid strategy may well be to do two surveys. A first survey would be the broad-based, multiple-choice option to gather initial information. A second survey would be shorter and based on the information gathered in the first, but with more specific questions requiring short or longer written answers from the students.

4. Survey Enough Students

How many is enough? How many are too few? Statisticians tell us that the best surveys are those from which at least 80% of those who take it respond. Such a return might be feasible in smaller school buildings or districts but impractical in larger ones. The basic rule, however, stands: A higher percentage of students who can be included in the results pool is likely to yield more accurate results. Lower percentages of students are more likely to be influenced by individuals providing incorrect information. If possible, survey everyone. If not, determine what is practical within the school setting and get as many as possible. I recommend surveying no less than 50% of any student group. In large school settings, it may be practical to survey every other grade or every other classroom in a particular grade. Be certain to include a wide spectrum of the student body in any survey that is conducted. Do not give the survey to groupings of students who are likely to be more representative of a particular segment of the school. In other words, a survey given only to high school students in eleventh-grade advanced placement classes will likely provide different information than a survey that is inclusive of all students within the school setting.

5. Ask the Right Questions

This is perhaps the most important part of any survey. It requires some first-hand knowledge and intuition about what kinds of student behaviors are occurring. If not already known, brief conversations with trusted students are likely to provide excellent ideas. First and foremost, make certain to provide a solid definition of the terms of which you are seeking information! It is of the utmost importance to have workable and easily understood definitions of "bullying" and "teasing." The 9 categories of information that will be useful in helping to determine the right questions are as follows:

- Has bullying/teasing been observed in the school?
- Has bullying/teasing occurred directly to the student?
- Who/which group is most frequently bullied/teased?
- Who/which group seems to be most likely to bully/tease?
- Where does bullying/teasing occur?
- When does bullying/teasing occur?
- Do those who are bullied/teased ask for help?
- What do other students do when they see bullying/teasing?
- What does the school do when students report bullying/teasing?

Students may be given the option of writing short comments. Remember, these are basic categories of requests for information. Each category clearly requires multiple questions to gather the kind of information needed to develop a response plan. It is clear to see how multiple-choice options provide an easy format for such categories. For instance, a single question may well take care of the category of determining where bullying or teasing most frequently occurs:

When bullying or teasing occurs to you or others, where is it most likely to happen? (Mark all that apply.)

(a) Restrooms

(b) Parking lot

(c) Classroom

(d) Bus or bus stop

(e) Gym

(f) Playground

(g) Home neighborhood

In a large school, the questions might need to be more specific.

When bullying or teasing occurs to you or others, where is it most likely to happen? (Mark all that apply.)

(a) First-floor restrooms

(b) Second-floor restrooms

(c) Third-floor restrooms

(d) North-end parking lot

(e) West-end parking lot

6. Act on the Information That Is Collected

Information that is collected and sits on a shelf or is reported only for the sake of reporting, with little or no intention of acting according to what such a needs assessment indicated, is of no use to anyone, least of all the kids. As soon as is possible, the data from the survey should be compiled and collated into some kind of intelligible reporting mechanism. Decisions must be made as to the interpretation of the data. What exactly are the kids telling us about their experiences? Is there a pattern to the information? Can specific targets of action be identified for a clear first step? It is important to share the information with the students in some form. At the elementary level, this could be something as simple as the following:

Boys and girls, you remember those questions you answered for us last week about bullying and teasing in our school? We have read what you told us and we are very grateful for your answers. Because you were so honest and gave us so much useful information, we have decided that we all need to learn some ways to help us cooperate with each other more and learn better ways of solving disagreements. So, starting today, and for each day from now until the end of the year, we will learn one new way each day to solve problems and settle arguments with one another.

USING THE SURVEY

With adolescents, the update on the use of the survey data might be more straightforward and could well be done not only in the classroom but also in the school newspaper. Parents too need to know that actions are being undertaken to improve the school climate. How much of the details a school building or school district will want or need to share is a local decision; but once collected, no effort should be made to "hide" the data from public scrutiny or "spin" the results if the information is not what a school would prefer that it was. No matter how disappointed we may be in the results of a survey, the focus must always be kept on the improvements that will occur as a result of receiving the information. It is better to know how bad a situation may be so that efforts can be designed to improve it, rather than ignoring it and having our children continue to be abused by things that we could prevent from happening.

I have consulted with and seen many different variations of surveys and results from school districts through the years. Additionally, my interns often gather survey data on the same topic. I never fail to be amazed at what those surveys reveal. Most of the first-time results reveal percentages of bullying and teasing behaviors far in excess of what was anticipated within the school. Depending on what kinds of and how the questions were asked, the kids were almost always unanimous in being able to pick out exactly where and when bullying and teasing were likely to occur within their school. Given the chance to provide additional information through an open comment option, they were even more explicit in the details of what was happening. Most schools are shocked by the raw numbers of students who report that they have been subjected to bullying and teasing themselves. It is important to make certain that those who review the results do not lose perspective of how percentages translate into actual numbers of students. While 5% may be a small percentage, when translated into a high school of 2,000 students, suddenly that 5% becomes 100. Depending on what is being measured—the number of students who want to take calculus next year or the number of students who are indicating that they have suicidal thoughts on occasion—small percentages take on great significance when put in the proper perspectives.

One school went so far as to ask of those who indicated that they had bullied others the reasons why they chose to do so. The top three reasons were that they "don't know" (third), "to get even because they were bothering me" (second), and because they "did not like" the person whom they bullied (first). This same school faculty pledged itself to tackling head-on the problem of rude and disrespectful behaviors among students. The survey data were used to design a plan of attack and within the first semester of increasing staff presence in the high-frequency areas of bullying reduced the behaviors by almost half! This occurred simply by redirecting staff resources to be visible in previously unknown unsafe areas of the school grounds. It cost no additional funds and created no additional workload for anyone. In fact, one teacher indicated that by merely walking 15 feet to the corner of the hallway during class changes, she was able to monitor a locker area that previously had been the scene of—until the survey results came in—a tremendous amount of harassment among a group of girls. The victims reported to the teacher that after she made this simple move, all of the teasing that they had received from the aggressors stopped, because when they were at the lockers was the only time during the entire school day that these two groups of girls had any contact with one another.

Of course, having the data on what is going on before an intervention program is in place is the basis for being able to discover how effectively the program has worked. It is essential at some later point to gather information on whether bullying and teasing have been reduced. Only with a first survey can such a determination be made.

I began my work with bullies long before I knew exactly what I was doing. Because I had shot my mouth off in the principal's office, I felt obligated to do something—I truly had no idea what—with both sides of the incident. Bruce needed help; there was no argument there. His plight was clear. What bothered me, though, was my growing conviction that kids like the Terrible Two must be operating out of their own set of desperate views about life. Why else would they be so ornery? Well, yes, each was "meaner than a junkyard dog." True. But what was it that made them act up so? Even junkyard dogs are not born that way. They start out as cute puppies. So why were the Terrible Two already junkyard dogs at the ripe old age of 13?

No one taught me diddly about dealing with bullies in undergrad teacher prep or during graduate school while training to become a school counselor. In fact, in the early days of my school counseling career, scant attention was paid to the issue of bullying or teasing. It was, remember, in those days just "kid stuff." I came back to school the day after the principal had inflicted his disciplinary decree on the aggressors and went to work doing—what? I had absolutely no idea!

I did know enough to check with Bruce again the next morning. By then, two days after the attack, many of the bruises were beginning to turn black and blue. His demeanor was quite cheery considering what he had been through. Bruce was the relatively easy part. We met for a few minutes that morning and set up a schedule to meet at least once each week for the next three weeks—more if he felt he needed it—just to talk about life in general. I did not feel compelled to press him about the attack and the bullying he had received through the years unless he wanted to talk about it. It was his time, I told him, and he could spend it with me talking about anything he wanted to.

After meeting with Bruce, I took care of a few office details that had been placed aside in the chaos of the past two days. The paperwork never ends as a school counselor. Everybody needs something filled out, a letter of recommendation written, a standardized test reviewed. And all the while kids' needs never cease. They just keep lining up in the doorway to talk about the travails of their lives. No wonder I never got the unimportant paperwork done until after the end of the school year.

I finished all the paper I could stand and then rushed out of the office and down to the in-school suspension room where, among a few more of the inmates, there were the three toadies to the Two. They were diligently working on classroom assignments. When the work ran out at about noon, I would not have wanted to be the in-school warden during the tenure of their sentence. The truth is, I had no idea what I was about to do, even when I got to the doorway of the suspension room. I just decided to start by what I had been trained to do as a school counselor—listen.

7

Strategic Intervention Point 2

Safeguard the Victim

Protection of the injured is the first priority when responding to an incident of bullying and teasing. Protection may mean different responses in different situations. In its most simplest of forms, it may be separating a bully from the target of verbal insults with a stern warning and the promise to discuss the matter later. In its ugliest form, it may well mean isolating a physically injured student from his attackers and acting to obtain emergency medical care on his behalf. In either scenario, when an incident of bullying or teasing is reported, the supervisory personnel are required to respond to the situation. To ignore an act of intimidation between students may be grounds for being held liable for neglect under state or federal laws. In either instance, a student request for assistance after a bully-victim interaction requires a legitimate response.

While frightening to all involved, an incident of bullying that involves physical assault is actually the easiest with which to deal. At its simplest, it may be a crime and the matter should be turned over to the police. Incidences of physical assault most likely have specific policies within school district rules or state statutes that require that physical altercations between students be reported to legal authorities. This is more likely to be the case with adolescents in middle school who are involved in altercations, particularly if a bully is clearly identified as the sole aggressor.

But what about a physical assault in the elementary grades? And what about the assaults on the integrity of a child's self-esteem through verbal abuse or behaviors that float "just under the radar" and do not rise to the level of a legal intervention, such as knocking the books out of a target's hands on a daily basis or the exclusion from peer groups? How do school personnel protect kids from these kinds of abuse?

PROTECTING KIDS WHO HAVE FILED REPORTS

We have already established that it is impossible to protect children 24 hours a day unless a bodyguard is provided for such a purpose. Protection of a child or adolescent who reports being victimized will require an analysis of several key factors.

Is the Individual Who Is Reporting the Abuse Medically Safe Now?

This includes such considerations as the determination of any obvious injuries that the individual may claim or are readily apparent. Clearly, in instances of physical injury medical attention of some kind is in order, be it a Band-Aid to cover a scrape or a call to emergency services for a broken arm. It is important for school personnel to remember that students who report being hit in the head or torso may have internal injuries that are not apparent by a surface contusion. If ever there is a doubt, refer a physically assaulted student to the school nurse or medical personnel for medical attention.

Is the Individual Who Is Reporting the Abuse Physically Safe Now?

This is more likely to be a problem for upper elementary–grade children and adolescents, because bullies at these ages are more capable of mounting a sustained campaign of terror against their targets than children in the earlier elementary years. It is important to know the particulars of the circumstances under which the abuse occurred, if it was a single incident or if this report is just the first time that long-term harassment is coming to the attention of an adult. Remember, by the time most adults learn of bullying and teasing from the victims, it has most likely been occurring for a long period of time. If the individual who is reporting the teasing is willing to provide the information, it is likely to help when deciding about holding the victimizers accountable, the likelihood of retaliation by them, and the relative safety of the abused both now and in the longer term.

Providing an immediate safe environment for a child might well involve rounding up the accused parties as soon as possible to place them on a "do not contact" order with the victim until all the facts are collected, which will help to determine how to proceed toward the next consideration in this strategic intervention point. *Immediate safety issues always come first.* Holding the responsible parties accountable for their actions can come only after all the facts surrounding the problem behaviors are known. This avoids a judgment or accountability action made in haste.

Is the Individual Who Is Reporting the Abuse Physically Safe for the Long Term?

This is a tougher determination to make, and it is one that will involve more time than is usually available in the immediate aftermath of a reported incident of abuse. Much consideration must be given at this point to *assessing the likelihood of retaliation* against the child who reported the teasing. Considerations of retaliation and of longer term safety within the confines of the school setting must take into account such factors as: Does the child reporting the victimization feel as if future incidents of abuse are likely to occur? Does the child want the harassment to stop? (As strange as this may sound, while wanting and needing immediate security and reassurance from an adult in the wake of the most recent unpleasant incident, children do not always want their attackers to be punished for fear of being further excluded from a peer group.) What are the chances of success that any intervention designed for use in the school setting will work?

School personnel can do only so much in the refereeing of disputes among children. They can be alert to potential problem areas and potential problem students, but they cannot—and should not have to!—personally escort victimized children from point to point during the school day as a 100% safeguard against further bullying or teasing. Ultimately we want a safe school phenomenon to emerge from a *total school philosophy*, where school personnel and students respect each other, where safe personal and behavioral boundaries are enforced by all, and where students know how to resolve conflicts peacefully and with the techniques to be effective in their assertiveness.

Is the Incident of Bullying or Teasing a "Reportable Offense" According to Local, State, or Federal Guidelines?

This consideration in responding to safeguarding an individual who reports harassment, particularly if it involves bullying, is one that students may not fully understand or appreciate, although it may be a factor in their consideration to not report such abuse. What is a "reportable offense"? It can mean anything from an offense that requires nothing more than documenting the incident within the confines of the local school disciplinary records to one that is a full-blown investigation by school and legal authorities designed to provide evidence for criminal or civil prosecution. As previously mentioned, most states today have statutory language related to how schools within their jurisdictions must handle incidents that have been determined to fall under the definition of specific types of harassment. Clearly some incidences of bullying or teasing will fall under these definitions—many reports related to sexual harassment, surprisingly, could be filed on behalf of males as a result of the blatant attempts by aggressors to denigrate other males' sexuality by both verbal and physical assaults, inclusive of statutory sodomy, which often occurs during athletic hazing incidents. Some states have moved directly to laws that specifically define the behaviors and conditions of bullying and teasing. Most local school districts have policies related to the types of accountability mechanisms that are to be employed if those involved with bullying and teasing continue to engage in such behaviors.

Does this mean that every little fracas between two kids is now a "crime"? No. Does it mean that every last little bump in the hallway that looks suspicious should be documented? No. To do so would be an overreaction and burden to everyone involved. There will be many times when school personnel will have to use their best professional judgment to determine how to proceed with an incident between students that has the appearances of victimization but not all the facts to back it up. There must always be room for teachers, administrators, and school counselors to use professional judgment. But, as I always tell my interns, once a professional judgment is made in a foggy situation, it had better be the correct one because everyone has to live with the consequences from that point forward. Worse, if the decision is made in error, those who are wronged have recourse to recoup their losses in the courts for many years after the original incident happens. There is no better example of this than the following case.

CASE STUDY: WHEN SCHOOL PERSONNEL FAIL TO ACT RESPONSIBLY

A high school girls' softball team had long practiced the hazing ritual of "depantsing" freshman-year players. Along with other aggravations thrown at the new team members throughout that initial year, the major event of depantsing involved catching the unsuspecting individuals at a vulnerable moment, restricting their movements so as to prevent escape (usually this involved several upper-level teammates gang-tackling the individuals or catching them from behind while holding their arms and legs), and pulling the pants down around the ankles or, if possible, completely off. This was always done in the presence of other team members (usually in the locker room). Everyone supposedly had a good laugh, and as is so often the **groupthink** ("Hey, everybody does it! We've always done it. Nobody's said anything to us before; what's the big deal now?") behind hazing, it was considered to be a "welcoming" tradition to their high school years. The depantsing of the new members never took place at the same time. Each new team member knew that her time would come; exactly when or where it would occur was a part of the stealth of the aggressors. Whether the coaches and other school personnel involved with the sport knew of the depantsing was unclear. It is hard to believe, however, that they did not.

Due to a rain delay at one away game, the team was waiting on the bus until conditions improved. The delay grew longer and the players began to resort to all manner of shenanigans to keep themselves occupied. Some did their homework, some read, and others engaged in horseplay. The coaching staff and the driver sat in the front portion of the bus and let the girls tend to their own business as long as it was not too noisy.

At some point during the delay, a decision was made to depants one of the new team members. A ruckus ensued at the back of the bus and soon, after quite a struggle, the deed was completed. The adults were aware that some kind of peer-on-peer hijinks was being undertaken in the back because of the noise level and laughter, but they allowed it to continue until after the depantsing had occurred and provided little in the way of discipline or structure to restore order or take an accounting of exactly what had happened to whom when things died down.

The next day, the ninth-grade girl who had been hazed reported the incident to her school counselor. The two of them talked about the episode and, according to the girl, about her feelings of being humiliated. After several more meetings with the student, the counselor felt that the player had accepted the incident as nothing more than a harmless ritual that all incoming players experienced. It is unclear if a report of any kind by any adults who knew about the incident was made to other school personnel in such a manner so as to warrant discipline of the responsible parties. It is also unclear what, if any, follow-up or additional investigation was done by the coaches.

Four years later, during the girl's freshman year of college, the school district was sued by the student over the incident. The suit claimed that school personnel had failed to seriously investigate the matter or consider the incident as a serious complaint. There were allegations that the district had encouraged the behavior through an atmosphere of institutionalized neglect toward such hazing. The students who had actually done the depantsing were not sued, but the coaches, the school counselor, and the principal were. The student's main contention in the suit claimed that she had been psychologically harmed from the humiliation she received in the hazing, and the trauma of the event had injured her abilities to play college sports or receive sports-related scholarships.

The suit asked for monetary damages. It was settled out of court for an undisclosed amount.

Say what you will about this case, but it has all the earmarks of a textbook example for school personnel of what *not* to do. Let us assume for the moment that the coaches actually were not aware of what had happened on the bus and that the school counselor was the first point of contact for the student's expression of distress about the matter. Should the school counselor have broken the student's confidence over the matter and reported the hazing to the coach and principal? It depends. If the student had agreed that she wanted the counselor to work with her as an advocate to redress the wrongs of the behavior, then the counselor would have had clear permission to use the student's confidences in taking the matter to other relevant school personnel. If, on the other hand, she had asked the counselor not to do so, the question remained, should the counselor have shared information about this incident with others, such as the principal?

In this instance there was a policy that defined the actions that took place on the bus as a reportable incident under the guidelines of harassment. It is unknown if the counselor actually followed through on the matter. The plaintiff claimed that it was not done; the school claimed it did.

The school did not do enough to prevent the depantsing ritual from having occurred. If nothing else, the disturbance at the back of the bus, had it immediately been thoroughly investigated on-site by the adults in charge, would have led to the discovery of the hazing rituals.

Should the school have been held accountable for the loss of scholarships and other claimed mental anguish as a result of the depantsing four years earlier? Whether it should have and whether the student who sued had a legitimate right to claim that the humiliation from the incident was the cause of her loss of prospective college sports opportunities became secondary matters to the prime grievance driving the case: negligence on the part of the school to act to prevent and stop behaviors that were considered harassment in the eyes of the court. Because the school personnel did not act on what the court considered compelling evidence of the existence of such hazing behaviors, which *should have been known* to school officials, the case was allowed to go forward. At that point, the student's claims of being harmed by the school's refusal or oversight to act to prevent such hazing from happening were considered to have enough merit so as to win judgment.

This case is a sobering reminder of what can happen when school personnel fail to act responsibly. Furthermore, it is a powerful reminder that aggrieved individuals have the right to ask that past wrongs be righted *years* after the fact of their occurrence. The statute of limitations on assault and harassment vary by state. The courts, however, are likely to be more lenient in accepting cases wherein adults sue over incidents that occurred when they were children and adolescents, especially when the wrongs happened under the scrutiny of caregivers.

One at a time, I quietly asked each of the Terrible Two's three coconspirators to come visit with me in my office for a while. Of course, it was such a captive audience, and it wasn't like they were going to be going anywhere anytime soon, so, yeah, sure, they were eager to come down. Anything to get out of in-school suspension for any length of time.

It became clear as I talked with the three that each of them had participated in the attack on Bruce for virtually the exact same reasons—because they thought they could get away with it; because they weren't the ones who started it; and because they weren't the only ones involved in it (and, by the way, why weren't the others being punished?). It was also clear that these three liked the intoxicating power of invulnerability they felt while in the presence of the Two. They began to vicariously experience the thrill of pestering other kids by first watching the Two do their voodoo. Then they began to join in on the actual taunting of targets. Eventually they helped to arrange situations that would victimize targets. In the beginning, they were the perfect ones for the setups, because no one knew they were in cahoots with the Two. Later their brazenness and boldness increased as the Two allowed them (and apparently others who had not been caught in this instance) to participate in their chaos. While they all had almost identical stories, one theme kept emerging from all of them that was exactly the same: They did what they did because they could. No one stopped them. Not peers or adults. Of course, it wasn't like they did their shenanigans in front of teachers on a regular basis. Most of the time the victimization was arranged to go on out of sight of adults who would most certainly have intervened. But there had been many times when smaller, less blatant behaviors were indeed overlooked or misinterpreted by teachers. Such times convinced everyone involved—participants, victims, and bystanders—that the adults really were not concerned about such things as shoves and bumps in the hallway, books that were "accidentally" knocked out of others' hands, classwork of targets crumpled by agents before it was turned in (if not outright destroyed), or "accidents" in the cafeteria that created a deluge of food on unsuspecting victims.

It was also clear that these three toadies were worried about the future. While the Two were out for a week, these three were now without their power base. Because they had been caught, the three were now under the scrutiny of the entire faculty—or at least they felt like we would be able to watch them all the time. A little dose of self-induced and short-term paranoia would not harm them any, I thought. But what bothered me the most was the sense that each one of them was just biding time until the Two returned so that they could start all over again. And that I was determined not to allow.

8

Strategic Intervention Point 3

Engage the Victim in Constructive and Supportive Interactions

This is perhaps one of the most important and hardest interventions to undertake, requiring a high level of patience and persistence. The level of difficulty involved in addressing this aspect of assisting the victim is matched only by the efforts and difficulty of the final point, that of assisting the perpetrators of such behaviors.

There are six critical aspects that comprise Strategic Intervention Point 3:

1. Listen to the story the victim tells.

2. Support the victim's efforts to belong to the school community in all its aspects.

3. Request permission from the victim to share necessary information (only!) with relevant school officials.

4. Determine when parents should be contacted.

5. Continue long-term supportive interaction for the victim.

6. Do not abandon the victim.

Some of these interventions can be done immediately after an incident of victimization is reported, while others are wide-ranging initiatives that could take months or years. Such is the magnitude of what is necessary to respond to the damaged psyches of those who are abused by their peers. Some students will respond more quickly than others to the remedies offered in this intervention. Each student will require monitoring to determine the extent of recovery.

1. LISTEN TO THE STORY THE VICTIM TELLS

Actually, it is more likely that victims will have many stories to tell, rather than just one. The key is in the listener's ability to hear what is being said.

Surface Stories and Inner Sagas

Every emotionally laden tale has two levels: a **surface story** and an underlying foundation, or **inner saga**, that always reveals far more than what lies at the surface. In counseling parlance, the inner saga is called the **metacommunication**. We will examine each of these story levels to help us understand how they are useful in learning to listen to the stories of those who come to tell us of their pain.

Listening is not easy. Well, "listening" may be easy, but do we actually "hear" what is being said? So much information passes through the air these days that we have grown to block out what we consider noise until we get to what we believe is the important part of the story, or to that part that is most relevant to us. This, of course, is **selective hearing**; and while it may be helpful for us to be able to ignore elevator music while conversing with our friend, it has tended to become the predominant form of listening that we do today, not just in selective settings, but in all environments and with all people, even with our closest family members.

For the vast majority of people who will work with victims of any kind of grievance, it is necessary to relearn the art of listening. Learning to listen so that we truly hear what a client is telling us is perhaps the cornerstone of the skills and techniques in the art of the counseling profession. While school counselors and related helping professionals within the schools may be the individuals best prepared to interact with victims who are tormented by bullies, *any* caring and sensitive adult in that child's life may well begin the process of healing by learning how to listen to the salient themes in that individual's story. *Every* adult in the school setting has the potential to begin that first step of the healing process. In the most kid-friendly and safe schools, they do. Adults in the school setting should never underestimate their abilities to influence kids for the positive.

When people tell a story about their lives, they reveal two things. In the surface story, they give details about "stuff"—things, people, and places. They give information about what they remember. They withhold information that they do not want others to know. Sometimes they honestly forget details. The surface story is filled with facts and fiction, but in the end, it is the primary picture through which people want us to view their world. It may or may not be accurate, but unless it is an absolute unabashed fabrication, it always contains some elements of the truth. The old Chinese proverb reminds us, "Even the clock which is stopped is right twice a day." That truth will be based on a canvas of the inner saga, which we will discuss in a moment.

The surface story can be viewed as an introduction to what people want us to know about them. Usually people in pain or desperation who seek help tell a more accurate surface story because it does them little good to alter the facts if true help is what they seek.

Here is a typical surface story:

I asked to see you, Mr. Young, because of what has been happening to me lately. I don't know who else to turn to. Yesterday I was cornered in the gym bathroom by a group of boys who have been bothering me and had my books thrown in the shower. It's not the first time that something like that has happened, but it's the first time they were able to ruin my books and now I don't have any books for class. I really don't know what to do. I need some help.

Opening surface stories are likely to be brief until further trust is established. Several important surface pieces of information are contained in this short interaction.

- The student had been having problems before this incident.
- This incident occurred in the gym locker room area.
- The incident involved a group of boys against one individual.
- The student's books were damaged.
- The student is frustrated in that he feels he has no other options available to him but to turn to an adult for assistance.

All of these things were clearly said by the victim of the shower incident.

The surface information provided here is enough to begin some type of response plan on behalf of the student. On this information alone, an immediate greater supervision of the boys' locker room by school personnel is warranted, as well as addressing the issue of the damaged books so that the victim's educational opportunities are not threatened. We still do not know who is responsible for these actions other than the fact that it involved a "group of boys."

How best, then, can we respond to this young man's request for assistance? We can certainly move ahead based solely on the surface information and ask questions on only what has been presented to us so far. However, to do so without responding to the "underlying canvas" of the "painting" will miss important opportunities to make connections with this student that will lay the foundation for longer-term assistance once the immediate issue is addressed.

What is the inner saga, or metacommunication, in this young man's presenting story? First, he feels he has run out of options for dealing with the situation. As such, he has had to resort to turning to an adult within the school setting for help. In Kid World, this makes it a serious matter. Second, he is likely frightened by the fact that he is outnumbered and overpowered. It is not a fair confrontation by any means. Third, he is afraid that losing his books will impact his school work and may well be worried about how the books will be replaced, especially if he knows that his family will be responsible for paying for new ones. Fourth, he likely has been living in fear of such behaviors for quite some time. This is not the first time that some kind of bullying or teasing has been directed toward him, and this incident may well be an escalation of what has occurred in the past.

All of these aspects of his existence are revealed on the canvas of the painting he presented us. None of it was communicated in words. But how can we be certain that any or all of these hunches are accurate? We have to respond at a level of empathy that conveys to him that we are trying to understand what it must be like to be in his predicament, while at the same time assuring him that we are prepared to help. For example:

> *John, I'm so sorry to hear that this happened to you and I'm very glad you came to me to ask for help. It sounds to me as if you have been putting up with this nonsense for longer than just what happened yesterday and I imagine that you're pretty frustrated and maybe even a little bit scared about what all of this means. I know I would be. Let's see what we can do, first of all, about getting you some books so that you don't miss any school work, and then let's chat about what we might be able to do to make this kind of misbehavior stop.*

Empathic Listening

Communicating to others that you hear them at a level beneath the surface of details and trivia fosters trust. It sends a message that you are trying to understand what it is like to be in their shoes. This is referred to as *empathic listening*. It is often received as comforting and reassuring, because most individuals who are victimized are made to feel as if they are so different and so outcast that no one understands them or—worse—that no one would want to understand them. Most importantly, it increases the likelihood that they will share more information in the future about their experiences and feelings when they believe that you truly "get" what they are trying to say. And in most instances of victimization, the involvement of adults is an approach-avoidance kind of situation. While kids may need adult intervention, so often they are afraid of what an adult's response will be or of the consequences of retaliation and additional ostracism from their peers once word leaks out that they have requested it.

2. SUPPORT THE VICTIM'S EFFORTS TO BELONG TO THE SCHOOL COMMUNITY IN ALL ITS ASPECTS

Kids have a right to go to school unimpeded by bullies, taunts, or slurs, and it is the responsibility of school personnel to ensure that this happens. If ever there was something that should inspire a little righteous indignation of teachers, administrators, and other school personnel to act, this is it. The key, of course, is to turn that righteous indignation into effective responses, not just to "even the score" on behalf of victims by meting out punishment to bullies.

Strong, Caring Messages

A major part of helping victims regain their self-esteem and a sense of security after an abusive episode or series of such is by sending a strong, caring message that this school is their school, that they belong here, and that the adults who work there will do everything that they can to help make the situation better. Kids should not be given the message, either directly or implied, that school personnel will be able to solve all of the problems associated with bullies, but rather that the adults will try their best to work with the aggrieved to implement a plan to prevent future occurrences. It is important that students know that they play an important role in gaining the power to prevent and avoid such behaviors from happening to them so that they gain the tools and confidence to protect themselves without adult assistance.

There are four main messages that a victim of bullying or teasing should receive in the aftermath of an abusive encounter and after the immediate health and safety needs have been attended to. These messages are that:

1. What happened (or has been happening to them) is not acceptable behavior and will not be tolerated in the school.
2. School is supposed to be a safe place so that everyone can learn to the best of their abilities.
3. With their help, a plan will be designed to improve the situation.
4. While the hope is that everything improves immediately, it might take time before the bullying or teasing stops (or is reduced).

No promises, outside of those that school personnel can actually guarantee (such as exactly what they can and will do), should be made. Victims need to understand that this is a *process* that takes time and there are a lot of uncertainties that remain to be resolved. A sample dialog might sound like the following:

Jackie, I wanted to meet with you again to follow up on what you shared with me yesterday about the teasing you've been receiving from your friends. You know that we've told Anne, Diane, and Joanne to stop what they have been doing, so for now maybe that will calm things down until we get a better understanding of what needs to be done.

Like I said yesterday, what they have been doing to you is not the kind of behavior that we allow here at Albert Ellis Elementary, and that has been made crystal clear to those three. We want everyone here to learn and to feel safe. You did the right thing by coming to tell me about what they have been doing to you. You are an important person here at Albert Ellis, and we want you to feel good about what you learn here, not to have to put up with unfair and unkind behaviors.

You said yesterday that you were eager for the teasing that you had been receiving to stop. I am, too. So, when the teachers here discover that teasing is occurring, we do everything that we can to help prevent it from happening again. We've already taken the first step by going directly to Anne, Diane, and Joanne and telling them to stop what they have been doing. But that is only a first step. What we need to do now is work out a plan so that everyone—you and the others—can learn how to get along with each other and to prevent those rude behaviors from happening again. If you want to do this, it will likely take some time before we get everything to work like we want it to, and the first plan we make may not work exactly like we want it to. I want you to understand at the very beginning that we—you, me, the school, Anne, Diane, and Joanne, and maybe even your parents—all have a part to play in this. I can't guarantee you how things will work out in the end, but I can tell you from experience that in almost all the other times I've worked with kids who have been in your situation, things have improved.

So, let's chat a little bit about what you think about all of this today. What questions or thoughts do you have?

In this sample dialog, the four main points are conveyed in as low-threat a manner as possible. The high value on the worth and dignity of the child who was teased was clearly stated. It was evident that school personnel had already begun some type of accountability program for the three peers who were responsible for the teasing. This, of course, puts words to action and relays to the victim that not only is the school concerned about what has happened, but also that it has taken immediate steps to stop the misbehavior. An offer of designing a plan was made. The prognosis for its success was realistic. Nothing from this sample follow-up discussion with the victim was unrealistic. Most importantly, Jackie was given the chance at the end of the dialog to begin expressing her concerns and gathering information to her questions. This is extremely important because plans that are imposed on individuals are less likely to be as committed to on the part of those individuals as the plans that they believe they have played a role in designing. **Ownership of plans** increases the likelihood that the individual will provide the follow-through. When it comes to implementing a plan, children are not different from adults in this respect.

It is so critical to help victims of peer abuse know that they really do belong to the school community, because the direct and indirect messages they receive through bullying and teasing are just exactly the opposite—that they do not belong, that they are not liked by their peers, and that they are worthless. These messages are reinforced if school personnel do not act to dispel them. Inaction is a powerful confirmation of adult endorsement of the status quo. It always works to the advantage of the bullies.

What interveners are likely to see and hear from those who have been subjected to long-term bullying and teasing is a very low self-esteem. The children may even make excuses for their tormentors and blame themselves for what has been happening to them. Helping the victim to reestablish dignity and self-respect is critical and will greatly increase the chances of the student's taking further steps toward learning the skills of assertiveness.

3. REQUEST PERMISSION FROM THE VICTIM TO SHARE NECESSARY INFORMATION (ONLY!) WITH RELEVANT SCHOOL OFFICIALS

This step and the next will likely be two of the most difficult parts of an intervention with a harassed individual. The tormented are often so afraid of retaliation from their attackers that they may have endured months or years of beatings, verbal haranguing, thefts, or vandalism. The mere act of sharing their abuse with a teacher is tantamount in Kid World to betrayal. No matter how onerous a particular bullying or teasing behavior may be, thou shalt not "narc" on thy peers! This becomes even truer as they grow into adolescence and strive to individuate, to handle their own affairs, and to be seen as capable of accepting the mantle of adulthood. Determining how to proceed through the entanglements of rules and statutes, then, while at the same time protecting the confidences of the victim is a delicate balance.

As previously discussed, this matter may not be negotiable. Students need to know this up front if such is the case. If school rules or state statutes dictate that any behaviors resembling bullying, teasing, or harassment of any kind are to be reported, then if school personnel fail to do so—even for good reasons (such as believing that to do so would further endanger the victim)—they are at personnel risk for criminal or civil charges, not to mention charges of neglecting to fulfill their duties as required by policy. Would I do the "paper chase" as required by such policies if I truly believed that doing so would result in a worse situation for a victim? No, I would not—at least not until I had better assurances that the child's safety issues were resolved. At the same time it is imperative to remember, as previously mentioned in the discussion about professional judgment, that once I make that decision to step outside the rules, I act alone and in jeopardy of all the consequences that would follow should I be wrong.

I can attest from professional practice in schools that to convince victims of the necessity or requirements of sharing their stories with other relevant school staff is often difficult. It takes a high degree of patience and trust on both parties' behalves to make it work. It is especially difficult when a student is torn between the need to talk to an adult and fear of the future when an intervention begins.

As an intervention proceeds, this sticky wicket has to be addressed. If a student is hesitant to agree to the release of information about the incident to others within the school, the establishment of certain guidelines may help.

Guidelines to Help Victims Report Abuse to Adults

First, students need to know the **rationale** behind how the sharing of information will work to improve the situation. For example:

> *I understand that you are reluctant to let me share information about this incident because you don't want to be seen as a crybaby among your friends and you are afraid that those who have been doing this will do it even worse the next time. Those are real concerns, and I don't blame you for feeling that way. But let me explain why I need to share this information with Mr. Principal and with the teachers on duty during lunchtime. First of all, because what has been occurring to you during lunch break is technically a fight—they are punching you, not that you are punching them—school rules say that all staff have to report that kind of misbehavior. And you know that is the rule because it's in your student handbook, right?*
>
> *If the teachers on duty know that there has been a problem in that area of the cafeteria and in that area of the school grounds, they are more likely to be able to keep an eye out to prevent that sort of trouble from happening. You said, didn't you, that you are not the only one who this stuff's been happening to? It seems to make sense to me that what you are asking me to do by helping to stop this kind of bullying from happening to you can also be of help to others.*
>
> *Every adult on this campus wants to stop the kind of bullying that you have told me about from happening to you or any other student, and a lot of those people have a lot of really great ideas about how to do it. If you will let me share just enough information, we all might even be able to put together a better plan than if just you and I try to figure one out ourselves.*

Second, students need to know exactly *what* information will be shared and with *whom*. They should also be given the opportunity to request exactly what pieces of information they would prefer be withheld.

> *I'm glad that you are willing to let me share some of this information with Mr. Principal. He and I do a lot of work together trying to stop this kind of stuff from happening, so I know that you've made the right decision.*
>
> *Now, here's what I need your advice on. I'm not sure that everything you told me needs to be shared with Mr. Principal and I will do my best to honor that. But I do think that he needs to be aware of what has been happening to you and others, who's been doing it, and where it has been happening. With those three bits of information, I think we can start trying to improve the situation.*
>
> *Is there anything specifically that you do not want me to share with him?*

Third, those victimized by bullies need to have some kind of expectation as to what *is* and *is not* likely to happen as an intervention moves forward.

> *I think we have worked really hard today to get started on trying to improve things. You have really given some careful thought to all of this, and that's great.*

I need to also share with you some thoughts on what might or might not happen in the future. As I said, there's no guarantee that things will get better. While we hope it will, it's important to remember that sometimes these things take time and we never know exactly what kinds of decisions those who have been treating you so poorly will make. They could back off and correct their behavior. They could keep doing what they have in the past. They might even make things worse. It's important to me that you understand these possibilities because I don't want to get your hopes too high too quickly that things will change overnight.

When I go to talk to Mr. Principal, I think I know what he will do. If the past is any indication, he will want to talk with you to make sure that you are okay. He has already spoken to the others and is deciding now exactly how best to hold them accountable for their actions. Probably, he and I will meet again tomorrow to discuss all of this and see how things are going.

Now, I also have to tell you that I do not know for sure that this is what will happen. He may have other ideas based on his meetings with the others and may feel as if other actions are necessary. What I will promise is to keep you informed as much as I can about what is going on. You also know that you can come and see me if you want to talk about all of this. And, if things do not improve or if they get worse, by all means come and see me quickly.

Are there any questions you have about what I just went over? Is there anything that you think we need to change or that you don't feel comfortable with that maybe we can adjust before I go talk to Mr. Principal?

There are details of how targets respond to their attackers that may not be relevant to share with those in the authority loop. I once worked with a tenth grader who had been cornered by a group of thugs who had been harassing him for quite some time. He confided in me that he had urinated on himself during the episode. While information of the intimidation and threats made needed to be reported to other school personnel, the fact that the young man had soiled himself out of fear had little relevance to the main facts of the incident. Any information that is not relevant to improving a child's situation and would do harm to the dignity or self-worth of that information should be kept as private as possible.

Retaliation and Revictimization

The primary obstacle likely to slow or stop a victim from asking for adult intervention is the **fear of retaliation**. It is a real threat, and the likelihood of its happening is the one thing over which school personnel have little control. Retaliatory actions against those who have reported being bullied or teased will most likely occur off school grounds, on the way to or from school, at extracurricular events where supervision is lax, or in some other venue wherein school personnel are absent. Retaliations are often brutal or worse than any previous harassment the victim has received to that point. From the bully's point of view, they are based on the premise that such acts are justified for the victim having gotten the aggressor in trouble. It is common that most bullies will back away from their targets when an adult intervention takes place. The motive of the bully's **retraction** of aggressive behaviors will be revealed in time. It could be that the intervention was at a level of effectiveness that caused the aggressor to change. It could also be a matter of the bullies reevaluating the landscape, determining how best to change tactics, and "laying low" until they feel the supervision is lax enough for them to strike again. I call this reassessment of attack strategy by bullies **remission**.

Those who are engaged in the intervention process need to be alert for retaliatory actions on the part of aggressors in the immediate period following the reporting of who is responsible for intimidating others. An intervention to stop harassment is an extremely stressful time for bullies. Their reputation as being in control of their world is challenged. The origin of that challenge, in their view, is the one or ones who reported the misbehavior; therefore those individuals have trumped (at least for a short time) the power of the bully. If bullies are to maintain or regain their status as "tough guys" among their peer groups, then some kind of behavior indicative of that status is in order.

There are two likely targets of a retaliatory action by a bully. The first and most obvious is an action directed toward the individual who "ratted out" the bully. That is why it is so important to keep close supervision over a victim who reports the intimidation in the immediate period following the report. Exactly because bullies are often astute enough to know that their previous victim is under more protective scrutiny than before, they are just as likely to act aggressively against either previous victims or new ones in an effort to send the message that "They may have managed to save that one (for a while), but I'm still who I am and look at how powerful and in control I remain!"

As terrified and frustrated as victims may be at the time of the initial telling of their story, the period immediately following the exposure of a bully can be even more tense. Threats may have been made (and usually are) throughout the intimidation as to what will happen to the victims if they ever tell. Worse, their peers may have observed a retaliatory action inflicted on someone who complained to an adult previously or someone who made an effort to stand up to the intimidation. That is why it is so important for those who are attempting to escape the cycle of abuse to know that they have adult resources within the school setting who are capable of assisting them in their journey through as uncomplicated a normal childhood and adolescence as possible.

A second obstacle to slowing or preventing victims from telling their stories, and one that receives less attention, is the possible consequences other than retaliation that might befall those who choose to ask for help. This is the possibility of **revictimizing the victim**.

Therapeutically speaking, revictimization can occur at any time an individual is forced to remember or "deal with" a traumatic event. This is particularly true if the individual is not psychologically ready or prepared to deal with the stresses of such therapeutic work. Those events that penetrate the psychological well-being of people are often difficult to discuss. In its most oppressive form, severe trauma can result in an individual's repressing either some or all memory of the event.

Posttraumatic Stress Disorder

Those who are subjected to intense and/or less intense but prolonged traumas may develop *posttraumatic stress disorder* (PTSD). PTSD is most characteristically seen in those who have experienced war or been involved in a natural catastrophe (tornado or flood), car accident, rape, or another life-threatening situation. PTSD is developed through a combination of exposure to trauma and preexisting personal traits. Any individual, young or old, under the right conditions is subject to developing PTSD or *PTSD-like symptomotologies*.

Individuals who are exposed to bullying or teasing usually do not become candidates for the development of PTSD. However, it is possible, and a far more likely possibility, that a child exposed to years of intimidation from peers may well develop PTSD-like behaviors or symptoms and be reluctant or unable to discuss all of the aspects of their mistreatment without reexperiencing many of the discomforts that accompanied the original abuse.

Forcing individuals to discuss what they choose not to is a form of revictimization. It is certainly understandable how people might choose to avoid talking about those events that terrified them, or about which made them feel powerless, or to face for the first time the ones responsible for their pain and misery.

While the concept of PTSD may have merit similar in context to how one might approach an individual who has been subjected to a life-threatening situation, when dealing with children and adolescents ensnarled in bully-victim relationships, it is usually more practical to determine how best to work with the victims without (a) exposing them to additional mistreatment at the hands of the bullies or (b) creating additional barriers and obstacles to normal and healthy peer relationships within the school setting.

The residents of Kid World have an incredible ability to be fickle in their loyalties even on the best of days. When it comes to dealing with adults, they may very well have what we might characterize as a love-hate relationship: "When I need you, I will let you know and you better be able to help me out; otherwise, just go away, leave me alone, act like you don't know me because my friends and I can take care of ourselves." This oxymoronic code becomes even more evident during adolescence. The desire to be independent of adult assistance manifests itself cruelly in children who actually do turn to adults for help, especially over matters of peer-to-peer disagreements. They may be looked upon with suspicion or deemed crybabies or narcs and be called all the derogatory names affiliated with such. And peer rejection, as we have already established, is a fate worse than death in Kid World.

What does all of this have to do with the concept of revictimization? *Everything!* The child's potential aversion to adult intervention for *anything* must be considered when designing *any* type of adult-imposed assistance. If the student is a willing and eager participant in the intervention, that is marvelous. If there is reluctance or resistance, a slower and more deliberative approach will have to be employed.

Forcing victims to act before they are ready is revictimization. Forcing victims to talk about their experiences before they are able is revictimization. Forcing victims to participate in a plan of which they are not in agreement or do not understand or cannot implement is revictimization. Increasing exposure to additional mistreatment at the hands of the bully by implementing a plan before all the pros and cons have been thoroughly assessed is revictimization. Creating a situation that further isolates or ostracizes victims from their peers is revictimization.

Yet policy may well require action before the victim is ready. In the rush to gather information about an incident of bullying, victims may be compelled to give embarrassing details. Hasty decisions may impose plans on both the bully and the victim that neither understands or are unrealistic to implement. Additionally, acting in the absence of consultation with the abused may create situations that place the victim in greater jeopardy than before the adult intervention began. Also, imposing sanctions and punishments on bullies that are viewed by peers as solely the result of a "tattletale" can further decrease the likelihood of victims's expanding their circle of friends.

Revictimization, then, is a much larger concept than the single concern about retaliation by bullies. The best way to avoid revictimization of the abused is to move as much as possible in concert with the readiness of the child. As noted, policy may preclude this from happening in the best of fashions, yet every effort should be made to incorporate the emotional and psychological readiness of the victims in taking back the power and self-esteem that was robbed from them. This may take time. Most likely, in the case of those who have been subjected to long-term bullying or teasing, it will take longer.

You know, you've shared a lot with me lately about everything that has been happening to you. You've been through such an ordeal, going all the way back to elementary school.

I want to keep helping you turn things around, and we've already started that process by your sharing your stories with me. But I will also tell you that I know from experience that it often helps if those who have been bullied can develop a plan to face those who have been dishing it out. I don't mean violently. Most of the time, when I've worked with kids on this matter, we've done the face-to-faces here in my office. The purpose is to give you the opportunity to firmly and calmly tell those who have abused you how their actions have been misguided. I am there to mediate the conversation. There are rules that everyone goes by so that what is said is done in an orderly fashion.

If you choose to do this, I want the decision to be yours. It's important that you know that you have the power to speak your mind and that they see that you are a capable individual. You don't have to make a decision today or even this week. I want you to think about it. Come back to me when you're ready and we can discuss the pros and cons of your decision.

4. DETERMINE WHEN PARENTS SHOULD BE CONTACTED

Unless policy mandates immediate contact with parents about all matters related to bullying and teasing within the school setting, careful consideration should be exercised before parents are contacted. Doesn't this fly in the face of a previous recommendation that the parents of the abused should be contacted if their children are being bullied? At the concrete level, perhaps. But let us examine this matter more in depth.

While parents generally have a right to know about what is happening to their children in any caregiving or educational setting, common sense and best professional judgment dictate that parents need not be contacted about every little stumbling block that may cross their child's path. Parents do not have the time to keep track of every hallway bump or rude comment that comes their child's way (and those who think they do—the "helicopter parents" who "hover" over their children every waking minute of the day—need to find some more mature ways of spending their days!). For that matter, teachers should not be expected to add piddly, everyday minor incidents to their already overburdened list of responsibilities. As a general rule, children prefer that their parents not know about everything that occurs in their lives, because adults' interpretations are quite often different from theirs. "It's no big deal" is the standard mantra to parents from the inhabitants of Kid World.

It does not do children well to "smother love" them to death by trying to protect them every minute of their lives. That is why parents should not be too antsy to overrule school personnel's judgments about how negative incidents are handled within the school environment—provided, of course, that the child either expresses no discomfort or does not display the outward signs of being negatively impacted by everyday peer-to-peer interaction. Additionally, constant adult intervention on behalf of a child may make them **codependent** for adult assistance and not allow them to develop or learn the skills necessary to manage their own difficult peer-to-peer interactions. While we want children to turn to adults for help when they need it, it is important for children to have reasonable expectations about under what conditions they actually need that assistance.

So, what are some of the issues that must be considered when contacting parents if no policy exists mandating that parents be automatically notified about such incidents?

If It Is Clear That the Mistreatment Is an Ongoing Problem, Contact the Parents

In instances where it is discovered that a child has been subjected to long-term torment, the parents need to know. They need to be assured that the school is acting responsibly to address the problem behavior and that efforts are being taken to safeguard their child. Failure to make contact with parents under these circumstances will lead to suspicion and mistrust on the part of the parents. Consider the following outreach to parents:

Mr. Adams, this is Roland's teacher, Ms. Hernandez. I wanted to let you know that today we discovered that Roland has been receiving some poor treatment from a few boys here at the school and that we are acting to stop the misbehavior in order to make this a safe place so Roland will feel better about being here. Let me tell you what we know and then, if you have any questions, I will be more than happy to answer them.

As far as we know, this behavior started about two months ago. Apparently, Roland and several other third graders were being cornered in the bathrooms at lunch break by some fifth graders and were jostled around, had water sprayed on them, and some of their school materials stolen. We know who is responsible and we have started the process of holding them accountable for their actions.

Roland seems to indicate that he didn't want to tell anyone about what was going on because he was afraid that things would get worse. Unfortunately, that is something that we hear time and time again on the few occasions when we find out about an incident of bullying here at school. I personally believe that there is more information that we have yet to learn as to exactly what the boys who were doing this did to the kids they were targeting. We are going to continue to find out all we can to prevent this sort of thing from happening again.

You might want to share with Roland tonight that you and I talked. I told him that I was going to call just to let you know the basic details of what we knew to this point. He may have other information that he shares with you. You might want to ask him if he feels comfortable telling us any additional information that he shares with you that he didn't with us.

If you would like to arrange a conference with me or anyone else here related to this matter, I will be more than happy to arrange it. Now, what questions can I answer for you?

Avoid providing the names of the abusers to parents. It may be a violation of state policy to discuss other children with nonschool personnel over matters of discipline. It could also set the stage for a parent to act impulsively against the children identified as the perpetrators. Oh, yes, it happens. More than likely, the child who was targeted will share the information with his parents.

If It Is Clear That the Mistreatment Is Negatively Impacting the Child's Education, Contact the Parents

The same basic concerns are relevant here as were in the previous scenario. Long-term negative behaviors impacting a child should be reported to parents, along with what plans are in place to correct the problems. Many times, appearances of the residual impact of long-term bullying or teasing will not appear until after the first intervention has taken place.

Mr. Adams, this is Ms. Hernandez, again. I wanted to get back in touch with you again as a follow-up to everything that we've been working on here at school related to that bullying incident that we stopped a month ago.

I have been talking with Roland's other teachers and we are all in agreement that something has changed for him since the bullying started three months ago. At first we weren't sure, but now we feel as if Roland's schoolwork has not been as solid as it once was before this problem came to our attention. When we've tried to chat with him about it, he says that he doesn't want to talk about it anymore. In fact, he told Ms. Smithson the other day that school isn't fun for him. I've watched his interactions with other students on the playground and I get the impression that he is telling us the truth—he really does not find school to be a fun place for him in any way, either in the classroom or at play.

We would like to get everyone together and talk with you about any other changes you may have seen in Roland. Is it possible that we might be able to arrange that this week?

Roland has probably not gotten the full attention he needed to help him deal with the negative self-esteem messages that he received at the hands of his attackers. That is a part of the **pernicious impact** of bullying. While bullies may go away, the scars they leave stay much longer, slowly eating away at the victim's beliefs about his place in not only Kid World, but the larger world as well.

If It Is Suspected, Yet Uncertain, That Mistreatment Is Occurring, Contact the Parents

As mentioned repeatedly, kids do not always choose to share with adults things that they should. Adolescents in particular make this decision in their efforts to individuate. Any child of any age, however, may choose to not tell about the bullying or teasing they experience if they are fearful of the consequences of sharing the information.

Parents and siblings may have observed behaviors or be aware of information that school personnel are not. Sometimes each group may have a piece of the puzzle, and until all the groups put those pieces on the table, the entire picture is not clear.

Ms. Hardy, this is Mr. Villagomez, Tyler's school counselor. I need your and Mrs. Hardy's help in trying to sort out a mystery we have here with Tyler.

We have been made aware that there is a group of upper-grade boys that has been going around and making life tough for the ninth graders, who have just come into the building. At this point, we don't know all we need to know and that is why I'm calling.

Several of Tyler's teachers have commented to me in passing that they have wondered if Tyler is one of the ninth graders being targeted by this group. His teachers have noticed that on some days he has all of his school materials, but on other days he doesn't, and that he has come to some of his classes with dirt and grass stains on his clothes, as if he's been pushed onto the ground. When I walked and talked with him just casually down the hallway today between class changes and briefly mentioned it, he quickly changed the subject and scooted on down to class in a hurry.

So, I'm calling to ask if you or any of Tyler's sisters are aware of anything unusual about his behavior of late. Has he mentioned anything at home about any of this or given an explanation as to how his clothes get so messed up during the day? Have you noticed any unexplainable behaviors on this part, things like his personal money being spent at a faster-than-normal rate or any of his other personal belongings being damaged or destroyed? Any information you have might well be something that is useful in helping us to figure all this out.

It is entirely possible that children do tell their parents everything about what is happening at school, but that the parents do not know how best to proceed. This may be especially true in the homes of first-generation immigrant families who do not understand how the school system works and may have limited English skills in which to express their concerns.

Parents as Partners

Parents should be contacted as partners in the solution to the problem. Children must see adults in *all* capacities as able and caring individuals during times of personal crises. One excellent way of doing this is to invite parents to work with the school in providing an around-the-clock sense of security for their children. We are not talking about providing around-the-clock-take-care-of-all-their-problems-act-as-a-security-guard kind of relationship, but rather a joining of school and home resources to increase the knowledge within the child that the world is truly a safe place, even though there are some people in it who misbehave.

Inviting parents to be a part of the solution keeps them in the *information loop* and gets them involved on the home front. Parents who are informed about the efforts being taken to help their children are far more likely to be willing to work longer with the school if a problem becomes more complicated than anticipated. Parents want to be able to do something to help their children deal with problems, and school personnel always need willing people to provide after-school assistance with a child's problem areas. On more than one consultation with parents and schools I have heard, "Just tell me what I can do and I'll do it!" The school can be just the resource for providing parents with ideas and suggestions about how best to work on the matter of bullying and teasing during the nonschool hours.

Ms. Hardy? Mr. Villagomez again, Tyler's school counselor. I am so glad that you and Mr. Hardy have worked with us on this bullying thing. It has turned into quite a mess. The more we dig, the more we find out stuff that we wish we weren't hearing.

I'm calling to let you know that since you and I started working on Tyler's situation, I've run across some materials that I think you and Mr. Hardy might find useful in working with Tyler's self-esteem. It's a series of one-page lessons that are designed to be discussed between a teen and the parent—each separately—about how they handled different kinds of teen problems in their days. It's really a rather interesting set of lessons, each one takes only about 10 minutes to read, and then however long a parent chooses to share their experiences is up to that parent. The parents who have used it have told me that they have had a lot of fun with it and that it has provided quite a few laughs. Whatever the family discusses is just for the family. It's not for me or anyone here at the school to know about.

If you would like me to send these over, I can catch Tyler before he comes home today and send them with him. Hopefully, these can allow you and Mr. Hardy the opportunity to help Tyler at home to regain some of that self-esteem we know has taken a downturn because of the mistreatment he received earlier in the semester.

5. CONTINUE LONG-TERM SUPPORTIVE INTERACTION FOR THE VICTIM

The stresses and strains associated with being victimized impact people at the very core of their being. As previously noted, it affects the way they think, the way they feel, and the way they act about themselves and toward the world in which they live. Responses to those who have been subjected to long-term bullying and teasing must address these three aspects of the victim's existence. If we fail to acknowledge that victims are impacted at these three levels and also fail to design strategies to act on each one, then there is a risk that longer-term issues will develop with a direct linkage to the bullying and teasing they received.

If there is a major shortcoming among those who are charged with supervising children and adolescents—second only to ignoring the problem in the first place—it is the failure to understand the opportunities that present themselves in the aftermath of the discovery of the occurrence of bullying and teasing. The window is open wide to address the cognitive, emotional, and behavioral deficits that may yet be forming in the psyche of the victim. It is incumbent on those who intervene to do so effectively in order to reduce the likelihood of the residual problems that accompany victimization from further development.

Intervening and Following Up

Who should best be involved in dealing with the cognitive, emotional, and behavioral impacts of bullying and teasing? *Everyone* in the school plays a role! From the first minute of the first intervention in the dyad (Teacher: "Bill, stop that this instant! I want to see you and Jerry immediately."), a message is sent to the victim as to the kinds of behaviors that will and will not be tolerated. This message is both *overt* and *subliminal*. The victim makes a determination as to the sense of safety within that environment: "The teachers here do not approve of that kind of behavior" versus "She looked right over here and saw what was happening and she didn't do anything. They don't care what happens to me or how anybody behaves." So, at the very beginning, those who stop a bullying or teasing behavior in the midst of its occurrence play an important role in the healing process that follows.

Afterwards, there must be follow-up. How the details of bullying and teasing are gleaned from victims and who does it sends another message. What role does the person obtaining information from the victim normally play in the school? Is it an administrator who is viewed by students as handling only discipline issues and not being too student-friendly? Or is it another staff member who is viewed by students as being more of a student advocate? While the business end of the discipline will have to be handled (the sad irony being that many times school policy dictates that both bullies and victims receive some type of punishment, especially if it involves a physical altercation and even if the victims were doing nothing more than defending themselves), both bullies and their targets are likely to provide more information if they trust the adult gathering the information. That information is critical in determining how best to proceed next with both parties.

By virtue of education and expertise, there are certain school personnel who are better prepared to deal with victims' psychological fallout from abuse. As previously noted, those who are trained in the behavioral sciences and helping professions—such as school counselors, school psychologists, and social workers—are likely to be better prepared than the average teacher or administrator to work with the damaged psyches of victims. The degree to which any type of helping professional will be effective depends on their relationship with kids and the special training they may have received in this area. Of course, all things being equal, how well the helping professional connects with kids probably has far more to do with the outcome of an intervention than does someone who knows a lot of psychobabble but makes kids feel uncomfortable or who seems to know little about what it is like to be an adolescent.

Effective long-term support means just that. It needs to work. It should be understood that it will be available as long as the victims choose to use it or until personal skills have reached the point of self-effectiveness. And it is designed only as *support*, not as the primary *crutch*, which does nothing to teach victims how to safely manage the conflict that may come their way in the future. Effective long-term support will address self-esteem issues, relationship enhancements, assertiveness training, alternatives to responding to aggressors, role play, and refusing to abandon the victim.

Self-Esteem Issues

Singular incidents of bullying or teasing will likely have less of an impact on their targets than those who have been subjected to a history of such mistreatment. It should be assumed that children and adolescents who are known to have been bullied or teased for lengthy periods of their lives will likely have lower self-esteem. Pay particular attention to those who have been abused as a result of racial or ethnic characteristics and mental or physical differences. These are cuts that go to the core of one's beliefs about self and are related to matters of which a child has no control. As one student told me, "I will grow out of the acne on my face, so when they make fun of my zits, I can deal with that. But I will always be black. What's wrong with that?"

Children who have low self-esteem must relearn how valuable they are. They need positive statements in their lives about themselves. They need to know that others see them as equal to their peers. They need to be able to talk about how they feel about themselves and to explore how they came to view themselves as they do. What most children who explore the origins of their self-esteem discover is that *they* did not do anything to create their negative views of self; rather, it was *other people* who gave them that message. Feedback is important in all social relationships, but it is not always correct, especially when it is malicious and designed to destroy another's self-esteem. Children and teens, however, live and die by the feedback they receive, particularly when it comes from their peers. Children are more likely to be impacted by the feedback they receive from adults. Adolescents are more likely to be impacted by what they hear from their peers. Helping victims to delineate between the feedback they get from others that is specifically designed to disrupt their daily living is an important aspect of regaining self-worth.

Challenging low-self-esteem statements is an effective tool in beginning the examination process with victims.

> *I know you said that you feel "ugly" and that you're not any good at "anything," but I'm not certain that those are true statements about yourself. What is it that makes you feel as if you are ugly? . . . Well, I think we successfully proved that when it comes to your physical appearance or clothes, you certainly aren't ugly by any stretch of the imagination. Now, what about that other thing—oh, yes. You're not supposed to be good at anything. Hmmmm, anything sure is a lot of stuff. Tell me those things that you think you're not so good at. . . . Well, we all have those things that we do that someone can always do better. But there are also a lot of things that we can do that we feel pretty good about. I happen to know for a fact that there are some things that you excel in. Want to take a guess at what some of those things are? . . . That's right, you got two of the very things I was thinking of. You're good at math and you do well in band. Well, let me tell you three other things you happen to be pretty good at that everybody around here knows. . . . So, what do you think about that, huh? Sounds to me as if you are good at some things, so I guess we can put that notion about you not being good at anything away!*

Self-esteem is the foundation on which our desire to strive emerges. If that is destroyed, we then lose a great deal of our inner drive, our enjoyment of life, and our reason to carry forth. That is why it is so tragic when the self-esteem of a developing child or adolescent is destroyed. That is why it is so essential to restore it once it is discovered to have been stolen.

Relationship Enhancements

Whether it was an issue before the mistreatment began or whether it occurred as a result of the abuse, quite often victims of bullying and teasing have certain deficits in their abilities to maintain peer relationships. Once mistreatment begins, children's belief in their ability to maintain normal peer relationships changes, as does the conceptualization of what constitutes a normal relationship. It appears to the abused that power is the socially accepted key to popularity. Because they do not have it, they then assume that they will be defective in their efforts to have relationships with their peers other than in the submissive caste role that they have been assigned. These individuals become quiet and isolated from the peer group in an effort to go unnoticed and receive additional mistreatment.

The opposite of this worldview is the individual who tries to counter the sense of powerlessness by acting as if the abuse is of no concern. They may well adopt the posture of playing the jester to the bully's advances in an effort to humor the aggressor and therefore to lessen the severity of any forthcoming punishment. Another behavior manifestation in the opposite direction of withdrawal is individuals who act out to draw attention to themselves in an effort to deal with the inner anxiety of being placed in the submissive role of the abused. Feeling the tension of future attacks and knowing that they are viewed negatively by peers, their actions often become boisterous and exaggerated. They are often called "pests" by their peers, and their overly excited efforts to find a niche within any peer group become the very reason that they are singled out. These are the provocative victims of which we spoke earlier. Peers reject them because of their pesky antics. Bullies use them as targets because no one will defend them among the peer group. Provocative victims often are very vocal in the punishments they receive from their aggressors. Subsequently, they are even more attractive to bullies because they give more "squeals per pinch" than the normal target.

Both of these groups of victims—the *withdrawn* and the *overly reactive*—need help in learning how to have normal relationships with their peers. However, both of these groups have different needs. Those who are withdrawn need help in learning how to reach out to others. Those who are overly reactive need to learn personal boundaries. Both groups will likely benefit from learning anxiety reduction skills.

Assertiveness Training and Recognizing Personal Boundaries

Assertiveness is an individual's ability to state to others the locations of their **personal boundaries**—both physical and interpersonal. The "boundaries" we speak of in this instance refer to many things: the boundaries of one's personal space and physical comfort; the identification of personal property; the limits of behaviors with which an individual feels comfortable. Most commonly understood among society, it is the ability to say "no" to others to let them know that it is time for them to stop a particular behavior (this is a response to an aggressor's **boundary challenge**). Assertiveness is not to be confused with **aggressiveness**, which is, in many respects, the antithesis of being assertive. The aggressive individual oversteps and disrespects another person's boundaries, both physically and interpersonally.

Being assertive is a learned trait. We are not born with it, but certain people may be more predisposed to implement its fundamentals than others. Assertive people most likely were raised with assertive role models in the home, but that is not always the case. Individuals who learn to be assertive have learned the differences between aggression and nonresponses to boundary challenges. They know that matching an aggressive response with the same will likely escalate the situation, and that aggressive people usually play that game very well. They know that a nonresponse in the face of a boundary challenge will likely encourage the aggressor to abuse the boundary again in the future.

The ability to be assertive confuses an aggressor. It sends a dual message. While not aggressive like the intent of the challenger, it states a limit in a calm and controlled fashion. It is a *nonemotional statement* of fact: "That's enough. I do not like it when you act that way toward me." It is also not a passive response. It meets the boundary challenge with a nonemotional statement of fact that explains that the person is aware when their personal boundaries are being encroached on, and that the aggressor should stop and proceed no further. Without responding in kind to the aggressor, the likelihood of escalation is reduced—but not eliminated altogether. In sending a message to an aggressor in the early stages of a confrontation, one that indicates that "I am capable of equaling your challenge" or "I know what you are doing," the bully is likely to seek less secure boundaries to invade. A bully is looking for the response to the challenge that says, "Please do not hurt me. Do what you will, then leave me alone." Of course, bullies gladly accept the invitation to have their ways with the targets, but they give no promises about not hurting them and most likely will be back again and again until they have a reason to leave.

Both groups of victims—the withdrawns and the overly reactives—will gain from assertiveness training. Both groups lack or have lost their abilities to set limits with those who want to challenge their boundaries. Those who are targets of bullies must learn the skills of assertiveness and put them into practice. This is one of the first true action steps that victims will need in the process of taking back the power that has been robbed from them.

Assertiveness skills training curricula are found within educational curriculum companies that deal with mental health– and counseling-related subjects (see Chapter 10 and the Recommended Resources section for suggestions).

Like any type of curricular materials, they should be previewed to determine which ones would be best for a specific school setting. Assertiveness skills modules can be applied as a teaching lesson for entire grades (as a preventive measure), or they can work in small groups. They are particularly effective with groups of individuals who have been victimized by bullies. They are most effective when practiced.

In addition to learning the verbal and behavioral skills necessary to defuse or match a boundary challenge, there are additional components that should be included in building skills to respond to intimidation. They include helping kids to learn as many alternative methods of responding to aggressors as possible, and the utilization of role playing as a method of practicing for the future challenges that await those subjected to victimization.

Alternatives to Responding to Aggressors

Learning to be assertive is certainly one way to respond to aggressors. Many of the curricular materials on the market today describe additional techniques, such as "verbal de-escalation," "escape mechanisms," "teaming," and "assertively ignoring" aggressive challenges.

Verbal de-escalation and **defusing,** aspects of which are incorporated into assertiveness skills training, are time-honored skills that have been practiced for years within law enforcement and correctional settings. The main goal of both is to stop an aggressive challenge from proceeding. In doing so, the forward momentum of aggression loses traction. If an aggressive challenger cannot advance a threat beyond the initial provocation, the aggressor typically leaves the initial subject alone in search of other, more easily aggravated targets. The bully remembers the implicit message from a potential target to the aggressor: "That one will not fall into my trap. She's no fun. I will find someone else who is easier prey."

The teaching metaphor I like to use to explain how aggression tends to take on a life of its own is comparing an aggressive interaction to two people climbing the same ladder. Both people are in a race to the top, but their goals on reaching the top are very different. For the target of the aggression, the goal is to climb up the ladder as far as possible so as to eventually outdistance the aggressor. For the bully, the goal is to chase the target as far up the ladder as possible in order to shove him off (Figure 8.1). Aggressors intend to entice their victims as high up the ladder as they can. They know the greater the escalation, the greater the fall, and they know just how to make it happen. Targets will rarely win once the climb up the ladder of aggression has begun, because the rules of the game are controlled by the bully. In fact, it is more often the case that bullies change the rules as they need to in order to make certain that they always win. The best that a target can hope for is to decode early in the challenge what is transpiring and refuse to climb the ladder. This I call **opting out** of playing the aggressor's game.

Figure 8.1   The Ladder Game. Aggressors like targets who respond to
their actions and escalate an interaction. The goal of the aggressor
is to push the target up a ladder of continuing high-risk interactions
so that the victim can eventually be shoved off. The "higher" up the
ladder a target can be manipulated, the greater the "fall."

Each rung on the ladder represents a higher level of challenge. Challenges, in this instance, may be encroachments on the personal boundaries of the target (similar to the boundary challenge discussed earlier); it may be verbal taunts; it may be physical contact; it may be a combination of all three. In order for the escalation to advance, the target must respond each time to an aggressor's challenge. In doing so, the target sends a message to the aggressor that they are still "in the game." Additionally, each time a target matches an aggressor's challenge, that response is likely to be perceived as a threat to the reputation of the bully. If the target has the abilities to actually respond in ways that turn the tables on the aggressor, the bully may feel threatened and feel the need to respond with an overwhelming next step. Woe be unto unsuspecting targets should they temporarily get the upper hand in an escalating situation in a public venue. The loss of face by a bully in the presence of peers is one of the most dangerous situations that can occur.

Kids must learn the techniques of verbal de-escalation and defusing (four examples of which will be discussed in greater detail in the following paragraphs). Knowing how to be assertive serves as an underlying foundation to increase the likelihood of using verbal de-escalation. Potential targets find it helpful to keep in mind the basic purpose of any kind of response they give to an aggressive invitation: "What can I say that will make this person lose interest in me?" Here are two examples of how a challenge by an aggressor can be handled:

A ninth-grade aggressor approaches a potential target in the school cafeteria during lunch. The aggressor is accompanied by three followers.

Bully (B):   Hey, Sarah. I heard you were kissing one of the cheerleaders yesterday in the locker room. What a lesbo!

Target (T): I did not! Who said that?

B: I did, and we're telling everybody that you're a lesbian!

T: If you do, I'll get you back!

B: Yeah, and how you going to do that?

T: I'll tell everybody that you're the one who was really making out in the locker room.

B: You do that and I'll put signs up all over campus that say you're looking for a lesbian lover! And I'll give your name and address to a bunch of gay magazines so that they start sending you all that queer stuff at your home!

T: You'd better not!

B: And how are you going to stop me? *[Turns to everybody in the immediate area and shouts]* Hey! Did you know that Sarah here got caught kissing some of the girls in the locker room yesterday? She says she liked it!

No matter what the target does in this instance, the aggressor always wins. When the target made an effort to match the intimidation by the bully ("I'll tell everybody that you're the one who was really making out in the locker room."), the bully responded by greatly upping the ante and, in the end, departing the scene with a loud pronouncement to everyone within earshot.

Who knows what would have happened if an effort to verbally de-escalate the situation by an assertive Sarah had occurred? Let's see. Now we'll look at the same scenario as before, but with a different outcome:

B: Hey, Sarah. I heard you were kissing one of the cheerleaders yesterday in the locker room. What a lesbo!

T: *[Looks at the aggressor matter-of-factly but says nothing.]*

B: What's the matter? The truth hurts, doesn't it?

T: *[Continues to look matter-of-factly at the aggressor.]* The truth is, Becky, that you do this to people all the time and it's getting old.

B: What are you talking about? I don't do this to people! You're just embarrassed because you're a lesbian!

T: I'm not going to play this game with you.

B: I'll tell everyone that you're the queen of a bunch of locker room queers!

T: Just go away and leave me alone, okay? *[By this time, Becky's followers are getting bored. One of them tugs at her arm and says, "Let's go, she's no fun."]*

In a perfect world (like one that can be constructed in this book!), the target's refusals to be intimidated by the aggressor's taunts encourage the bully to go elsewhere. Unfortunately, that is exactly what will happen. The aggressors will move on down the tables in the cafeteria until they find someone else who will react to their intimidation. In this scenario, the target showed a great deal of maturity by not verbally reacting to the very first taunt. Often, eye-to-eye contact with no accompanying facial cues give the impression that what was just thrown toward the target made little impact. Nothing that the target responded with was anything other than factual information, and it was stated in a calm manner. The *voice intonation* of a response to a challenge is as important as the content of the response. The tone needs to match the wording and the intent of the message. If I look unfazed, sound unfazed, and my words indicate that this interaction is not bothering me, then I have gone a long way toward de-escalating a situation designed to do just the opposite to me.

Defusing a situation is often a combination of verbal and physical responses. In the examples just given, words were the tools of de-escalating a tense situation. The goal is to stop the climb up the ladder of tension and aggression. However, there are more ways than just verbal to defuse an aggressor's challenge. These include learning escape mechanisms, ignoring the challenge, leaving the scene, and teaming with peers.

Escape Mechanisms

Escape mechanisms refer to methods of getting away from situations where verbal de-escalation may not work or has not worked in the past. Targets have a great need for a wide array of techniques at their disposal that they can employ during challenging situations, especially because the overdependence on any one technique will eventually fail to work. Escape mechanisms often include nonviolent physical means for terminating an escalating situation. Perhaps more wisely, one can also "escape" a situation by not getting in it to begin with. This can be accomplished by avoiding problem areas where abuse often occurs or arriving late to those settings that cannot be otherwise avoided. Certain actions are likely to work better with different age levels than others. As a general rule, the older the child, the more persistent and devious the abilities needed to bring mayhem to a target.

Ignoring the Challenge

Ignoring a challenge means just that. It is a failure to acknowledge by word or action a challenge that has been thrown toward the target. It is easier to ignore verbal challenges than physical threats. Ignoring a challenge often works best in concert with some of the other alternatives we are discussing in this section.

In the second scenario, Sarah employed a degree of ignoring Becky's challenge when she looked matter-of-factly at Becky after the first taunt and said nothing. Ignoring can mean either *absolute nonrecognition* of a challenge (in Sarah's case, that would have meant no eye contact and no verbal response to the offensive challenge), or it could mean *limited nonrecognition,* such as eye contact but no other response. Absolute nonrecognition works best when the target has an immediate safe place in which to focus. It is easier to ignore a taunt in a crowded hallway, where there is much activity and everyone is moving within a specified time limit, than it is to avoid the same in a setting such as a cafeteria or on the bus ride to and from school.

Using the same pair of students in the same situation as before:

B: Hey, Sarah. I heard you were kissing one of the cheerleaders yesterday in the locker room. What a lesbo!

T: [*No verbal response. Sarah does not look up from her meal. She turns to another student at her table.*] Would you pass me the salt, please?

B: Hey, don't be giving her anything. Hey, Sarah, I'm talking to you! What do you say about what I just said you were doing?

T: [*Finishes with the salt and passes it back to the student who gave it to her.*] Thanks.

B: You just going to sit there and act like you don't care?

T: [*Turns to another student at the table behind her.*] Did you say that Mr. Hogan gave a pop quiz in third hour today? He didn't give us one.

In this scene, absolutely no recognition was given to the aggressor. If successful, the bully will tire of the nonresponsiveness and move to other aggravations.

Ignoring challenges as a single tool to combat bullying works well in the elementary grades. Children tire more easily. At the age level in the scenarios we have been using—ninth grade—the likelihood of absolute nonrecognition working this well would be suspect.

Leaving the Scene

If ignoring a challenge does not work, then leaving the scene of the aggression may be in order. *Leaving the scene* of a challenge is not running away. Though bullies may choose to characterize it as such, leaving the scene is doing exactly what the phrase describes—leaving the area of the harassment. When targets leave the scene of an aggressive challenge, they do so *calmly* and with *dignity.* It is important that targets have a safe destination in mind when they begin to leave. Walking away from one area into another that does not provide any more safety than the last one will not do the target much good.

Helping targets plan how to leave the scene of aggression is important, because when individuals are faced with threats, the mind has a tendency to go into biological survival mode and anything not typically done by rote may not be created in the midst of the moment. Remember, fight, flight, or freeze? Targets need to first and foremost be encouraged to avoid the areas where intimidation most frequently occurs. Reducing exposure to such behavior makes sense. If they cannot avoid these areas, then they need to know the nearest safe havens wherein they are likely to be able to increase adult supervision or be in some kind of neutral zone where bullies do not act. In the situation between Sarah and Becky, there are specific classrooms just outside the cafeteria that remain open for students as study rooms. The library, as well, lies across the hallway from the cafeteria. There are adult supervisors in each of these locations. Usually, after a good dose of assertive de-escalation, followed by ignoring, and topped off with a departure to a safe area—especially if this is a response applied by many students—most bullies find that they have to look harder for their victims.

B:	Hey, Sarah. I heard you were kissing one of the cheerleaders yesterday in the locker room. What a lesbo!
T:	*[No verbal response. Sarah does not look up from her meal. She turns to another student at her table.]* Would you pass me the salt, please?
B:	Hey, don't be giving her anything. Hey, Sarah, I'm talking to you! What do you say about what I just said you were doing?
T:	*[Finishes with the salt and passes it back to the student who gave it to her.]* Thanks.
B:	You just going to sit there and act like you don't care?
T:	*[Turns to another student at the table behind her.]* Did you say that Mr. Hogan gave a pop quiz in third hour today? He didn't give us one. *[Sarah and her peers at the other table begin to discuss that issue.]*
B:	*[Walks over to the other table and interrupts the group to whom Sarah is now talking.]* Listen, you can't get away from us that easily. We're talking to you. Hey, did you all hear that Sarah here has been French-kissing the cheerleaders?
T:	*[Sarah still does not respond and continues talking with those at the table behind her. No one at that table responds to the challenge, either. She finishes that conversation, says goodbye to her friends at both tables, tosses her lunch bag in the garbage, and walks to the library, where she finds a book and starts to read.]*

It was helpful that no one at either of the tables responded in any way to the challenges thrown at Sarah. Whether this occurred by chance or because of a previous effort at a group response makes little difference. The bottom line was that it served the same purpose: It gave no feedback to the aggressors that their behaviors were endorsed or desired.

Teaming

Teaming is when a group of students concerned about the mistreatment of others band together during times of challenge to offer a buffer against the behavior. It is not the forming of a gang of retaliators. In fact, it may not be viewed as any structured group of specific peers. Teaming occurs when a target utilizes those in the immediate vicinity to neutralize the threats coming from an aggressor. It is the same strategy employed by schools of fish to escape their predators. Schools of fish provide greater protection to those in the middle; they give the appearance of being a much larger (and potentially challenging) foe; and they confuse the attacker. If Sarah left the cafeteria and moved into a common area populated with many students, found a group of her friends, and began to interact with them, that would be a combination of leaving the scene and teaming. It could happen accidentally. If Sarah left the cafeteria and moved into a large crowd of students and became lost in the crowd, that is another form of teaming.

The best teaming occurs when all students are sensitive to the issue of bullying and teasing and are committed to stopping it. In this positive school environment, students actively combat the behavior by speaking out against it. When they see it occurring, they move toward it in an effort to stop it. The presence of a group of peers who proactively attempt to stop a misbehavior is a powerful weapon, perhaps one of the most powerful in the arsenal of stopping bullying and teasing. Their message may be the same as the one delivered by adults, but when it comes from their own, however, it takes on a new urgency.

Continuing with our scene in the cafeteria:

T:	*[Turns to another student at the table behind her.]* Did you say that Mr. Hogan gave a pop quiz in third hour today? He didn't give us one. *[Sarah and the peers at that table begin to discuss that issue.]*
B:	*[Walks over to the table and interrupts the group to whom Sarah is now talking.]* Listen, you can't get away from us that easily. We're talking to you. Hey, did you all hear that Sarah here has been French-kissing the cheerleaders?
Friend 1:	Becky, no one appreciates what you're trying to do.
Friend 2:	Yeah, you know you said the same thing about Melissa last year. It wasn't funny then and it isn't funny now.
B:	*[Says nothing. Assesses the situation.]*

Friend 3:   If you don't mind, we were having a discussion about something important here. We're going to continue now.

B: Yeah, well, what I said was true. For all I know, you're all a bunch of lesbians! *[Turns to her followers.]* Come on, girls, let's leave this table full of flaming faggots before they try to take off all our clothes!

In this instance, the teaming took place without Sarah's having to leave the scene. Although it did not lessen the verbal taunting by the aggressor—as is common, the bully then spewed her venom on all of those in opposition to her behavior—the message sent was clear: "We do not approve of what you are doing, and we are going to try to stop you from doing it." In joining with Sarah to verbally confront the efforts under way to escalate the intimidation against her, the bullies were met with nonviolent words that effectively prevented them from gaining further traction on the aggression ladder.

Intentional teaming, which involves other students actively and nonviolently intervening on behalf of their targeted peers, is a method of solving the issue of *involved* and *noninvolved bystanders.* By their inaction, bystanders contribute to the problem. Remember the concept of vicarious learning circles? In this example, outside the immediate area of conflict between a victim and an aggressor are differing levels of bystanders. Those closest to the victimization are likely the most interested in supporting the aggressive action and become de facto participants through taunts and support of the actual aggressor. The farther away a child is from the center of the activity, the lower the level of involvement, knowledge, or concern.

As noted earlier, inaction is an endorsement of the status quo—and that includes kids, too. When bystanders who have the ability to intervene, either by verbally defusing a situation or by providing a teaming effort, and they do not, their inaction endorses the bullying. Schools need *positive involved bystanders* who are willing and able to prevent or intervene assertively and nonviolently to stop acts of intimidation directed toward victims. Schools do not want *negative involved bystanders*, who actively encourage misbehavior.

Finally, if they are unable to get away from an aggressive challenge themselves, students can always turn directly to adults and ask for assistance. It is always better, however, when peers can work out their problems among themselves without adult intervention. Self-solution can then be applied by children and adolescents 24 hours a day and in multiple settings both in and out of school. That is empowerment at its best.

The Importance of Role Playing: Practice Makes Perfect

The title of this section says it all. Students need to practice the techniques of bullying and teasing intervention in order to increase the likelihood that they will succeed in applying them. They need to hear themselves say out loud the words that are designed to respond to an aggressor's taunts. They need to physically do the actions necessary to extricate themselves from tense situations. The best method for preparing students to utilize the techniques that we want them to have to combat bullying is to have them practice via *role playing*.

When done right, role playing is serious business. That is not to say that it is not fun or educational. Role playing allows individuals the chance to learn how to do what is needed in order to perform some kind of anticipated behavior. It also applies to practicing specific words or phrases designed to impact change. It is not enough to talk about what should be done in a specific circumstance. That is only the first step. The brain learns much better when a person sees something, hears it, and does it.

Role playing is particularly effective when used with those who have been targeted by aggressors. Many times these individuals believe they have lost, or never had, the ability to do what is necessary to escape their torment. In some instances, they actually might never have had the knowledge of what to do. Other times, they have been so beaten down for so long that they have given up trying. Remember learned helplessness?

In doing consultations with schools and working with my interns, who implement many bully intervention efforts within schools, it has become apparent that the practice of role playing the techniques of how to ward off aggression is a powerful experience for victims. Besides the comments they make during small-group sessions about the pain of their experiences, targets get very excited as they are given the intervention tools designed to decrease the probability of their being further abused. It is an uplifting experience to watch young people's self-esteem improve as they learn that they are capable of saying the phrases to defuse tense confrontations. It is a wonderful moment in the lives of those who are trying to help these young people when we watch their entire body language change, when they hold their heads up and go out to become engaged with their peers—some for the first time.

Effective role playing works best when the participants are willing to try it and when the environment feels safe for them. That is why so often role playing in a general classroom does not work. The focus of role-playing exercises in classroom settings often is not so much on the goal of the lesson, but more on the nonparticipants finding something to laugh at among their peers. Role playing is far more likely to be a meaningful learning experience when undertaken in small groups. For victims of bullying and teasing, this is especially true. Because they are accustomed to being put on the spot in front of their peers, they need no more of that, and that is exactly what is likely to occur in a classroom session where half the people are not interested in participating.

One of the most important aspects of role playing surprises many, and it is one that is often overlooked by those who are in charge of it. Those who are learning a specific behavior in role playing must understand clearly that when practiced in the real world, it may not work the first few times. This is a critical understanding that participants must have. I have observed role-playing participants, who were so enthused by the skills they learned in lessons, come back in tears after they tried to use the same skills the first time with the results being less than what they thought they would be. With those who have been tormented for long periods of time, their tolerance for coping with additional disappointments and failure in their peer relationships may be very low. It is imperative that everyone learning new skills understand that perfection rarely occurs on the first try.

> *Jeff, I am so proud that you have worked really hard at all that we have done in learning new ways to assert yourself. You, of all people, have had some of the most difficult things to deal with. I also want you to remember that very important thing that I said when we started these lessons. Do you remember what we said about taking these lessons and applying them in the real world? . . . Yes, that's right. They may not all work the first few times. But if we keep trying, and if we try several of the different kinds of skills that we learned, chances are things will start to improve. In the meantime, you can always check back with me for a tune-up, right?*

And we must be ready to shore up the disheartened when their early attempts at putting practice to reality fail:

> *Andrea, your disappointment is written all over your face that those first few efforts at verbal de-escalation didn't work as we had planned. Let's go over again exactly what happened and what you did to try to resolve the conflict. . . . Well, you certainly get an A for those efforts. It sounds to me as if you did everything that you were supposed to do. But did you remember some of the other techniques we learned if what we were trying didn't work out? . . . Okay, well, let's see if we can't go over some of those again because it seems as if you've forgotten some other tools in your tool kit that you might find useful. Let's start with ignoring those who are attempting to annoy you. Then we'll go over the other options we learned: leaving the scene of the problem for a safe place and looking for someone to team up with.*

One of the most powerful tools to stimulate change within the school setting is live theater or motivational speakers. Many a new student initiative has been launched in the immediate departure of an inspirational thespian troupe that has performed some kind of play about a contemporary issue in the lives of kids. Effective presentations of this kind can serve as a catalyst for encouraging victims to take an active role in their predicaments. Some programs offer away-from-school retreats for specific grade levels or peer helper groups. Others come into the school and provide programs for the entire student body. Two groups worthy of further investigation are Youth Frontiers (www.youth-frontiers.org) and Climb Theatre (www.climb.org/index.html), both of which offer programs related to respect, self-esteem, and bullying. My endorsement of these two particular programs is based on experience and the recommendations of colleagues, whose reports of the positive impacts that these groups have had on their respective schools is a testament to the good work of the organizations. Is there a cost involved? Sure. But it is worth the money to bring these powerful groups into a school because of the changes that begin among the student body after their performance.

6. DO NOT ABANDON THE VICTIM

I cannot emphasize this point enough! Once the target of bullies has turned to adults to ask for assistance and we have responded, it triggers the beginning of a long-term commitment to ensure that we see the task through to its conclusion. **Abandonment** can mean several things and be done in several ways. In its purest form, abandonment occurs when we neglect to respond to a child's initial cries for help. Assuming that we do respond, we cannot simply walk away from working with the victim once an immediate threat has been eliminated. In truth, the chances are good that the threat has not been eliminated but has more likely gone dormant until it can resurface again when supervisors are looking the other way. Abandonment also occurs if we leave the child defenseless. To do so sets the child up for future attacks. It sets the stage for revictimization.

Support Systems

In order to prevent such revictimization and abandonment from occurring, one of the first steps in ensuring longer-term success for targets in recovery from their abuse is through the establishment of some kind of support system. This can be done in several ways. It is important that victims know that they are not alone in their concerns and that, unfortunately, there are others within the school who are dealing with similar concerns and issues. Arranging for victims to take part in counseling support groups is one way of normalizing a target's experience.

Counseling Support

Counseling support groups for victims of aggression are designed first and foremost to give those who have been targeted the chance to voice their thoughts and feelings in a safe environment. In the safety of the school counselor's office, victims have the opportunity to speak freely about their experiences and how the misbehaviors directed toward them have impacted their lives. Counseling support groups are often formed to address specific deficits in the lives of victims. Almost all of the victims of bullying and teasing have low self-esteem. Sometimes they need help with learning how to better form relationships with their peers, especially provocative victims or those who have had little or no peer interactions. While counseling support groups of this kind are designed to allow the participants to talk about the emotional side of their lives at the hands of bullies, that should not be the only focus of the sessions.

They should also be educational, in the sense of teaching skills and techniques to help the victim respond to the overtures of the bully.

Role Models

Another method of providing support is through the pairing of victims with positive role models. This is the concept behind such peer support networks as a "big brother" and "big sister" or "student ambassador" program. Such big brother–sister programs pair students with specific needs with other students in the school who have volunteered to help others. Student ambassador programs go under many names and serve to assist needy students in many ways, such as welcoming new students to the school and helping them find their way around, or teaming with students who need a companion during difficult times. Students who are selected for such ambassador-type positions clearly must be trained to understand how their stature as a positive role model is helpful to others.

Student ambassadors may well come from the same mold as those students who wish to serve as peer helpers in a school. The major difference is in the training that peer helpers receive as compared to the average student ambassador. Peer helpers typically are selected because they want to help their peers during times of crisis. As such, they may have received training in conflict resolution skills. Many elementary schools employ this concept with their "peacemaker" peer helper groups. Peacemakers are specially trained students within the school to whom other students turn for help in resolving disputes before they require adult assistance. They have proven especially helpful in reducing problems on playgrounds during recess. Whatever the name of a peer helper group, when effective, they are often responsible for a direct reduction in peer-on-peer abuse incidents.

Students who have turned to others for assistance in the bully-victim relationship must know who they can turn to after the initial reported incident has subsided. They must be told that the support network that they relied on for help in that instance is there for them in the future, should they need it. And likely they will. That is, unless we are totally effective in the implementation of Strategic Intervention Point 4, in which case the entire problem just magically goes away! Unfortunately, that likely will not happen in my lifetime, but you will see what I mean in the next chapter.

Because listening is the primary tool of the counselor, I began a journey to accompany the toadies and the Two, after they returned to school, into their world. Even though I had been the one who had caught all five of them in the act—and hence was responsible for their being punished—I was lucky in that within Kid World my reputation as an "okay guy" was solid, even with these five. I scheduled individual meetings each week with all five. Even though working with bullies was new to me, I had enough common sense to know that I would not have stood a chance with all five of them in the same room together at once. The principal kept close tabs on me, not in an interference kind of way, but because he was intrigued by what I was up to, especially because it was his goal to catch the Two in another suspendable offense in the near future and leverage that into a more lengthy "vacation" for them. I truly did not have any reason to doubt that that very thing would occur.

Even though the Two were now trying to become best buddies with me—they were quite charming and manipulative—I let them know at the outset that probably I was their best bet to avoid getting booted out of school for good and that a part of the principal's willingness to let them back in was that they would agree to meet with me on a regular basis. They laid low on their return to all school functions, but it was clear to me that it was just a matter of time before they were back to their old tricks.

All five got the same treatment. I met with them individually each week. We talked about not just their behavior, but about their interests, their school work, and how they saw themselves in the school environment. I had a video about aggressive kids and why they acted out that I showed them segments of some weeks as a stimulus for discussion. Of all the topics we covered, the video seemed to be the one that created the most discomfort for them. They could see via the video what actions like theirs did to others. While their first response was to try and laugh the video away ("Ah, man, that stuff's just fake."), I refused to let them off the hook that easily.

I pressed them for a more personal answer. "The video may be fake with the actors in it, but what do you think about how realistically they portray the topic?"

One by one, each of them began to open up to me that semester. All I did was listen and occasionally zing them with a question or comment to try and make them think a little more about what they had said to minimize or justify their behaviors. And almost every one of them (the more I remember, it may have well been every last one of them), at some point, said words to the effect of, "You know, nobody around here [translate that to the adults] ever took the time to talk to me before. Everybody always sees me as trouble, not like a normal kid. So that's what I give them. Trouble. If that's what they think I am supposed to be, then I guess I will."

9

Strategic Intervention Point 4

Engage the Bully in Constructive and Supportive Interactions

This is, as far as I am concerned, the most important part of this book. No matter what we do to help the victims of intimidation, no matter how much comfort we give them or how well we teach them the skills of assertiveness, *unless we give as much attention to the bully as we do the victim, we will never solve the problem of the bully-victim dyad.*

Bullies are kids, too. Like it or not, they need and deserve our full attention, just as much as, if not more so than, the victims they torment. That is not to say that those who intervene have to excuse bullying behaviors. Far from it. One of the main goals for bullies is for them to learn that they are accountable for their actions and that we intend to make certain that they are. But, as with victims, we have an obligation to get beyond the surface story and work to discover the inner saga of this troubled young person.

Bullies are not easy people with whom to work. In all honesty, they push our emotional buttons. As previously mentioned in Chapter 5, we almost instinctively respond defensively in their presence. It takes much willpower and self-control to work with those whom we want to believe have no redeeming qualities and who do not want to improve their station in life. The bully, aware of this psychological mind-set in adults, will often act accordingly and thus, perpetuate a self-fulfilling prophecy.

Readers may find it surprising that I offer the same basic intervention steps with the bully as I do the victim. My premise is that it is the bully's surface behavior that we find intolerable and that we must get beneath it if we are to understand the child who resides underneath. I characterize it as washing the mud off a child with a garden hose to reveal the real person beneath the yuck. Interventionists hold the hose. The hose and its stream of water represent the skills we employ to change the child's negative behavior (the mud).

Working with bullies is not an easy proposition. It takes a tremendous amount of patience and willingness to withstand bellicose behaviors. Like working with victims, a strategy may not work the first time. But unless we are willing to not give up on the bullies, there will be no change and the bullies will be doomed to assume that the same behaviors that they employ with their peers *now* will work with adults *later*. After all, in their minds, when they direct those behaviors toward us and we leave them alone, they get reinforcement that what they're doing must be right.

There are eight critical aspects that comprise Strategic Intervention Point 4:

1. Understand the rationale and logic of the victimizer.

2. Listen to the story that the bully tells.

3. Educate aggressors on boundaries and acceptable behaviors.

4. Take a team approach in reducing aggression, but work with aggressors as individuals during the accountability phase.

5. Contact the parents of the bully.

6. Make sure that effective bullying and teasing policies are in place—and enforced when necessary.

7. Provide violence prevention education, support, and positive initiatives on behalf of the individual aggressor.

8. Do not abandon the bully.

A detailed look at each aspect follows, to help us get inside the heads—and hearts—of bullies.

1. UNDERSTAND THE RATIONALE AND LOGIC OF THE VICTIMIZER

Like victims, the perpetrators of aggression do so for a reason. They may be aware of why they do what they do. They may also not be aware. In either instance, effective intervention will help to explore the basis for the bully's behavior.

Many of the things that make the bully tick can be found in Chapter 5. However, do not automatically assume that bullies are products of their immediate home environment. As previously noted, there are plenty of nonpoint and floating resources to which kids are exposed today that encourage them to misbehave and act aggressively. Sometimes kids will tell us why they acted to way they did: "He dissed me in front of my friends so I hit him to put him in his place!" or "He made me mad, that's why!" Actions to avenge perceived slights are likely the number one reason that aggressors will give as to the reasons for their surface behavior. Because American society has always placed a high premium on its people's ability to take care of themselves—particularly men—revenge for perceived slights is one assumed way of "evening the score." This is true for both boys and girls. More likely, though, is this response to inquiries as to the rationale behind attacking others: "I don't know. I just did it." And they may truly not know why they behave in the aggressive manners in which they do. This is certainly true of children and adolescents who act impulsively or out of a foundation of anger.

Knowing the reasons behind a child's aggressive behavior serves as a foundation for designing a more effective intervention. It does little good to tell a young person to simply stop behaviors fueled by a deep, underlying need to deal with the frustrations created by the heavy-handed discipline meted out by parents. Until we know the real reasons for a child's misbehaviors and begin the efforts to deal with the roots of the thought processes, little we do will be effective. The counseling dialog in the next section will demonstrate how we can ascertain the bully's rationale.

2. LISTEN TO THE STORY THAT THE BULLY TELLS

Bullies and their targets share some amazing similarities. As with victims, bullies have a lot of stories to tell. As with their targets, bullies may never have had the opportunity to tell those stories. They probably have never felt safe enough to tell them. Even more likely is the possibility that no significant adult in their lives has ever asked or shown concern.

Bullies, like victims, have that surface story and an inner saga. Surface stories will revolve around the immediate stressors that caused the actions of the bully. This is where it takes patience and persistence to get beneath the veneer of "stuff." Most likely, we will already know the surface story by the time an incident comes our way. Amanda was caught sending threatening and slanderous text messages to Karla. That is what happened, but it does not tell us Amanda's reasons.

Intervener (I):   Amanda, yesterday we dealt with the problem of you sending threatening messages to Karla, and we said that today we would spend more time trying to understand what was going on between you two. So, I have to ask, what were your reasons for doing that?

Amanda (A):   I just did it. [She says nothing else.]

I: That's it, you just did it? Well, we know that, but my question to you is, what caused you to feel as if you had to do it?

A: *[Long pause before responding.]* She just makes me so mad, that's all.

I: So you were mad at Karla and that is what caused you to send her the messages?

A: Yes.

I: My hunch is that there is more to it than that. Is what was making you mad something that happened recently or long ago?

A: It's been going on since elementary school. She spread some rumors between me and some other friends that caused us all to hate each other. I've hated her ever since.

I: That's quite a long time to be mad at someone.

A: Well, it was worth it if I got her back with those messages I sent.

Now we understand Amanda's logic for her actions. She was seeking revenge for what she perceived as the theft of friendships from elementary school. The basis for the messages is deep-seated: Amanda has never forgiven Karla for the rumors she blames Karla for starting years earlier. With this information, we now have some foundations on which to build toward analyzing Amanda's inner saga.

I: That's quite a long time to be mad at someone.

A: Well, it was worth it if I got her back with those messages I sent.

I: So, the reason you sent those threatening messages was because of something that happened over three years ago. I see. You know, sometimes we go straight to "mad" when we are really experiencing some other feelings inside us, things like hurt and sadness. I wonder if what you really feel inside is actually more sadness and hurt because you feel as if Karla stole some of your friends.

A: *[No response. She is deep in thought.]*

I: Amanda, often it's hard for people to say what they may really be feeling because we live in a world where we're supposed to be tough and not admit that some things actually are hurtful to us. I don't know what's really going on in your head, about what's making you think the way you do about Karla. That's for you to decide. But I do know that it's not an admission of being a sissy or of being weak when we honestly talk about things like losing friends and how sometimes that hurts.

A: *[Still no response.]*

I: Why don't you think about what I've said and we'll meet again tomorrow to talk some more, if you'd like. I know that you and Ms. Principal have another meeting today to talk about all of this. You may have some more thoughts about this whole thing after today.

A: *[Leaves the room without saying anything and goes back to class.]*

In this scenario, the intervener is trying to be as nonjudgmental as possible in talking with the aggressor. Someone else will clearly be making judgments later that day—Ms. Principal—and whatever accountability is imposed is not the role of the intervener in this case. It is always important for kids to have **neutral third-party adults** with whom they can share their thoughts, adults who are not in the discipline loop and who will not be the ones handing down sentences for whatever the bullies have been accused. The intervener here also did not press Amanda for answers beyond what she was willing to talk about. The door was left open for her to think about what was discussed and to further explore it the next day if she chose to do so. So often when working on long-term and deep-seated issues, conversations of one day do nothing more than plant seeds for another day's harvest.

The next day, Amanda does come back to see the intervener, even before the intervener has the chance to touch base with her.

A: I've been thinking about what you said yesterday, about maybe I was really hurt and sad about what happened in fifth grade.

I: And . . . ?

A: You may be right. I remember I was really hurt that Karla had stolen my friends away from our group. And I was sad, too. But I was also angry that she did it the way she did.

I: Then it was all three of those emotions that you were dealing with—hurt, sadness, and anger?

A: I guess so.

I: And anger won out?

A: I guess. All I wanted to do was get her back for what she'd done to me because it hurt a lot. When Karla got that new cell phone for Christmas, I knew that I could get her back as much as I wanted to by sending those messages.

I: You just forgot that with each one you sent, your phone number went along with it and showed up on her caller ID!

A: *[Laughs.]* Something like that.

I: Well, I'm glad you've thought about some other reasons why you might have done what you did. It's important to be honest with ourselves, even when the truth may be difficult to admit. So, I'm wondering, is this the first time that you've acted out of anger when you were really feeling something else inside?

A: You know, I was thinking about that last night, too. I think that maybe there are a bunch of things that I've done because I was mad when really I felt something else.

I: And if you had to put feeling words on those examples you are thinking about, what might they be?

A: Well, one time I was babysitting my little brother and . . .

Amanda has accepted the intervener's invitation to explore other examples of her behaviors in the past and how she might have acted with anger instead of the real emotions she felt. The basis is now set for Amanda to begin major self-exploration on the motivations behind her bullying behaviors.

3. EDUCATE AGGRESSORS ON BOUNDARIES AND ACCEPTABLE BEHAVIORS

This is a very important aspect of interventions with bullies, particularly boys. Bullies need to know when their behaviors cross other people's interpersonal and physical boundaries. They need to be told explicitly that their aggressive behaviors are not welcomed and will not be tolerated in the school setting. Likewise, they need to get the message that their misbehaviors also may not be appreciated among their peers outside of school. Believe it or not, many aggressive kids have never understood the concept of boundaries, especially if they come from a home where everyone's boundaries are not respected or are entangled. **Enmeshment** is the equivalent of "everyone messin' in everybody else's' business." If one member of the family has a problem, everyone becomes involved in either attempting to solve it or adding additional fuel to the fire to aggravate the situation. If misbehavior at school is not frowned upon at home, children likely perceive this as receiving tacit approval from their parents to continue such behaviors.

Let us take the easy one first: the explicit declaration that bullying behaviors will not be tolerated at school.

Intervener (I):   Toby, this morning Mr. Principal shared with me that you and some other boys were throwing rocks at Rick on the playground and that he was going to be meeting with you and your parents later today.

Toby (T):	I guess. Whatever.
I:	Doesn't sound to me that you're too concerned about it.
T:	Nah, I'm not worried. It's not my fault he moved into the direction I was throwing the rock. We were just fooling around, that's all.
I:	Maybe so. But Rick's got a cut on his head from that "playing around," and I don't think he thinks you were playing. That's something that you and Mr. Principal will have to work out later. The only reason that I'm in on this is because, as you know from what's in the student handbook, if one of our students is involved in an act of bullying others, the policy says that I am to talk with them to see what's really going on before Mr. Principal makes a decision about what to do.
T:	Whatever. I really don't care what he does. I'm not scared.
I:	That's fine, Toby. That's between you and Mr. Principal. But I do have a feeling that you and I are going to be spending some time together in the coming weeks talking about all this.
T:	Whatever.
I:	I'm willing to help in any way I can to make this a safe place for everybody—including you, Toby. So, if there's something going on that I need to know about, I hope that you will share that with me or Mr. Principal later today.
T:	I won't be sharing anything with either of you.
I:	That's okay with me, but you and Mr. Principal will have to work out a deal as to how the two of you decide to get along. Again, I want you to know that if you ever want to talk to me about stuff, you can. But I have to make this crystal clear with you: At this school, we do not tolerate abusive behaviors to others. No one does. This school deals very quickly and firmly with students who bully and tease others, and if you continue to do things like you did today, Mr. Principal will continue to hold you responsible for what you do and each time that visit will likely get more unpleasant. Do you understand what I just said?
T:	Yeah, yeah, yeah.
I:	Then let me know in your own words what I said about your behavior in school.
T:	If I get caught bullying, you people are going to punish me and if I do it enough, you'll kick me out.
I:	Well, that's not exactly it, but it's a starting point for us to begin . . .

Toby displayed the **defiant behavior** of the stereotypical bully. He feigned concern about what might happen to him. He *minimized* the rock-throwing incident. He indicated his intent to not be cooperative in future intervention and accountability efforts. He exaggerated the explanation of what were acceptable behaviors in the school setting and placed blame for any accountability action that might come his way on "you people." Bullies are astute manipulators in blaming others for their problems.

Explicit statements about which behaviors will not be tolerated are essential. Make certain that they are *simple, direct,* and expressed in a *tone of seriousness,* but never in a tone that invokes sarcasm, mockery, or shows abuse of power. These are self-confirming prophesies on the part of the bully about how adults view them and may actually mimic the behaviors that help create the bully in the first place.

Working with bullies to help them understand the concept of boundaries takes time. They need to understand the concept of personal space and that their behaviors may be misinterpreted by others when they act in belligerent ways, even though they do not believe that what they are doing is harmful to others. Many bullies actually have no concept that their aggressiveness is perceived as such by others, particularly if they were raised in a home where aggressiveness was the family standard.

Boundary education with bullies requires that time be spent with them. In doing so, other insights into the bully's world will likely be exposed. This is another excellent opportunity to discover the inner saga of the aggressor. Like the interaction with Amanda, learning to identify the **metacommunicational themes** of the bully is quintessential in developing the most effective intervention plan. Typical themes may include such buried expressions as *fear, sadness, hurt, anger,* and *loneliness.* It has been my experience that some or all of these five themes are the motivating factors for both bullies and victims. They respond to them, however, in completely different ways out of the matrix of their life experiences and within the confines of how much control over the world they believe they have.

Boundary education must begin with some kind of understanding of how the bully views the limitations of the world. It is important to ascertain under what conditions the bully would not entertain the thought of crossing the boundaries of others. This may be discovered by simply asking questions revolving around the known aggressive behaviors of the bully.

Intervener (I):   Toby, in working with you over the past few days, I've noticed some interesting patterns about who you seem to have trouble with, and I'd like to ask you to help me figure all of this out. You up for that?

Toby (T):   I don't have trouble with anyone until they bug me.

I: That's what I mean. It seems as if certain people bug you more than others.

T: Well, it's true, they do.

I: It seems as though the people whom you find bothersome to you the most are always the ones who are physically weaker than you and who you can easily frighten.

T: *[No response.]*

I: Toby, that makes me wonder if there are other people in the school who you don't bother and, if so, why you don't.

T: Because I like them. They don't bug me.

I: Is it also because they tell you when to stop behaving in ways that they don't like and to back off?

T: Well, yeah. Sometimes. I'm not afraid of anybody, though.

I: I'm not talking about being afraid of anybody. I'm talking about who it is that you tend to pick on.

T: I pick on the ones that bug me! I told you that, already! You deaf?

I: *[Ignores the taunt.]* What I also think I understand is that you pick on those people who don't tell you when to stop. And it doesn't help that you're bigger than they are. At least it doesn't help them.

T: Well, if they wanted me to stop, I guess they'd tell me. If they're too stupid to tell me to quit, then they must like it!

I: Not everybody has the ability to speak up like you do and tell others what they want. You see, Toby, each person carries with them something like an invisible shell that surrounds them. It's like an invisible bubble.

T: *[Laughs.]* That's the dumbest thing I've ever heard of. An invisible bubble!

I: Maybe so, but we all have that invisible bubble. It's called a boundary—some people call it a limit—and it's that amount of distance we like to keep between ourselves and others because it makes us feel secure and comfortable. You have a boundary around you, I have one around me, everyone in this school has a boundary around them. Are you with me so far?

T: Yeah, but it still sounds dumb.

I: Toby, we all work hard to protect that invisible boundary around us because when someone begins to push on it, we feel threatened. Those boundaries are a lot like huge soap bubbles that you can make with one of those big plastic bubble rings. We like our boundaries to keep their shape because if they are pressed on too hard, they will break.

T: *[Looks at the intervenor but says nothing. It is clear that his interest is piqued.]*

I: Sometimes, people will tell us when to back away from those boundary bubbles. Some people are very good at doing it. I bet you know some people in your friendship groups who are good at asking people to move away from their personal boundary.

T: Yeah. Me and my friends are good at it. We'll kick your butt if you try and bust our bubbles! *[Laughs again.]*

I: Well, we don't want anyone to settle their disputes by fighting, which is one of the big reasons we're in here now. But we do want our students to be able to be aware when they think that they may be overstepping their boundaries and beginning to get into someone else's bubble. Have you ever had anyone push your boundary to the point that you felt uncomfortable?

T: *[Thinks, then answers.]* Maybe.

I: And who might that be?

T: Well, people who are bigger than me can almost always scare me away.

I: Just like you do to the people you pick on?

T: *[Thinks. Says nothing.]*

I: What do you do when someone pushes too closely on your personal space?

T: I move away and get outta there.

I: Because . . . ?

T: Because I know that they're about to hit me or steal my money or something. I'm not stupid, I know when somebody's out to get me! Besides, the closer they get to me, the uneasier I get because I know something's about to happen.

I: Toby, my money says that you've learned to do what you do because you've had it done to you. I bet that you know when you're crossing other people's boundaries, and that you know the ones you're able to keep pushing on and those who will tell you to get lost. Why don't we talk some more about all of this boundary stuff and you can tell me what it is that you think is happening inside those whose boundaries you step into . . .

The door is now wide-open for further exploration into Toby's world. While the intervenor in this instance pushed Toby's own psychological boundaries a bit by encouraging him to think about who he did not intimidate and the reasons why, at no time was there an accusatory tone taken toward him to make him feel more uncomfortable than he probably already was about having to talk about his actions. The key to working with those who are being held accountable for their actions is to find that balance between making them *think* about what they have done without making them so uncomfortable or defensive that they shut down or act out. It is not an easy balance to find, and it takes patience and persistence on the part of the intervener to make it happen.

4. TAKE A TEAM APPROACH IN REDUCING AGGRESSION, BUT WORK WITH AGGRESSORS AS INDIVIDUALS DURING THE ACCOUNTABILITY PHASE

Taking a team approach to aggressive children and youths means that the entire staff—including Bob the custodian, Mabel the cook, and Burt the bus driver—is on board with efforts to combat bullying behaviors within the school. Unless the entire school commits itself to fighting such behaviors, the bullies will find the weak spots in the school's efforts and exploit it there.

Team Approaches

A school that I consulted with had a staff that was divided over their willingness to stop bullying and teasing. About three-quarters of the teachers agreed that it was a worthwhile thing to do. The other quarter of the teachers thought it was silly to be wasting their time on trying to stop what was "kid's stuff" and behaviors that "kids would sort out among themselves" without "adult interference." As the year progressed, you guessed it, virtually all of the instances of bullying and teasing occurred in locations and time periods under the supervision of those teachers who were not convinced of the "worthiness" of being involved in intimidation reduction. When the staff met at the end of the semester and was shown the data, there was quite a lively discussion about what it all meant. But there was no arguing about the fact that there was a great disparity between when, where, and under whose jurisdiction bullying and teasing behaviors continued.

Another school district had a special inservice training for all staff, substitute teachers, playground monitors, and noninstructional staff on the issue of violence reduction. At the conclusion of the training, everyone had been exposed to what the school was attempting to do. Reports of intimidating behaviors soared from bus drivers in the days following the opening of school. Afterwards, the number of bus incidents was virtually eliminated for the remainder of the year. When asked about the change in reporting from past years, the bus drivers indicated that while they had known that they could report incidents of behaviors that were distracting to them, they had not been reporting instances of peer-on-peer abuse because they were of the belief that those kinds of behaviors were normal and that they did not know that such behaviors could have such long-term consequences for its victims. Problems that were solved on the front end—in the past, many on-bus conflicts later spilled over into the hallways—and were addressed first thing in the morning did not fester and continue or explode later in the day. Likewise, the number of reports of aggressive behaviors from playground monitors during recess and from the food service staff during lunch increased. The custodial staff reported instances of graffiti within the school that seemed to have direct intentions to harm or were disrespectful toward identifiable students. As the year progressed, the number of disciplinary referrals for instances of intimidation plummeted. At the beginning of the second year, fewer instances of aggressive acts were reported because the kids knew that everyone—*everyone!*—within that particular school did not tolerate such offensive behaviors. The aggressive kids from the year before were less aggressive the second year—at least in the school environment.

As in the first case study, a school that is not totally committed to violence and intimidation reduction will encourage such acts to continue within the corridors and under the supervision of those who do little more than give lip service to the cause. It does not have to be a large percentage of school personnel who do not buy into a violence reduction plan to sabotage the safety net for all the kids in the school. I am aware of schools wherein all faculty but a few actively participated in efforts to reduce bullying and teasing, and the only places where it ended up occurring was in those specific faculty members' jurisdictions.

In taking a team approach against intimidating behaviors, kids get the message that all staff in this school are against bullying and teasing and will act immediately and persistently to stop it when it comes to their attention. The team approach eliminates any doubts among the student body as to what is and what is not acceptable behavior. From a disciplinary standpoint, there may be a spike in referrals for intimidating behaviors at the beginning of the year, but that spike should be well worth the preventive maintenance as fewer incidents of bullying and teasing occur throughout the remainder of the year.

Individual Approaches

While the team approach with all school staff is necessary to reduce the likelihood of intimidating behaviors among students going unnoticed or being ignored, the exact opposite is advised in working with those who are being held accountable for their aggressive behaviors. Work individually with those responsible for bullying and teasing. There are both therapeutic and commonsense reasons for this.

Therapeutic Reasons

Bullies are used to being dealt with as "problem children." They have learned that if they are caught, they will be punished, and other than that, scant attention will be paid to them. Their modus operandi, then, becomes one of stealth. They may well be used to receiving harsh punishment at the hands of adults, particularly if they have learned those behaviors in the home environment. As such, they believe that the only attention paid to them is when they behave in the manner of a bully. "No one sees me unless I am tough," they reason. "Adults are concerned about me only when they catch me acting up. They never try to figure out what else I'm about. They know me only as a bully, so that's what I give them."

We must be willing and able to turn that paradigm on its head. How better to do so than to do *exactly the opposite* of what the aggressors believe we will do—*see them for who they are beyond the repulsive behavior that gets our attention.* That is best accomplished by spending **one-on-one time** with the perpetrator. In doing so, the aggressors learn that we are interested in them beyond the rumors they were caught spreading; beyond the graffiti on the locker; beyond the threatening e-mails they sent to their victims. In doing so, we learn about the children *beneath* the behaviors whom we have lost track of by the distracting behaviors that they have engaged in.

One-on-one time between an aggressor and an intervening adult will likely first be met with resistance from the agent unless and until there is a level of trust between the two. One-on-one time may best be spent between the aggressor and a school-based helping professional such as the school counselor, who has the skills to communicate beneath the surface story and may well be viewed by the bully as the least threatening and judgmental staff member within the school. Until bullies believe that they are safe to discuss the real person beneath their overt behaviors, it is doubtful that they will do so. That is why bullies seldom give their inner saga away to those in the disciplinary chain.

Commonsense Reasons

As mentioned, there are commonsense reasons for dealing with bullies as individuals. Do you really want to sit with a room full of aggressive kids and try to discuss the basis of their behaviors? I don't, and I don't advise it to anyone. While small groups are perfect for individuals who have been the targets of bullies as a way to discover the commonalities of their predicaments and raise their self-esteem by learning that they are not the only ones who have experienced such treatment, groups with bullies are accidents waiting to happen. Aggressive kids in groups tend to band together in a resistant knot to any effort to crack their bravado. Furthermore, it is an excellent way for them to learn new ways of misbehaviors and new tricks for their goody bag of mayhem.

One of my interns once tried to do this very thing at the elementary level. Even though advised not to, she formed a group of four boys who were known to bully and intimidate others throughout the school. Interns are supervised by both an on-site supervisor in the school and a university supervisor (in this instance, me). They have to submit tapes of their sessions to their university supervisor to be reviewed as updates on how their counseling skills are progressing. It was her time to submit a tape for my review, and she decided that she would tape this group.

Her experience with these fourth-grade boys was everything you could imagine! They were rude, wild, and darn near uncontrollable. With every suggestion or activity planned by the intern to explore the issue of their behavior, they laughed. "We do what we want because we can!" one of them proclaimed. "Yeah, nobody here is big enough to stop us," said another. Before the intern could wrap up the session—early, as you might expect—the boys had regaled her with tall tales of all their many abusive exploits within the school. Several left with new shenanigans to try out at lunch. The group had truly proved every point I made to the intern before she tried to do what she thought she could handle. At the end of the session she was frazzled and frustrated, much like the victims of the bullies themselves!

After we consulted over the disaster, she went back to the school the next day and met with each of the four boys individually to begin a long-term relationship with them as individuals. What she found was remarkable. In a one-on-one setting, each of the boys was very different. They were less belligerent (though clearly still not angels) and much easier to talk with. Each of them made the same observation as her meetings with them progressed: No one at the school had ever taken the time to talk with them individually unless they were about to be disciplined. Even during the administration of discipline, though, there was no discussion about anything other than what they were being disciplined for and the type of accountability that was being assigned to them.

Such one-on-one sessions provide a gateway to understanding the inner saga of the bully. Do not expect the aggressors to open up immediately. They may choose to remain forever encased with the real reasons for their behavior. But it has been my experience that the more time that is spent in a nonthreatening interaction between an adult and a child whose behavior is problematic, the more it will likely encourage that child to take the risk and talk about issues beyond the surface behaviors that they exhibit.

By the way, I ended up giving the intern credit for the tape because she was brave enough to bring it for the two of us to review and figure out what went wrong. Sometimes the best learning experiences are the ones that we mess up. At least then we know what not to do the next time!

5. CONTACT THE PARENTS OF THE BULLY

The parents of bullies should be notified in cases where it is clear that a child is *consistently* behaving in a manner designed to intimidate others. Not every act of aggression between children is an act of bullying, so it is very important that school personnel know what they are dealing with before they label a behavior as an effort at bullying others. The key is with the consistency of the behavior.

Intervener (I):   Mr. Kulland, this is Mr. Archer, Dan's principal. We have a little problem here at school that we need your help with to try to fix. Dan has been observed on three occasions now taking food from other kids' trays in the cafeteria without their permission. He seems to have a dislike for two kids in particular. We've spoken with him on each occasion and assigned him to in-school suspension after today's incident. Would you be able to come to school this week so that we could spend some time trying to determine how we all might work together to stop this behavior?

The parents of children who bully need to know *specific information:* First, the school has identified their child as engaging in consistent behaviors that seem to indicate the intent to bully others; second, the school is engaged in attempting to stop the behavior; and third, the school is enlisting the aid of the parents in being a part of the solution to the problem. Parents need to know when their child is engaging in behaviors that have long-term negative consequences. They may very well be capable of applying additional resources in the effort to stop the behavior before it grows worse.

But what happens when parents are contributors to the problem? They should still be notified unless there is reason to believe that to do so would create a situation harmful to the child.

Intervener (I):   Would you be able to come to school this week so that we could spend some time trying to determine how we all might work together to stop this behavior?

Parent (P):   I really don't have the time to do that. Why don't you just handle the situation up there? Can't you give him a couple of whacks or something if he does it again? That's what we do here at the house when he misbehaves.

I: Mr. Kulland, we believe that Dan needs to see all of us working together on this to impress on him the fact that his bullying of others is not acceptable.

P: Well, he told me about some of this and made it sound like he was getting back food from the others' trays that they had stolen from him.

I: I assure you that that was not the case, Mr. Kulland. Three different teachers independently observed what he was doing on each occasion. But I really would prefer that we conference on this face-to-face so that we can be more successful in helping Dan.

P: Dan is just fine! All he's doing is what we tell him here at home—don't let people push you around.

I: Mr. Kulland, will you come to meet with us about Dan's behaviors?

P: No, look, you just deal with it, okay? But you be fair, too. Don't just pick on him because he doesn't take any crap from other kids.

I: I assure you we will treat him fairly. But I also have to be very up front and let you know that if Dan continues to bully and tease others, we may have no other options but to send him home for a few days to think it over, and we don't want to have to do that.

In this instance, the parent is hesitant to be a part of the solution and may well be a part of the reason why Dan acts as he does. Nonetheless, the principal who is contacting the parent has made it clear what the problem is and what may have to be done if Dan's behaviors do not improve. Hopefully, his father or mother will eventually understand the role they can play in solving the problem and go to the school as requested.

School personnel should also be aware that for some parents the *only* time they are asked to come to school is when there is a problem. These parents have an aversion to parent-teacher conferences of any kind. After all, if all that one ever receives from the school is news about how awful one's child is, why go? I wouldn't want to go, either. School personnel must be very cognizant of this fact, especially when dealing with parents whose child has been the focus of behavioral disruptions in the past.

I: Mrs. Kulland, thank you so much for coming. I understand that this may be a little awkward because it seems as if the only time we talk is when there is a problem with Dan. Well, before we begin to work on what we originally called about, I'd like to share with you some positive reports that the teachers have been giving lately on Dan. We don't see him just as a "problem child." We actually see Dan as a very talented individual who, with a little guidance both here and at home, will come to understand how some of his behaviors are getting in the way of his having a more enjoyable time at school. . . .

Once engaged, the parents of children who bully should be given background information on how those behaviors negatively impact the child's peers and educational opportunities. Parents, just like the kids, should be given the opportunity to discuss their concerns about what is occurring. They should be encouraged to ask questions of the child at home about how their peer relationships are conducted at school, if they have fears about anything at school, and about their motivation as to why they bully others. Parents must also be firm in making it clear to the child who bullies that they do not condone such behaviors and that they intend to work with school personnel to stop it. Parents who scorn the school's request for assistance must be told the consequences that may await their child if such behaviors do not stop. Sadly, in the end, it is sometimes left up to the school to manage the problem of a child's bullying behaviors without parent involvement.

6. MAKE SURE THAT EFFECTIVE BULLYING AND TEASING POLICIES ARE IN PLACE—AND ENFORCED WHEN NECESSARY

This may seem like a no-brainer at first glance. Most schools will have policies in place dealing with general student misbehaviors and that delineate the penalties for violent eruptions. Most schools likely have policies related to harassment or intimidation. Exactly what kinds of harassment or intimidation are covered in the policies may determine whether they are applied to instances of bullying or teasing. If the policy deals exclusively with sexual harassment, then it might apply only in matters of gender or orientation victimization. If a school does not have policy language that will cover incidents of bullying and teasing, then it may be setting itself up for legal challenges by both sets of parents whose children are involved in a bully-victim relationship. The parents of a child who bullies could challenge the discipline meted out if the child is held to a rule that is too vague. Likewise, the parents of the child who is a target of bullying could hold the school liable for its failure to have any policy.

But it is not enough to have policies designed to prevent or respond to acts of bullying. Those policies also must be enforced when such incidents occur. Failure to do so once again sends that message to kids of the tacit approval of misbehavior that is viewed as never being addressed by the adults in authority.

You may have noticed that I have tried to avoid the use of the term "punishment" throughout the book, because I prefer to speak of holding those responsible "accountable" for their actions. **Accountability** for everyone is the acceptance of responsibility for one's actions and being able to explain the logic behind them. Whether that is a punishment may be up to the interpretation of the individual being held to account for their actions. Being held accountable for one's behavior does not mean that some kind of distasteful measure is not applied, but whatever the price bullies pay for their behaviors, *it must always be done in a context of reason* so that the person being held liable for those actions understands the reasons behind them.

Both punishment and accountability are types of different disciplinary actions, and, as I said earlier, bullies must be held accountable for their misdeeds. **Punishment**, however, implies something different than being held accountable because it is often synonymous with pain. Its implications are that one must have an equal pound of flesh extracted in order to right a wrong. The history of the use of punishment within schools is one fraught with ugliness. We have tried beating students with paddles, sitting them in the corner with a dunce cap on the head, suspending them from school, and humiliating them in front of their peers as methods to redress misbehaviors. Punishment has been administered on evildoers without an effort to see if they even understood the reasons behind the need for such treatment. The metacommunication that they get in this instance is quite clear: If you get caught doing something wrong, you will be punished, so just don't get caught. But what exactly should the basis of punishment be? Shouldn't its recipient learn something from the encounter so as to be better able to live as a productive citizen?

Therein lies the difference between a disciplinary action that is designed to punish as opposed to a disciplinary action that is designed to hold people accountable for their actions. One explanation of the origin of the word "discipline" is "follow the example of an exemplar." When I am held accountable for my actions, I am given the chance to *understand the rationale* behind the decisions made by those in power to hold me as such. In being held accountable, I learn that when I violate the rules, the strings that are attached to that violation are *logical* and *designed to improve the situation for all,* not just to give me a noxious medicine to watch me gag. More importantly, I am given the *chance to watch how those in power respond rationally and nonviolently to my infraction.* Look at that origin of discipline again. What kind of example will my exemplar provide for me: anger and punishment or guidance and redirection?

Intervener (I):	Phillip, you know why you're in here today?
Phillip (P):	Because I'm going to get punished for what I did to those kids during recess?
I:	Let's say it's more like you're going to get the chance to prove how responsible you are.
P:	*[Says nothing. He has a puzzled look on this face.]*
I:	This morning you were caught spitting from the upper balcony on the two new students in our school. We do not tolerate that kind of behavior, Phillip. You know that, don't you?
P:	I guess, if you say so.
I:	One of the things that marks maturity in a young person is when they accept the responsibility for what they do and make efforts to correct the harm they might have caused others. I've never heard any student in this school say that they wanted to be treated like a child. Everybody always says that they want to be treated with dignity and with the respect they deserve. I've even heard you say that before, Phillip. Just last week I overheard you complaining to Ms. Principal that she never treated you as if you were in the sixth grade. You had that conversation with her didn't you?
P:	Yeah, I guess.

I:	Well, how do you think she is likely to treat you after this incident?
P:	Like a little kid. Like she always does.
I:	Maybe. Maybe not. What do you think might be something that you could do that would be a sign of maturity in this incident?
P:	*[Says nothing for a long time.]* Be responsible?
I:	Yes, I think that just might be the thing. And how could you do that?
P:	*[Hesitates.]* Apologize to the two kids I spit on?
I:	I think that's a good start. What do you think about me bringing each one of those students up here, one at a time, so that you could personally apologize to them?
P:	I wouldn't know what to say.
I:	We can practice that before they get here . . .

Here the intervener is helping Phillip to own up to his behavior and taking the first steps toward **restorative justice**. Here the concept of a **restorative discipline** is applied in an attempt to get Phillip to take responsibility for harming others and to "right the wrong" as much as he can. A **restorative action** will be designed to let the aggrieved parties know that Phillip accepts responsibility for and regrets the misbehavior. A third step will be to *make amends* for the wrong. Some wrongs are easier to address than others. If property is stolen or broken, returning or replacing it would be part of a restorative action. But the premise of restorative justice is much more than merely replacing a tangible object. It is the opportunity, albeit one that may be forced on a perpetrator, for an aggressor to *think* about what they did in an effort to *generate empathy* and *compassion* for the person who was harmed. In this instance, Phillip did not break an object that can be purchased for tangible restoration. What Phillip "stole" from the two new students in his demeaning act was their dignity and sense of security in their new school.

I:	Phillip, now that you've had the chance to meet with Ian and Heath, my guess is that you've probably learned some things.
P:	Yeah. Maybe.
I:	Could you share some of those thoughts with me?
P:	I guess I've learned that I shouldn't have spit on them because it hurt their pride a great deal.
I:	I think that's what we both learned from what they told us.
P:	And I guess I also learned that I'm responsible for what I do.

I: Yep. Anything else?

P: I learned that even when I apologize for something that I did, it can't always make things even. It's not like I stole something from them. I embarrassed them in front of a whole lot of people.

I: That you did.

P: I also know that I wouldn't want that to have happened to me, and that I have a responsibility to try to make up for what I did.

I: Phillip, I think you said that very well. And you did a good job offering a sincere apology to Heath and Ian. I think you meant it. More important, I think they believe you meant it. Now, let's brainstorm some ideas about ways that you might be able to get things back to the way they were before you did what you did. What do you think is fair to try and right that wrong?

There is a responsibility incumbent on the intervener to help aggressors who are sincere in the desire to apply a restorative action to the wronged. It is not enough to leave the nabbed perpetrators twisting in the wind to think in ways—compassionate and empathetic—that to this point they may never have. We must **role model** the kind of sincere compassion that we want the aggressor to exhibit. This is not always easy. Bullies will likely not want to do this on the first try, or, if they do, they may just try and go through the motions with an insincere and flippant apology so as to "get it over with." We must be willing to be patient with the aggressor. We must remember that impatience is probably the kind of treatment from adults that the bully is most accustomed to.

Let me reiterate one more time so that no one misunderstands: *Bullies must be held accountable for their actions!* I cannot stress that enough. But the accountability that we *teach* them is different from the accountability that we *inflict* on them. Accountability works best when it genuinely comes from *within.* However, for those who do not self-correct their behaviors, isolation by suspension of some type might well be in order. At the end of the day, we have a responsibility to ensure that school is a place where students are safe and can learn. If delinquent behaviors threaten to disrupt the learning process, then those who engage in such shenanigans might well be in need of being denied the privilege of attending classes. Do I advocate suspending students? Only as a last resort. Suspensions are tantamount to the death penalty in Kid World, whether they know it at the time or not. *Every minute that a student is out of a classroom, even serving an in-school suspension, is a minute that the student is not receiving the full benefits of an education.* Out-of-school suspensions are horrible for everyone because they tend to be only short-term solutions to long-range problem behaviors.

Figure 9.1 suggests a continuum of recommendations I make in dealing with students who engage in bullying behaviors.

Figure 9.1   Suggested Guidelines for School Personnel in Responding to Bullies

Behavior of Aggressive Student	Response Warranted
First reported incident of teasing or bullying	Direct warning that such behavior will not be tolerated. Student held accountable for behavior. Restorative effort on the part of aggressor.
Second reported incident	Same response as the first incident. Parents of aggressor notified of concerns.
Third reported incident	Mandatory conference with parent(s). Develop long-range behavioral contract for aggressor. Aggressor held accountable and restorative action for incident enforced. Consideration of suspension alternatives.
Fourth reported incident	Mandatory conference with parent(s)/guardian(s). Consideration of suspension alternatives.

Of course, one should not assume that Figure 9.1 implies that aggressors always get "four chances" before they are suspended. A severe incident of bullying or victimization may require an immediate in- or out-of-school suspension on the first occurrence.

7. PROVIDE VIOLENCE PREVENTION EDUCATION, SUPPORT, AND POSITIVE INITIATIVES ON BEHALF OF THE INDIVIDUAL AGGRESSOR

Why on earth would we want to show support for a bully? It is quite simple, really. First, because it is likely that no one else has. Second, because by showing support, we stand a greater likelihood of being able to impact long-term change in a bully's behavior. Third, because if we drive the bully out of school, then we just have one more angry kid roaming the streets of our world.

When I say provide support for aggressors, I am not talking about praising them for what they have done to others. To the contrary, I am advocating providing bullies with the right kind of support that will most likely be the antithesis of what they are used to receiving. The support I am talking about is the *support of the positive characteristics* of the bully rather than dwelling on the negative ones. It is the *provision of positive role models* to bullies rather than the negative ones that they have likely been exposed to throughout life. It is the willingness of adults in the school environment to *refuse to give up* on the kid who is trying so hard to drive us away.

As with interventions of those who have been victimized, we must address the cognitive, emotional, and behavioral aspects of how the aggressor views the world. The more time that is spent individually with a bully by someone respected, the more likely it is that this will occur. Getting to understand how victimizers view their world will likely give insight into the emotions and behaviors that follow those views.

Aggressors likely need help in developing *coping* and *new survival skills* within what they view as the harsh world in which they live. Below are some key areas with which bullies may need assistance.

Provide Anger Management Strategies

Bullies often operate out of a **worldview of anger.** Those who operate from this perspective have learned that anger is the emotion through which people get what they need. Perhaps they have learned it through firsthand experiences in the home. They certainly have likely been exposed to enough anger-driven role models through the media. Anger becomes the hammer and all problems become nails. If I can get what I want by raising my voice in anger, I will. If I am not afraid of using physical contact with a person whom I judge to be in the way of my goals, then I will. The more I am successful in using an anger-based solution in my approach to the problems I encounter, the more I will use that approach in the future. Nothing succeeds like success in the continuation of a behavior, even if that success is a negative behavior.

Kids who operate from an **anger base** often can identify when they are beginning to become angry. Many report that they can "feel it rising" or that they "start to get hot" or feel their bodies "start to tense." In some respects, children who have the luxury of a *physiological cue* signaling that they are getting angry have the opportunity to learn to back away from those situations that anger them. Other aggressive kids report that they act on *impulse*. Typical are variations from the genre, "I didn't think about it, I just did it!" and "He made me mad, so I hit him." These impulsive behaviors imply action without thought to consequences.

Many bullies claim that they wish they did not act aggressively, but that they do not know how to stop themselves before doing just that. Helping children to identify the cues that signal the likelihood of acting aggressively is important in the overall self-discipline that they must ultimately develop.

There are many anger management curricula tools on the market. Sunburst Visual Media (www.sunburstvm.com/svm.jsp) and Boulden Publishing (www .bouldenpublishing.com) offer several videos and other resources with accompanying guides designed to help angry kids identify the situations and cues that serve as catalysts for aggressive actions. It is particularly important to assist boys in the development of management strategies to handle anger, especially during the middle and junior high school years, because these are the peak ages and grade levels when bullying occurs.

While it might be feasible to do a broad-based, in-classroom curricular module on techniques for dealing with anger with all students in a school—and that is something that I recommend—it would not likely be as effective as with a small group of boys or girls who have been identified as prone to acting in anger for the reasons previously stated. What works best with these angry children is that one-on-one interaction with an intervener:

> *Today, Lance, we're going to talk about some of the things that happen to us when we get angry. I've got a pretty good video that we're going to watch called* When Anger Turns to Rage. *It has some scenes and situations in it that I think you can relate to, and what I would like you to do is ask me to stop the video when you have questions or see things in it that are similar to your life. There may also be some times when I stop the video to ask you what you think about what we just watched. We may not get through the entire thing today because of the discussions that we have, but what we don't finish today, we will finish during the next times we meet.*

Do not assume that the only angry people within a school are boys. Girl bullies are just as likely to act out of a framework of anger as boys, though as we know, the tactics they employ against their targets are often much more discrete. While boys are more likely to act out of a sense of anger based on a perceived macho need to exert power and force to prove their toughness and "manhood," girls are more likely to act in anger from perceived slights to their social status within the peer group. The results for the victim, however, are quite the same—humiliation and excommunication from the in-group.

Provide Alternate Strategies to Violence

Bullies need assistance with two main aspects of their behaviors, especially those who act from an anger base. First, they need help *identifying when they are getting angry*. Second, they need to *know what to do with that anger* once it begins to build.

There is some debate among researchers over the historical advice to aggressive individuals that when they feel the need to hit others, instead of doing so, they vent toward other targets that will not be damaged by their rage. This is the basic concept behind **displacement theory**. Displacement is supposed to allow the individual to find a more positive or safer venue for anger. When the man who is mad at his boss, but knows that if he yelled at him he would lose his job, comes home and yells at the dog, that is **uncontrolled displacement**. It is uncontrolled in the sense that the pent-up aggression is spewed at an innocent victim. While not human in this instance, the recipient is still a living entity that will be negatively impacted by the displaced anger. When the adolescent male who is angry at another student chooses to hit a punching bag or pillow instead, that is **controlled displacement**. It is controlled because the anger is consciously directed toward an inanimate object that, in receiving the outburst, is less likely to be negatively impacted by the rant. When the elementary girl runs around the playground to exhaustion in the effort to deal with her anger toward another girl who did something that she did not like, that is also controlled displacement.

Of these three examples of displacement, only the last displacement attempt is the one that I would prescribe. The controversy over displacement learning techniques for people who are angry revolves around the substitution of one aggressive act for another. For years we have encouraged individuals to substitute their aggression with aggressive acts on inanimate objects such as punching bags, pillows, foam bats, or kicking the beanbag chair. I have even encouraged these behaviors myself in the early days of practice. The problem is that by substituting one aggressive act for another (albeit an improvement to hit a punching bag instead of the nose of a rival), we are still allowing individuals to vent in a negative and violent fashion. Venting by **equivalent displacement** (i.e., hitting something else instead of hitting the desired target) does not deal with the problem of the method in which an individual chooses to express the anger—by hitting. The angry male who kicks the door on a car in the parking lot is exhibiting both uncontrolled and equivalent displacement. While no human target was attacked—good—the venting of rage on the car door still has negative consequences attached to it for the angry kid—not good.

If displacement learning techniques are to be advocated, they must be accompanied by a **cognitive approach** that "talks out" the pros and cons of such displacement with the individual. A displacement approach must help the aggressive individual to *think* about the actions about to be undertaken. I recommend today that the best displacement is one of **inequivalent displacement**, or a substitution in which a venting can still take place but not with the same kind of action that an individual wishes to do to an intended target. The third example above is a way of allowing an individual to vent frustration in a nonviolent fashion. Encouraging exercise to vent, such as running until tired or shooting baskets in the gym until a frustration subsides, has some residual health benefits as well. History is filled with famous people who vented their frustrations in nonviolent and creative ways. The cognitive focus in employing a displacement strategy with an aggressor should be on *exploring the reasoning behind* the perceived need to hit in order to obtain what the agent wants.

If paired with displacement, *counting techniques* may reduce the frustration before a displacement action is needed. For those who "feel" or "know" the cues associated with an anger reaction, exiting the scene of the tension and counting upward slowly to 100 (or beyond if necessary!) or backward from 100 (this one usually makes people think about what they are doing, which may provide a longer distraction to the stressor) may provide the needed emotional buffer to allow emotions to return to a more manageable state. Exiting the scene is an example of using a previously discussed escape route action. Like exiting the scene, escape routes are designed to move the aggressor away from the area of a likely tense and escalating interaction. Escape routes, however, work only if the angry individual knows when to leave. That may take training.

Dana, here's what we're going to try to work out for you. It's the best deal I could make with your teachers and the principal, so work with me on this. We've spent a great deal of time talking and practicing ways to help you to cope better with the anger you feel sometimes toward certain people in school. I also want to offer you this option. When you feel or think that you are about to lose it, and none of the other methods we've practiced are working for you, all of your teachers have agreed to let you come immediately to my office to see me before you do something that we'll all end up regretting. All you have to do is quietly whisper to your teachers where you are headed and come down. If I'm tied up with another student when you come down, then you can sit in the waiting area until I'm free. It's much better for you to come down here and rant and rave with me about what's bugging you than for you to do it in class and run the risk of getting kicked out of school. But here's the catch: If you choose to do this, you can't wear out your welcome with me or abuse this option. We can't have you down here 20 times a day. This option is available for you only if you really and truly feel as if nothing else is working and you're about to blow a gasket.

Now, I want to make certain that you understand this idea, answer any questions you have about it, and discuss any problems that you think might happen if we do this. So, first, would you please tell me in your own words how this plan is supposed to work.

Interveners should be especially alert to the *desires of an aggressor to leave a negative peer group* that engages in bullying behaviors. Many of the tag-alongs, the **peripheral bullies** or **peripherals**, who follow a bully around are just that— toadies who are not leaders but followers, who have gotten sucked into a negative group. Does a follower of a bully get something out of it? You bet. They get to live the vicarious thrill of being viewed as powerful people. As they hang around with the aggressive group longer, they may even get to participate in an intimidating action against another led by the ringleader. And if they hang around long enough, they may even one day branch out and start their own group of bullies, and, like mold, the cycle of violence just continues to perpetuate itself until acted on by a greater force.

Many of the peripherals would actually like to leave the negative peer group, and they would if given the chance. It is particularly important to help to make this happen in the early stages of a group in formation. The longer peripheral bullies stay in a group, the harder it is for them to leave. One of the best methods to help a toadie leave the gang is by one-on-one interaction. The strategy is to divide and conquer the group by depriving the bullies of their junior members. But such a strategy must provide a new direction for the peripherals to move in or they will likely gravitate back to the people with whom they are most familiar and who, in their own way, meet their self-esteem needs.

Intervener (I):	Yolanda, I've asked you to come to visit with me today because I've noticed some things going on with you lately that I'm concerned about.
Yolanda (Y):	Like what?

I: Well, for openers, Mr. Principal tells me that your name keeps coming up along with several other girls who have been harassing another group of girls lately. Is that accurate?

Y: Might be.

I: I get the impression, though, from all the years that we've known each other, that that kind of behavior is not the real Yolanda.

Y: *[Listens, but says nothing.]*

I: I'm wondering, Yolanda, if you have been more of a follower of that group of girls than a ringleader.

Y: Maybe.

I: I hear a lot of "maybes" and "might bes" coming from you. That makes me think that you're not too committed to staying with that group.

Y: *[Says nothing.]*

I: What if I were to offer you the chance to—instead of going off with that group at lunchtime to look for people to bother—go and work with some of the older students in the science lab who are preparing for the upcoming science fair? I know that you like science. You told me one time that you wanted to be—

Y: *[Interrupts.]* A marine biologist.

I: Right, a marine biologist. I know that some of those students are preparing experiments with fish. When I was down there yesterday, they were complaining about needing some assistants. Would you be interested?

Y: I might.

I: *[Laughs at another "might" kind of answer.]* Well, I'll tell you what. You think about it, and if you decide that you want to do it, let me know and I'll introduce you to some of those upperclassmen down there. You "might" want to think hard about this offer. It "might" beat getting assigned detention or worse for pestering other kids, don't you think?

Y: *[Laughs.]* It might . . .

In this instance, the invitation is made for Yolanda to participate in a positive *near-peer group activity*. What the intervener knows, but not Yolanda, is that several of the upperclass science students have agreed to act as positive big brothers and big sisters for students in the lower grade levels who have specific interests in certain academic areas. If Yolanda chooses to help those working on their science fair projects, she will be pulled out of the negative peer group—at least during lunch. If the plan is successful, there will be other such enticements coming Yolanda's way to provide additional opportunities to keep her away from the negative peer group. The secret to pulling kids out of negative peer interactions is to provide positive alternatives for them that match their interests. This may take some calculation on an intervenor's part, along with consultation with other school staff who might know the students better and know more about what interests them.

Long-Term Support

Aggressive kids need to be *supervised, redirected* toward more positive behaviors, and *supported* in their efforts to change the negative ones. Far too often we block the doors of change that a young person might make with barriers of assumption. "A leopard does not change its spots," we say. That one is just a "bad apple."

While past behavior *is* a good indicator of how one may act in the future, the past may influence that future only if nothing about the now is changed. If we do not intervene with aggressive youngsters and alter the negative influences in their lives, then, of course, their futures will likely follow the same paths because those negative influences are still in place. *That is why it is so necessary to break the behavioral inertia of the bully.* It needs to be disrupted, not only for the sake of safeguarding the victims now but to decrease the chances that the young bully will grow up to be a bigger one later.

In school settings, the best kind of long-term support that we can provide the bully is by keeping a constant positive pressure on to behave in positive directions. Supervision is in order, but not a punitive supervision. The best monitoring of those we are concerned about can be done when we keep them *near* us, *not away* from us.

That is a lesson I learned in my very early years of teaching. I taught for 10 years in a small rural school. It was one of those environments where everyone knew everyone else—one of the advantages (and disadvantages) of working in a small school district. In this particular school, there was a young man, Jack, who had created quite a reputation for himself by the time he left elementary school. Jack had already had several run-ins with the local police. He had vandalized property in town, some of it belonging to school personnel. He was charming enough when he wanted to be. He could also be devious. And he had all the classic behaviors of a bully.

As the school year progressed, Jack's behaviors became more burdensome to everyone. We teachers were ready to revolt when the middle school principal made Jack an office monitor.

"An office monitor!" we cried. "Has that man lost his mind?!? Only good kids get to be office monitors!" Revolution was in the air, and I drew the short straw to get to be the one to go to the principal and complain.

So I did. I expressed the sentiments of the faculty to the principal calmly and ended with the observation, "Most of us think that the last thing Jack needs is to be rewarded by being an office monitor. In fact, we think that he should have been kicked out of here long ago."

The principal smiled at me from behind the hands that had been in front of his mouth.

"Walt," he began, "let's just think a minute about that last suggestion. I'll grant you that Jack is a handful. He's got quite a reputation to live up to, that's for sure. But if I kick him out of here, where do you think he will be?"

"Who cares? Out of here! Home," I answered.

"Jack? No way," was the reply. "You know just as well as I do that nobody looks out for Jack except Jack. Half the time I'm not even sure his parents know where he is, and the other half of the time Jack's trying to get out of his house because his old man is pretty rough with him. That's one of the reasons why Jack is who he is. He's just imitating what he gets from home.

"No, Walt. If we kick Jack out of school, he won't be at *his* house, but he's likely to visit *yours* while you're here at school. For that matter, he's likely to visit *all* of our houses while we're here at school!

"A wise man once told me that if you've got a boy in trouble, you need to keep your eye on him because it lessens the chances that he'll get into more mischief."

He then walked over to me, asked me to stand, put his arm across my shoulder, and pulled me close.

"So, Walt, you tell me. Where is Jack *least* likely to get into trouble? When I can watch and reach him at the end of my arm like this, or . . ." He gently shoved me toward the door. "When I kick him out of school and I can't see him at all?

"I'll talk to the rest of the faculty tomorrow about what's going on and what I'm trying to do. I'm trying to do the *exact opposite* of what Jack is used to. I'm trying to keep him *in,* when everybody in his world is trying to keep him *out.* I don't know if I'm right or wrong, or even if it will work, but I'm willing to give it a try."

I never forgot that conversation. It is a lesson that I repeat to this day to anyone who will listen when I speak about the necessity of working with the bully. It was such an eye-opening moment for me as a young teacher. While I saw Jack only as trouble, the principal saw him as troubled. Where I did not know what Jack's home life was like, the principal understood that Jack was largely who he was because of that home. While I wanted to stop giving Jack any more chances, the principal was always willing to give him one more in the hopes that maybe the next one would stick and Jack would start coming around.

We made it through middle school with Jack. Some of his behaviors modified for the better, and others stayed the same. Jack's relationship with the principal, I am convinced, was the only thing that kept him in school, off the streets, and out of jail.

Enhancing Personal Deficits

Bullies are not always the traditional brutish oafs they have been portrayed as throughout history. Today's bullies in particular are often savvy about the many ways to manipulate and control the lives of their victims, as evidenced by the use of technology. While some aggressors do appear to be the stereotypical comic strip kind of dimwitted slug, most have a requisite number of social skills and intelligence to allow them to hide behind enough charm and wit so as to go undetected by supervisors. Indeed, many of them may be raised to the canons of sainthood within Kid World when they occupy the adult-sanctioned thrones of the athletic hero, the cheerleader, or the kid who throws the best parties in town because his or her parents are never home.

The biggest personal skills deficit that aggressive youths are likely to have is in the previously identified and discussed area of interpersonal boundary abuse. Another area to explore may have to do with *grandiose thinking.* Power bullies, because they have tended to use physical power as a means of dominating others to get what they want, often adopt an *inflated self-esteem.* This often masks the true inner feelings of deflated self-esteem or of feeling powerless, especially for those who experience bullying domination from the home. Grandiose thinking and inflated self-esteem are nourished by continued success through bullying behaviors.

For those who consistently act in intimidating ways, it will be necessary to teach them new methods of obtaining their goals without aggression. This will most likely be achieved through first *exploring the origins of their aggressive thoughts* and *learning new ways to deal with anger,* because anger is beneath so much of the rationale of the bully. Bullies often do not employ nonaggressive social skills because they either do not know how, have never been forced to do so, or both. Social skills training is especially useful at the elementary level because the interruption of aggressive patterns of behavior in the early years is essential to reducing their occurrence later.

Exploring the Family of Origin

This one is a minefield. While knowing about the conditions of the home and how they might impact the learning process for a student is important for school personnel in designing strategies and techniques to best reach them, how that information is discovered and who uncovers it is fraught with all sorts of pitfalls.

There is a legitimate concern among parents about how other people learn of the home life of a child. Supervisors need to know the right kind of information, not just information for the sake of being gossipy. Knowing too much about a difficult family situation may compel an adult to have reason for reporting questionable home situations to social services. It is one thing if information about the private lives of students crosses a teacher's desk in the form of a student statement, an overheard comment, a request for assistance from a student in need, or that student's friend who is asking on another's behalf. As I always say, when someone leaves a baby on your doorstep in a driving rain, you just cannot leave it there and wait for someone else to deal with it. There are times when adults will have to act on information they receive about the home life of a student, especially if such information appears to be accurate and the health and safety of the child are in question.

But what kind of information is the right kind and who is best positioned to obtain it? Do school personnel have the right to pry into the home lives of students for whom they are concerned? For that matter, what is the definition of the word "pry"? Is it prying if a teacher asks about a bruise on a student's arm? No. Is it prying if that same teacher, on learning that the bruise was the result of a father "wrestling" with his child, asks the child if such activity occurs often and if there have been other occasions of bruises that resulted from it? That answer could be yes or no. If the purpose of following a genuine lead is to make certain that a child is not in danger from abuse in the home, then I would agree that inquiring about such instances would be in order. If the teacher is asking only to further the "did you hear this one" database as something to gossip about in the teacher's lounge without concern for the child's welfare, then that borders on professional voyeurism and is unprofessional.

The people most likely within the school who are best equipped to learn about the home life of an aggressive child and the family interactional patterns that might contribute to those behaviors are those trained in the helping professions. The average teacher education program does not equip teachers to understand some of the nuances and implications of the personal and social factors impacting the lives of their students. I do not say this with malice, it is just a fact. Teacher education programs focus on the skills to be an effective teacher, on curriculum, on discipline techniques, and on a gobzillion other things that they have to learn before being allowed into the classroom. While they may be required to take a course on human development, one course does not a human development specialist make!

Helping professionals in the school—the school counselor, school social worker, school psychologist, and school nurse—see and hear personal information every day. They are known, by virtue of what they do inside schools, to have skills that are different from those of the average classroom teacher. Notice I said *different*. I did not say *better*. Both teachers and school-based helping professionals form an invaluable team when it comes to the mental health needs of children. They are all professionals in their respective fields of study. Teachers have daily contact with students. They know the **homeostatic nature**, or everyday behavior, of each child in their classrooms, and because of this, they know when a child is acting differently from normal or seems preoccupied with matters distracting them from learning. School-based helping professionals, on the other hand, do not see all students in the building every day. Their focus is largely driven by students who come or are sent to them for assistance, sometimes in times of crisis, other times for issues more mundane. Often these student-related issues require lengthy interventions involving both time and energies that the classroom teacher is not prepared to offer and that they likely cannot provide due to the nature of their daily duties and responsibilities. Teachers should refer those students for whom they have personal and social concerns to the helping professionals within their school.

Exploration of the "family of origin" is in order when a legitimate need is identified due to the behavior of a student. The **family of origin** refers to the caregivers and family members in both the current living situation and any other past living situations that might have played a role in the development of a child. Such exploration can be detailed or less formal. It could obtain relevant information solely from the child or in collaboration with the parents. Notice, the key is on the concept of obtaining *relevant* information. Following are two examples of efforts to explore the family of origin situation of Jack, the student we just discussed. One example is an abomination, the other clearly justified.

Intervener (I):	Jack, we've been working for some time now to make things better for you here at school. How do you think things are going?
Jack (J):	Better, I guess. I'm not getting into as much trouble these days.
I:	That's great to hear. I know that your teachers have commented that things seem to be going better for you.
J:	Yeah, they have.
I:	Jack, what I wanted to meet with you about is something that has been on my mind for quite some time, but I thought I would wait until some things settled down a bit before I asked you.
J:	About what?
I:	I have some concerns that perhaps there are some things going on at home that may have contributed to some of your behaviors.
J:	*[Says nothing. Looks to the floor.]*
I:	Sometimes kids do some things at school that they learn somewhere else. I know, because you've told me in the past, that home life has not always been easy for you. Am I right about that?
J:	Yeah. Well, maybe so.
I:	Can you give me some more information about what life is like for you at home?
J:	*[Pauses before speaking.]* Well, my dad drinks a lot. When he gets really bad off, he yells at everybody in the house. That's about it.
I:	Is that all that happens?

J: Well, sometimes he pushes us around when he's mad.

I: He's a pretty big guy, isn't he?

J: Yeah.

I: Can you tell me more about that pushing around?

J: He only does it when he gets mad, but then he stays that way most of the time. We just try and stay out of his way when he gets that way.

I: Has your dad ever been in trouble with the law?

J: You mean here?

I: Anywhere.

J: Before we moved here, he was in jail for beating up a neighbor.

I: Over what?

J: Dad asked to borrow his lawn mower and then tore it up. When the guy asked for it back, Dad started yelling at him about how crappy a lawn mower he had and before we knew it, he hit him.

I: Does your dad have a mean swing?

J: He does when he wants to.

I: I bet he could pack a punch. He looks like he could knock a ball out of the park.

J: [Waits for the intervenor to ask another question.]

I: Have any other members of your family ever been in jail?

In this instance, while the approach may have started effectively, all too soon the intervener has abandoned the focus about Jack and gone on to asking about other details that do nothing to increase an understanding of Jack. The intervener has become focused on gossipy details. A real concern must be raised as to the exact purpose of the questions being raised by the intervener.

In the next instance, we take the opening of the approach with Jack and increase the levels of empathy and reflective listening to keep the focus on him.

Intervener (I):   Jack, we've been working for some time now to make things better for you here at school. How do you think things are going?

Jack (J):   Better, I guess. I'm not getting into as much trouble these days.

I: That's great to hear. I know that your teachers have commented that things seem to be going better for you.

J: Yeah, they have.

I: Jack, what I wanted to meet with you about is something that has been on my mind for quite some time, but I thought I would wait until some things settled down a bit before I asked you.

J: About what?

I: I have some concerns that perhaps there are some things going on at home that may have contributed to some of your behaviors.

J: *[Says nothing. Looks to the floor.]*

I: Sometimes kids do some things at school that they learn in other places. I know, because you've told me in the past, that home life has not always been easy for you. Am I right about that?

J: Yeah. Well, maybe so.

I: Can you give me some more information about what life is like for you at home?

J: *[Pauses before speaking.]* Well, my dad drinks a lot. When he gets really bad off, he yells at everybody in the house. That's about it.

I: That must be difficult for you and your family.

J: Yeah, well, you get used to it after a while.

I: I imagine, though, that some of the things that he says and does when that happens are not too easy to forget.

J: Yeah.

I: I'm truly sorry to hear that that happens in your house. I don't know what that's like for you, but I would guess that it probably hurts you inside and makes you sad. I think I'd be afraid and maybe even a little bit angry about getting treated like that.

J: *[Looks up from the floor.]* Sometimes I get so mad at him for what he does to me and everybody else.

I: I think I can certainly see why you would feel that way. You know, Jack, what I said earlier about sometimes kids learn things in other places and then they bring it to school? I'm wondering if maybe some of that anger that you feel toward your dad sometimes comes to school with you and gets taken out on other people.

J: *[Does not respond. Looks at the floor again.]*

I: Maybe we could talk about that some more later, if you'd like to. I know that in the past I've talked to a lot of kids here at school who are in similar situations as yours, and they have told me some of the same stories as you have about how icky feelings at home spill over to school and sometimes creates some problems for them. Sometimes they have difficulty concentrating on their schoolwork. Sometimes they are just so angry about things at home that they find reasons to take that anger out on other kids here who don't have anything to do with the cause of the problems at home. I don't know if any of this makes sense or not, but it's something I've been thinking of lately and I wanted to share it with you.

J: *[Is quiet for a while.]* Maybe I would like to talk some more about all this sometime.

I: I'll be here when you need me.

Here the intervener kept the focus on Jack through making efforts to reflect back to him the intervener's interpretation of how Jack must feel when life at home goes haywire. He also did not get distracted about the gossipy details of Jack's dad's arrest record or how hard he could hit. While those details may be important to know, too much detail tends to distract from the focus of what is likely to solidify a connection with others and to keep the channels of communication open. If I think that you are interested in me, I will likely be willing to share more with you. If I think that you are interested in me only for the "stuff" I can tell you about me, then I am more likely to be inclined to be convinced that you are interested in me only for entertainment purposes. If it's entertainment you want, then rent a DVD.

8. DO NOT ABANDON THE BULLY

Bullies need support in their efforts to break away from old habits. Do not abandon them in this effort! Because bullies are so used to being rejected by people and as a person, a caring adult can be the key to unlocking the potential within. The principal who worked with Jack knew this because a "wise man" once told him. That wise man cared enough about both Jack and me to share the secret. Both Jack and I are better today because he did.

Not abandoning aggressive children means staying with them through thick and thin after the intervention begins. It means not writing them off even though they have managed to alienate everyone in the school. It means holding them accountable when they mess up—holding them to account *fairly*. It means that in holding them to that accountability, that they be asked to provide the logic for the actions when they need to explain. It means that we, too, must provide a logic for the administration of that accountability, not just assign a disciplinary action because the bully got caught doing something wrong.

Perhaps most importantly—and the most difficult of all—it means that we have to *see beyond the behavior of the bully to the child within*. That child is held captive by defense mechanisms designed to protect him from something that he is afraid of within his world. By growling and barking, he can keep people away from that inner pain and fear. By acting out, he can repulse those around him and ensure that they never come near.

We cannot give up on bullies, no matter how much they try to drive us away. We do not do them a service either by overlooking their behaviors and not holding them accountable, or by ignoring them out of the misguided belief that they are hopeless and will never be able to change. The only prediction that is most likely to come true with kids in trouble is that when we adults do nothing to intervene or break the behavioral inertia that guides their path, most likely they will continue to do more of the same. *Tough kids demand* **tough love**. Tough love demands *persistence* from those willing to accept the challenge to try to administer it. There is nothing easy about stopping a train wreck, but if we don't apply the brakes at some point, that train just builds steam and keeps sailing right down the tracks, mowing over everything in its path.

Without a doubt, some of the most poignant stories I have ever heard, both as a practitioner and through the review of my interns' tapes, have come from aggressive children. Many of those stories are textbook examples of the very things we have discussed in these pages—aggressive children, coming from aggressive homes, taking out their frustrations and anger against those who get in their way with the only methods they know—yelling, hitting, fighting. The image, however, often belies the child beneath who is often afraid and feels as if there is no safe adult in his world to whom he can turn. Adults, they believe, exercise abusive power as a means to get what they want, be it quiet in the house or discipline in the classroom, and if that's what it means to be an adult, then they can do that, too. If not in the presence of adults (at least, not now), then among the peer group.

Subverting this belief among children and adolescents who are aggressive is one of the best gifts we can give them. In the midst of chaos, somebody needs to act like an adult, but it is not always so easy to do. Like with Jack, we have to be willing to pull those who want us to push them away closer to us. It takes time to work with kids in trouble. It takes patience. It takes the ability to bite one's tongue and hold on to that gut-level response that we most likely would prefer to give when "that darn kid" pushes our buttons. And they know where our buttons are and how to push them, take my word for it.

We managed to get through *The Year of the Terrible Two* without any additional mobbing from the main culprits or their toadies. Keeping a close eye on the whole lot had proven, if not therapeutic for them, at least aggravating enough to their modus operandi that they avoided similar behaviors the remainder of the year. It became a point of mutual good-natured antagonism between the principal and me that my intervention with the Two had somehow managed to work. Every day he would crack some joke toward me to break my cautious glee that we had somehow put a damper on a behavior that had negatively impacted the school. There were plenty of other behaviors that warranted our attention, mind you. The Two were not responsible for all the ills of our little piece of bliss known as a school.

In April the principal collared me in the hallway as I was headed to a classroom to check up on the progress of a student who was having academic problems. He put his hand on my shoulder and grinned. It was never a good thing when he did that. It usually meant that he either had won a bet that I had made with him or that he had some kind of deviously, fiendish kid conundrum for me to resolve.

"When you get back from your errand," he began, "be sure and stop by your office. There's a couple of your good friends who will be there for you when you get back."

Oh, great! The Terrible Two! He'd been waiting all year for them to act up again. What had they done now? My mind went straight to catastrophe.

I hurried my visit with the teacher in whose class I had been scheduled and then scampered back to the office. Where are those Two, I thought to myself. After everything I've done for them this year, all the sweat equity I've put into them to keep their noses clean, how dare they do this to me! To say that I had a little emotional investment in the future of My Little Science Project was an understatement.

I rounded the door to the waiting room outside my office. No one was on the couch outside. Must be in the office, already. I pursed my lips in expectation.

But the Two weren't there. Nowhere to be scene. Not even close.

In my office that day sat Bruce and his closest friend, Will. Neither of them said anything. Their heads were bowed, they were sheepish, and if it had been within their power, they would have just as soon melted into the couch.

Bruce and Will had become best friends that year. Will had been one of the first kids to help me help pick Bruce up and dust himself off after the initial attack by the Two outside my office window in the fall. They were as different as night and day. Bruce was huge; Will was tiny. Bruce struggled academically; Will excelled. Together that year they had forged quite a bond, and from all appearances, to me at least, it seemed a good match. Bruce got some badly needed self-esteem from someone who looked up to him as a big brother, not to mention help with his homework.

I sat down in the chair across from the couch where they both slumped. "Soooooo?" I asked. They knew exactly what my question meant.

"The principal told us to come down here," Bruce said. And nothing else.

"Foooooooorrrrr?" I felt as if I was trying to milk a rock.

Will and Bruce looked at one another, then back down at their shoes.

"Come on, guys, help me out, okay? I'm not a mind reader, but I appreciate your vote of confidence."

Had they been attacked by the Two or somebody else? I did not see any bruises, dirt on their clothes, or any rips indicative of having been pummeled.

Slowly Bruce spoke. "We did something wrong."

I said nothing for a long time, just letting them dwell on Bruce's admission of having done "something wrong," the likes of which I could not possibly have imagined coming from these two.

Finally, curiosity killed the cat. "And that would beeeeee . . . ?"

They began to piece together the most incredible story—at least for me, at that time, it was. Now, of course, I understand that the whole cycle of bullying was just playing out before me.

Bruce and Will had been called down to the principal's office after receiving reports from the elementary school principal that they had been threatening and intimidating elementary students at the bus stop and on the bus. Apparently, it had been going on for several days. None of the elementary kids that they had been harassing ever told. The bus driver ended up reporting several bits and pieces of observed bullying to the elementary principal, who had transferred the information to the high school principal for follow-up.

I was stunned. And disappointed. And incredulous. It was clear, however, that as stunned, and disappointed, and incredulous as I was, they were as equally genuinely apologetic, guilt-ridden, ashamed, and embarrassed.

I said nothing for several seconds. What in the world were these boys thinking, I wondered to myself. So I asked, "After everything we've been through this year, what on earth were you boys thinking?"

There was another long silence. "I guess I wanted to see how it felt to do that to somebody else," Bruce quietly said, little more than a whisper. Will said nothing. He didn't have to. I knew that by virtue of his marginal status among his seventh-grade peers, he was just one step ahead of peer abuse and had, at times, received disrespectful comments among them. His accompanying Bruce was a vicarious adventure. Will the brain; Bruce the enforcer.

"So what do we do now?" I asked. "How much trouble are you two in for?"

That's when both of them started to cry. Apparently, where the Terrible Two were fearless and conniving when confronted by the principal, Bruce and Will had no life ahead of them as hard-core criminals. "He said he's going to kick us out and that we ought to be ashamed of ourselves for picking on little kids!" Will sputtered between snorts of sobbing. I didn't know what hurt Will worse—the threat of being kicked out of school or being accused of "picking on little kids." After all, he wasn't much bigger than them himself, and it had been less than a year since he had been in elementary school.

"Think there's anything that the two of you might be able to do to make things better?" Long before I had ever heard of restorative justice, its principles made good practice.

And from that point, in the days to come, the three of us began to brainstorm ways to make it up to the elementary students they had been intimidating. As for their punishment from the principal, the irony of school district policy was that Bruce and Will were in much deeper trouble for having committed their offenses toward elementary children at the bus stop and on the bus than the Terrible Two had been in their attack on Bruce earlier that year. School policy dictated removal from bus service for a full week (of which I didn't have much argument) and automatic three-day suspension from school (of which I did). While the principal had a lot of leeway in most disciplinary matters, on bus infractions he had very little.

Bruce and Will served their sentences, carted to school that spring week courtesy of their parents after being booted out for three days (and who reminded them each and every mile and every day as to the inconvenience that they were enduring because of their children's misbehaviors). It was not without great faux umbrage that the Two relished Bruce and Will's errant behavior. After they got wind of Bruce and Will's escapade, they appeared in my office wanting to know what was going to be done to the new errant pair.

"Are they going to get suspended like we did?" they demanded to know.

"You know what the rules are for acting up on the bus," I responded.

"Good!" they squealed in delight. "Serves 'em right for picking on little kids like that!"

It was important for Bruce and Will to develop some kind of apology to the elementary students for their misdeeds. When they returned, the three of us developed some workable ideas as to what the two of them might be able to do to right the wrongs they had done. They decided that the best thing to do was to personally apologize to each of their targets at the elementary school in the presence of the elementary principal and me, and to write a letter of apology to the elementary students' parents and the bus driver.

The year ended without any further violence or intimidation from either the Terrible Two or the Terrible Two Wannabes. The Terrible Two transferred out of the district that summer and were never seen again. Bruce and Will came back and never hassled other kids again—at least not that we were aware of at school.

As for the principal, he never let me forget my hard work on behalf of those seven kids that year.

"Fine job, Walt. Fine job," he would say to me as he slapped me on the back from time to time, usually in front of a crowd of school board members. "Turned our victims into bullies and runs our bullies out of town!" he would laugh. "What do they teach you in those universities of higher education these days?"

I always just laughed along with him and continued my role in the Good Cop, Bad Cop routine. And we got along just fine. Little did I know that that year would be the beginning of a lifelong journey to try to prevent and reduce the cycle of violence emerging from the likes of the Terrible Twos of Kid World and their targets.

10

What Now? Taking Those First Steps

EFFECTIVE VIOLENCE PREVENTION REQUIRES AN EFFECTIVE CURRICULUM

Through the years during my workshops across the nation, the most asked questions that I always get are, "Which resources do you recommend?" and "What are the best videos that you think we should get for our school?" and "What's the best program out there to prevent bullying and teasing?" All of these are great questions, and they all deserve answers.

My answer is that there are many great resources out there that deal with bullying and teasing. There are lots of great curricular modules, really flashy videos, wonderful workbooks for kids, and a lot of neat related books and articles that adults can read about the topic to help them understand how to better the lives of children and adolescents. There are also a lot of products floating around out there that I have seen that I do not believe would be very effective in either the classroom or for working with small groups of kids who are in need of building their assertiveness skills. At least *I* would not want to work with some of those products because I do not believe that they would fit my style and approach.

Notice what I am emphasizing here. What works for *me* may not necessarily work for *you*. What *I* like, *you* might not. What would work for my kids in our setting might be a disaster with yours.

Curricular selection is an entirely personal matter based on factors that are peculiar for that specific environment. While I have opinions about what makes for effective curricula, and will share them momentarily, ultimately the people closest to the problem that they are trying to solve are likely to know more about what types of materials will most likely work in that setting.

Here are five main points that I recommend be considered in the selection of materials for use with kids when dealing with violence prevention and intervention topics.

Curricular Consideration 1: The Material Must Be Relevant for Its Intended Audience

Besides the grade-level match, what is portrayed or suggested in the materials must be believable by the audience for whom it is intended. I know of a great video that I highly recommend, but it is dated. It covers a tremendous amount of the key points that are dead-on for its topic. The problem is that no updated version of the video has been made in 15 years. This particular video I am referring to is for adults. As such, they are less distracted (even though every time I use it, somebody in the audience always says, "I can't believe we used to dress like that!" and "Look at that hair!") than adolescents would be with a video with similar datedness. They would die laughing. Relevance, then, is both *content* and *perceived merit* on behalf of the audience.

Curricular Consideration 2: Those Who Intend to Teach the Material Must Screen It

Never purchase any kind of material without either having reviewed it first or, if that is not feasible, having great credence in its reputation either because of past experience with its producers or because of the trusted recommendation of a colleague. The best guarantee of predicting the likelihood of success within a particular setting is to observe its use with an audience similar to the one for which it is intended. Many materials are selected on the basis of professional recommendation and comments about its effectiveness. Conferences and professional listservs often prove useful in soliciting colleague experience and opinion of curricular materials. Materials that are evaluated should meet the relevance standard as described above.

Decisions must also be made as to the "part-value" of the material. **Part-value** refers to a determination as to how many "pieces" or **segments** of a specific curricular item might be usable, and if the item would lend itself to multiple lessons or in additional ways beyond what is suggested in its guidelines. The most common part-value used with educational materials is the breaking up of videos into smaller, stand-alone units. For example, I have shown videos on how to avoid being teased to children who were targeted for such behaviors. The video ran a total of no more than 20 minutes and came with suggested activities after viewing it in its entirety.

What became evident, however, was that the emotions and behaviors displayed by the child actors on the video elicited strong reactions on the parts of those who watched it. Victims felt as if the depictions were very true and they wanted to talk about their experiences in light of having seen their experiences portrayed so vividly in the video. So, I just began to stop the video after each vignette and ask the group what their thoughts were in relation to the segment they had just seen. In doing so, that 20-minute video became three 50-minute small-group sessions' worth of material. And we never even got around to doing most of the suggested activities with the accompanying guidebook, so rich were the discussions and activities we designed on our own just from the vignettes portrayed in the video. For my money, that video was worth its weight in gold! It is sometimes worth paying the higher price of a specific curricular item that has more applicability of a smaller segment within it (hence, high part-value) than spending less on materials that kids do not relate to or that do not entice them to learn.

Curricular Consideration 3: If Possible, Ask for the Opinion of Students on the Material

The ultimate experts about Kid World are the kids themselves! Why should we not ask their opinion about educational materials before we select them? Kids see things differently from adults and, given the chance, will more than gladly point out the things that work or do not work for them. Some things even adults will catch, as exemplified in that late 1980s video I was talking about earlier. But Kid World changes so quickly. What was relevant just 5 years ago may not be so important today. What might have been fashionable to them yesterday has changed today. This is an important consideration in choosing materials that may be extremely flashy and hip and very relevant *right now*. Will what was cool when it was purchased in 2005 still be able to hold kids' interests in 2007? We adults may think so. We may also be oh so wrong, too. It is also important to *ask student opinion* about whether the activities included with a particular curricular item would be of interest to students. Would they be interested in doing workbook pages, or role plays, or discussing the suggested questions in the guidebook? *When all else fails and we really want to talk to the experts, ask the kids!*

Curricular Consideration 4: The Material Should Be Based on Some Kind of Legitimate and Effective Foundation

If I have one major criticism about the proliferation of violence prevention–related curricula, it is this: It has proliferated simply because there is money to be made in it. But what evidence exists that a particular piece of violence prevention material works? On what was the basis of its creation—to make money or to actually provide a product that works?

The most effective violence prevention products on the market typically have been around for a while. That is a testament to why they are still around. Because they work, people keep buying them. Effective materials will tell the consumer up front what the basis for the success or intended success of the product is. Does the product promote a specific frame of reference for its approach? For instance, are the materials designed to increase resilience among youths, implement recognized conflict resolution methodologies, or teach youths the skills to solve their own peer-to-peer disagreements? These are important considerations in the review of materials before utilization within the school.

How does one know what makes for potentially effective materials? Professional journals are filled with such information. Examples of such journals will be found in the Recommended Resources and Reference sections of this book. Spend some time online for additional information (be sure to go to credible sources!). The Office of Juvenile Justice and Delinquency Prevention (www.ojjdp.ncjrs.org) and the U.S. Department of Education (www.ed.gov) both have extensive databases within their respective jurisdictions. Plug in the phrases "conflict resolution" or "violence prevention" and see what comes up. Of course, if one has the rest of one's life to read it all, a Google search of either of these phrases plus other related key words will generate more than enough to facilitate the decision-making process. Just the term "conflict resolution" generated nearly 11 million hits on Google alone in 2005 (and Google wants us to know that it found them in only 0.11 seconds!).

Curricular Consideration 5: Know the Reputation of the Company That Sells the Material

Legitimate companies that have a reputation to protect do not intend to squander it on get-rich money schemes through the sale of poor-quality merchandise. How long has the company been around? One method of determining the quality of materials offered through a company is to ascertain its history. In this day, a lot of one-decade wonders come and go in the business world. It is also helpful to know if the company has had a history of financial instability or has ever renamed itself after declaring bankruptcy. What has been the company's primary sales focus? Does it offer a variety of educational materials or just one type of product? Companies that are pieces of corporate conglomerations and sell a diversity of products not related to one specific area may be less concerned about their customers in some of those divisions, especially if its board of directors intends to sell it off for tax purposes very soon. My experience leads me to believe that smaller companies with a narrower focus may offer the better product because their time and energies are devoted to that one specific issue. What are the purchasing and refunding policies? What types of guarantees are provided for the return of merchandise, particularly if found to be faulty? It is important to be able to return materials found to be defective or swap materials of equal value if it is found that the original purchase did not meet expectations as advertised. I never do business with companies that do not allow me to preview materials first or those that have a nonrefundable fiscal policy—and companies with those types of business policies are still out there. Most importantly, what do colleagues say about their experiences with the company? In the end, when all is said and done, that may well be the clincher for most people.

HELPING SISYPHUS: GETTING KIDS OVER THEIR VICTIMIZATION

The ancient Greeks told the myth of Sisyphus, a cruel king from the city-state of Corinth who, when sent to Hades, was doomed to roll a huge stone up a hill, only to have it escape his grasp near the top and roll back down. Such is what many adolescents believe about life during those grueling teen years, particularly those who are bullied. Every day, they attempt to get their personal boulders—the victimization—over the hill to freedom, only to have it escape from their grasp and have to endure it all over again the next day.

So now, what do we do when it comes to the topic of helping our kids, ourselves, our families, and society deal with bullying and intimidation in our schools? How do we help Sisyphus over the hill? That remains entirely up to you and us. We are all in this together. We all stand to gain or lose by virtue of our actions.

Perhaps the first step we have to take is one of *courage*. The kind of courage I am talking about here is not the courage of rescuing small children and puppies from a burning building or disarming an armed robber, but the kind of courage that comes from following through on what we know is the right thing to do. We know that it is the right thing to intervene on behalf of those who are victimized by aggressive acts in our schools. We know what consequences befall the victims of our failure to make our schools safe from bullying torment. We know what the long-term prognosis is for the perpetrators of such behaviors.

If we know all of these things, then why don't we do something? Because it takes that courage I just mentioned. It takes courage to make that first step toward actively stopping harassment in our schools and in our children's lives. It takes courage and *willpower* to move toward the agent provocateurs of mayhem. It takes *restraint* in resisting the temptation to use our positions of adult authority to use punishment as the sole means of responding to those who use aggression against innocent victims. And it takes *time* to formulate strategies that will work with *both* victims and aggressors to address the cognitive, behavioral, and emotional needs that emerge during the deadly dance of the bully-victim dyad.

GO AHEAD, MAKE MY DAY

Every child has the potential to be the next savior of humanity. Who among us can say which one will make engines that run on seawater, discover a cure for cancer, or find the cure for AIDS? That person may well be the child in our classrooms right now—the child who is hungry or hurt, the child who is angry, the child who acts out. Our mission is to reach out and touch those who need us—those who push us away, who are used to feeling the backhand of power—and to show them that there is a better way, that life holds great things for the future. We must go upstream and find the cause as to why our children, our brothers and sisters, are falling into the river. We must build new bridges for those who have lost their way and help them find that future, their future, our future.

It is up to you, now, to take that first step, whatever it may be. You have devoted the time to become more knowledgeable about the topic of bullying and its effect on children. But knowledge, in and of itself, means little without action. So go ahead, make my day. Do something to make life better for kids who are bullied and intimidated. In doing so, you will not only be making my day; more importantly, you will be helping to make their day better, as well.

Time's a-wasting! I'll be out there with you! Let's go!

Recommended Resources

The following list is offered as a *starting point* for schools and related interested parties to "grow their own" bully prevention/intervention initiatives. Each school should review any materials listed to determine which is most appropriate for its particular setting. A brief annotation follows each resource or resource category.

Many curricular-related companies sell a wide range of educational materials related to safe school environments, violence prevention, and conflict mediation. Just count all the catalogs you get each year! *Be cautious in purchasing materials based on appearances.* The best advice is to obtain any potential curricular materials on a preview basis. One of the best companies that allows previews of materials and has a solid reputation in the area of violence prevention materials is Sunburst Visual Media (www.sunburst.com). If local Web access allows, Sunburst can also provide online previews of their products, inclusive of videos and software. Another company that provides excellent resources is Childswork Childsplay (www.childswork.com).

VIDEOS

Chasnoff, D. (Director), & Cohen, H. S. (Executive Producer). (2003). *Let's get real* [Video]. San Francisco: Women's Educational Media.

Fantastic video for adults to help them to understand what it's like to face bullying and intimidation in schools today. Also relevant for kids as a stimulus for discussion in class.

Cohen, H. S. (Producer), & Chasnoff, D. (2003). *Lets get real* [Motion picture]. San Francisco, CA: Respect for All Project.

Excellent resource for adults to understand how kids feel about being bullied. Real interviews with real kids. Grades 7–12.

Ferguson, S. (Producer), & Stephens, R. D. (Executive Director). (1988). *Set straight on bullies* [Video]. Westlake Village, CA: National School Safety Center.

Though somewhat dated by the style of hair and clothing worn, this video is an excellent inservice learning experience for adults and faculty. It provides basic background on the bully-victim relationship.

Perlman, J. (Director), & Page, M. (Producer). (2000). *Bully dance* [Video]. Oley, PA: Bullfrog Films.

Expensive, but worth every penny! This nonverbal cartoon video runs approximately 10 minutes. Featuring nondescript figures, it is perfect for grades K–8 and may well be usable in the high school grades. Perfect for students whose first language is not English or for those with limited reading proficiency.

Twisted Scholar (Producer). (2003). *Gum in my hair* [Motion picture]. Seattle, WA: Twisted Scholar, Inc.

The coolest video ever for middle schoolers. Fast, funny, and great kid music.

Yarrow, P. (Producer/Director), Lazar, F. (Director), & Roerden, S. P. (Writer). (2000). *Don't laugh at me: Creating a ridicule-free classroom* [Video & Compact Disk]. New York: Operation Respect, Inc.

If still available, the price is right—*free!* Go to http://www.dontlaugh.org for details. Complete curriculum includes guidebook and videos. Two different grade levels: 2–5 and 6–8.

BOOKS

Please note: Not all of the books listed below are designed for student use. Many are listed as background for adult reading.

Beane, A. L. (1999). *The bully free classroom: Over 100 tips and strategies for teachers K–8.* Minneapolis, MN: Free Spirit Publishing.

A curricular guide with great suggestions for the classroom.

Berenstain, S., & Berenstain, J. (1995). *The Berenstain bears and too much teasing.* New York: Random House.

Our favorite bears tackle a tough subject. For the wee people, of course.

Bodine, R. J., Crawford, D. K., & Schrumpf, F. (1994). *Creating the peaceable school: A comprehensive program for teaching conflict resolution. Program guide.* Champaign, IL: Research Press.

One of three curricular books I highly recommend for use in creating and maintaining conflict resolution skills among students.

Brown, B., & Merritt, R. (2002). *No easy answers: The truth behind death at Columbine*. New York: Lantern Books.

An absolute must-read for adults. Written by one of the shooter's close friends, it gives a riveting picture of the dynamics leading up to the Columbine shootings.

Carnes, J. (Ed.). (1999). *Responding to hate at school: A guide for teachers, counselors and administrators*. Montgomery, AL: Teaching Tolerance.

Another free resource. Filled with examples of nonviolent responses to racial, ethnic, and religious discrimination. Go to http://www.tolerance .org for details and other resources, many free.

Drew, N. (1995). *Learning the skills of peacemaking: A K–6 activity guide on resolving conflict, communicating, cooperating* (Rev. ed.). Torrance, CA: Jalmar Press.

The second of three excellent curricular books for creating and maintaining conflict resolution skills among students.

Elliott, S. N., & Gresham, F. M. (1991). *Social skills intervention guide: Practical strategies for social skills training*. Circle Pines, MN: American Guidance Service.

Practical suggestions for working with students who have social skills deficits. Think: the provocative victim.

Father Flanagan's Boys' Home. (1989). *Working with aggressive youth: A sourcebook for child-care providers*. Boys Town, NE: The Boys Town Press.

Resource book with activities and ideas for responding to aggressive kids.

Garbarino, J. (1999). *Lost boys: Why our sons turn violent and how we can save them*. New York: Free Press.

A hard look at how American society teaches males to be aggressive.

Garrity, C., Jens, K., Porter, W., Sager, N., & Short-Camilli, C. (1994–1995). *Bully proofing your school: A comprehensive approach for elementary schools*. Longmont, CO: Sopris West.

One of the first practical curricular guides for use in stopping bullying. Lots of hands-on materials. A companion guide exists for the middle school grades.

Hoover, J. H., & Oliver, R. (1996). *The bullying prevention handbook: A guide for principals, teachers, and counselors*. Bloomington, IN: National Educational Service.

Another curricular guide. Less hands-on materials than the Garrity et al. manual.

Johnson, D. W., & Johnson, R. T. (1995). *Teaching students to be peacemakers.* Edina, MN: Interaction Book Company.

The third recommended curricular book for use in creating and maintaining conflict resolution skills among students. Possibly the best of this genre.

Langan, P. (2003). *Bullying in schools: What you need to know.* West Berlin, NJ: Townsend Press.

A small, readable book for students in the upper elementary through middle school years. Some schools have purchased this book in bulk and provided it to their entire student bodies as one part of their bullying prevention programs.

Mikaelsen, B. (2001). *Touching spirit bear.* New York: HarperCollins.

Upper elementary and middle school. A "guy" book. Fiction dealing with restorative justice, Native Americans, and bears. Perfect for angry boys.

Ludwig, T., & Marble, A. (2004). *My secret bully.* Ashland, OR: RiverWood Books.

One of the best books I have ever read on girls and relational aggression. Grades 3–5.

Naylor, P. R., & Malone, N. L. (1991). *King of the playground.* New York: Aladdin Paperbacks.

Grades 3–5. A male version of the Ludwig and Marble book.

Newman, D. A., Horne, A. M., & Bartolomucci, C. L. (2000). *Bully busters: A teacher's manual for helping bullies, victims, and bystanders.* Champaign, IL: Research Press.

Another excellent resource for starting one's own program. Note the title. It takes into account those who are not directly involved (the bystanders) but who play a role in the problem.

Null, C. (2002). *Half mast.* San Francisco: Sutro Press.

Fiction or fact? A novel for adolescents, but one that adults should read before recommending to them. A realistic portrayal of life as a long-term target of bullies. It ain't pretty.

Nuwer, H. (2000). *High school hazing: When rites become wrongs.* New York: Grolier Publishing; and Nuwer, H. (1999). *Wrongs of passage: Fraternities, sororities, hazing, and binge drinking.* Bloomington: Indiana University Press.

Two important works for adults on the true brutal nature and psychology behind hazing rituals at the high school and college levels.

O'Neill, A., & Huliska-Beith, L. (2002). *The recess queen.* New York: Scholastic Press.

Whoa! Look out for the Recess Queen! But she meets her match in this book for lower elementary grades.

Pollack, W. (1998). *Real boys: Rescuing our sons from the myths of boyhood.* New York: Henry Holt .

Similar to Garbarino's work, this book takes another look at the messages we send to males in America as to who they are supposed to be. Real boys don't cry, do they?

Pollack, W. S. (2000). *Real boys' voices.* New York: Random House.

The *Reviving Ophelia* of boys. Interviews with boys and how they view themselves and their place in our culture.

Romain, T. (1997). *Bullies are a pain in the brain.* Minneapolis, MN: Free Spirit Publishing; and Romain, T. (1998). *Cliques, phonies, and other baloney.* Minneapolis, MN: Free Spirit Publishing.

Both of these books are great for the middle and upper elementary grades. A look at how exclusionary groups and bullying behaviors hurt kids, along with practical ways to respond.

Schrumpf, F., Crawford, D. K., & Bodine, R. J. (1997). *Peer mediation: Conflict resolution in schools. Program guide* (Rev. ed.). Champaign, IL: Research Press.

The manual for creating a conflict resolution program in schools. Comes with background information for the program leader and hands-on materials for kids.

Simmons, R. (2002). *Odd girl out: The hidden culture of aggression in girls.* New York: Harcourt; and Wiseman, R. (2002). *Queen bees and wannabes: Helping your daughter survive cliques, gossip, boyfriends, and other realities of adolescence.* New York: Crown Publishers.

These two books were best-sellers in 2002. Both have excellent information about life in Girl World. The style of writing is different in each.

Wilhelm, D. (2003). *The revealers.* New York: Farrar, Straus, & Giroux.

Middle schoolers will love this book about three outsiders and their efforts to expose the bullying in their school.

References

This book contains a compilation of over a decade of theoretical and practice applications by the author. Below is a list of reference materials that were used in writing this book. If previously noted in the Recommended Resources section, it is not referenced again in this section. (Note: At the time of final preparation for the book, electronic links were active. Readers may find some links inactive today at the decision of the hosting Web site.)

5 girls injured in savage hazing. (2003, May 7). *CBSNews.com.* Retrieved May 7, 2003, from http://www.cbsnews.com/stories/2003/05/07/national/printable552828 .shtml

10-year-old boy charged with murder. (2003, March 28). *CBSNews.com.* Retrieved April 1, 2003, from http://www.cbsnews.com/stories/2003/03/29/national/main 546752 .shtml

48 hours investigates: Dangerous minds [Video]. (2004, April 14). CBS Worldwide.

Alford, W. R. (2003, December 29). California school district faces lawsuit over harassment. *The Washington Dispatch.* Retrieved January 11, 2004, from http://www .washingtondispatch.com/article_7479.shtml

American Psychiatric Association. (1994). *Diagnostic and statistical manual of mental disorders* (4th ed.). Washington, DC: Author.

Anderson, C. (Speaker). (2003, October 28). *Circle dialogue: Building relationships and addressing harm* [Handout]. Workshop on circle dialogue: Building skills for adult-youth communications, Council for Health Action and Promotion (CHAP), North Mankato, MN.

Anderson, M., Kaufman, J., Simon, T. R., Barrios, L., Paulozzi, L., Ryan, G., et al. (2001). School-associated violent deaths in the United States, 1994–1999. *Journal of the American Medical Association, 286,* 2695–2702. Abstract retrieved April 20, 2003, from JAMA & Archives database.

Anti-bullying bill advances in state senate. (2004, January 14). *TheIndyChannel.com.* Retrieved January 14, 2004, from http://www.theindychannel.com/education/ 2765889/detail.html

APA HelpCenter. (n.d.). *Children and television violence.* Retrieved May 23, 2003, from http://helping.apa.org/family/kidtvviol.html

Arce, R. (2001, March 8). Study: Kids rate bullying and teasing as "big problem." *CNN.com.* Retrieved July 29, 2003, from http://www.cnn.com/2001/US/03/08/ violence.survey/

Aronson, E. (2000). *Nobody left to hate: Teaching compassion after Columbine.* New York: W. H. Freeman.

Asidao, C., Vion, S., & Espelage, D. (1999). *Interviews with middle school students: Bullying, victimization, and contextual factors.* Paper presented at the 107th American Psychological Conference, Boston, MA.

Askew, S. (1989). Aggressive behaviour in boys: To what extent is it institutionalized? In D. P. Tatum & D. A. Lane (Eds.), *Bullying in schools* (pp. 59–71). Hanley, Stoke-on-Trent: Trentham Books.

Baker, R. L., & Mednick, B. R. (1990). Protecting the high school environment as an island of safety: Correlates of student fear of in-school victimization. *Children's Environmental Quarterly, 7*(3), 37–49.

Ballard, M., Argus, T., & Remley, T. P., Jr. (1999). Bullying and school violence: A proposed prevention program. *NASSP Bulletin, 83,* 38–47.

Bandura, A., Ross, D., & Ross, S. A. (1961). Transmission of aggression through imitation of aggressive models. *Journal of Abnormal and Social Psychology, 63,* 575–582.

Belsey, B. (n.d.). Internet usage: Facts and news. *www.cyberbullying.ca.* Retrieved August 7, 2003, from http://www.cyberbullying.ca/facts.html

Berg, E. (2002, December 9). Dealing with bullies: Students feel helpless by adults' inaction. *Daily Press.* Retrieved August 25, 2003, from http://www.vvdailypress.com/cgi-bin/newspro/viewnews.cgi?newsid1039451512,29561

Bevin, E. (2003, November 26). Bullying pushed girl to the brink. *NEWS.com.au.* Retrieved November 25, 2003, from http://news.com.au/common/story_page/0,4057,7980557%255E13569,00.html

Beyond punishment: Restorative discipline in schools. (2000, Spring). *Conciliation Quarterly, 19*(2).

Blyth, D. A., Thiel, K. S., Bush, D. M., & Simmons, R. G. (1980). Another look at school crime: Student as victim. *Youth and Society, 11*(3), 369–388.

Bonding or brutality: High school hazing more sadistic and dangerous. (2003, June 1). *ABCNEWS.com.* Retrieved June 29, 2003, from http://abcnews.go.com/onair/2020/2020_000601_hshazing_feature.html

Boodman, S. G. (2001, June 5). Teaching bullies a lesson. *The Washington Post.* Retrieved June 26, 2001, from http://washingtonpost.com/wp-dyn/health/childrenyouth/focus/bullies/A19097-2001Jun4.html

Bowers, C. (Reporter). (1999, September 2). *Untitled news clip* [Television broadcast]. CBS Evening News.

Brody, J. (2004, January 20). Future is bleak for bully, victim. *The Ledger.* Retrieved February 2, 2004, from http://www.theledger.com/apps/pbcs.dll/article?AID=/20040120/NEWS/401200303/1021

Brody, J. E. (1996, March 31). School bullies aren't born that way: They're made. *Star Tribune* [Minneapolis, MN], p. E3.

Brody, J. E. (2004, January 13). A bully's future, from hard life to hard time. *The New York Times.* Retrieved January 12, 2004, from http://www.nytimes.com/2004/01/13/health/psychology/13BROD.html?ex=1074574800&en=9f8a796887db4cb8&ei=5062&partner=GOOGLE

Brown, K. S., & Parson, R. D. (1998). Accurate identification of childhood aggression: A key to successful intervention. *Professional School Counseling, 2,* 135–140.

Buckley, F. (2000, March 31). Experts say hazing on the rise at U.S. high schools. *CNN.com.* Retrieved May 6, 2003, from http://www.cnn.com/2000/US/03/31/hazing/index.html

Bullard, C. (1993, April 15). School cited in teen's death: Counselor didn't prevent his suicide, father claims. *The Des Moines Register,* p. 2A.

Bullying case costs Oregon school district $10,000. (2004, January 18). *The Seattle Times.* Retrieved February 2, 2004, from http://seattletimes.nwsource.com/html/education/2001839182_bullying18.html

Bullying in schools: Harassment puts gay youth at risk. *National Mental Health Association* [Fact Sheet]. Retrieved from http://www.nmha.org/pbedu/backtoschool/bullyingGayYouth.cfm

Bullying is widespread, often ignored in schools. (2001, April 25). *Star Tribune* [Minneapolis, MN], pp. A1, A9.

Bullying led to suicide attempt. *RainbowNetwork.com.* Retrieved December 13, 2003, from http://www.rainbownetwork.com/content/News.asp?newsid=4055

Byron, P. (1998, June 22). Complaint by gay student triggers historic civil rights. *Lambda Legal.* Retrieved March 8, 2005, from http://www.lambdalegal.org/cgi-bin/iowa/news/press.html?record=252

Byron, P. (2000, November 7). Mother can take police to court over son's suicide. *Lambda Legal.* Retrieved March 8, 2005, from http://www.lambdalegal.org/cgi-bin/iowa/cases/record?record=136

Carroll, M. R., & King, V. G. (1985). The peer-helping phenomenon: A quiet revolution. *Counseling and Human Development, 17*(9), 1–8.

Center for Media Education. (n.d.). *Children & television: Frequently asked questions.* Retrieved May 23, 2003, from http://www.cme.org/children/kids_tv/c_and_t.html

Cervantes, N. (2003, May 26). Senior's taunting of freshman investigated. *The Buffalo News.* Retrieved May 30, 2003, from http://www.buffalonews.com/editorial/20030526/1004868.asp

Cervantes, N. (2003, May 28). Meeting to focus on swim probe. *The Buffalo News.* Retrieved May 30, 2003, from http://www.buffalonews.com/editorial/20030528/1000758.asp

Cervantes, N. (2003, May 29). No decision on swim staff in harassment. *The Buffalo News.* Retrieved May 30, 2003, from http://www.buffalonews.com/editorial/20030529/1011431.asp

Childhood viewing of TV violence affects women as well as men. (2003, March 3). *Newswise.* Retrieved May 23, 2003, from http://www.newswise.com/articles/2003/3/HUESMANN.UMI.html

Clarke, E. A., & Kiselica, M. S. (1997). A systemic counseling approach to the problem of bullying. *Elementary School Guidance & Counseling, 31,* 310–325.

Classmates react to alleged hazing. (2003, May 7). *NBC5.com.* Retrieved May 7, 2003, from http://www.nbc5.com/news/2186362/detail.html

Cloud, J. (2001, March 19). The legacy of Columbine. *Time, 157,* 32–35.

A community and its shooter. (1998, December 8). *The Courier-Journal.* Retrieved February 1, 2003, from http://www.courier-journal.com/cjextra/schoolshoot/SCHglimpsesofwallen.html

Coloroso, B. (2003). *The bully, the bullied, and the bystander.* New York: HarperCollins.

Cox, A. (2001, February 19). School bullies take their attacks to the Internet. *Star Tribune* [Minneapolis, MN], p. E3.

Craig, W. M., Peters, R. D., & Konarski, R. (1998). *Bullying and victimization among Canadian school children.* Applied Research Branch Strategic Policy, Human Resources Development Canada. [Online]. Available: http://www.hrdc-drhc.ca/arb/publications/research/abw-98–28e.shtml

Crawford, D., & Bodine, R. (1996). *Conflict resolution education: A guide to implementing programs in schools, youth-serving organizations, and community and juvenile justice settings.* Washington, DC: US Department of Justice.

Cummins, H. J. (2002, December 13). Gay slurs are now most common type of school bullying. *Star Tribune* [Minneapolis, MN], p. A14.

Cyberbullying. (n.d.). *urban75*. Retrieved August 7, 2003, from http://www.urban75 .org/info/bullying.html

Cyberspace bullies plague kids. (2003, March 10). *Health News*. Retrieved August 7, 2003, from http://12.31.13.29/HealthNews/Reuters/NewsStory0310200325.htm

The dark side of school life. (2003, September 17). *telegraph.co.uk*. Retrieved September 17, 2003, from http://www.telegraph.co.uk/health/main.jhtml?xml=/health/ 2003/09/09/hbu1109.xml&sSheet=/health/2003/09/17/ixhmain.html

Davidson, J. (2002, August 28). Groundbreaking legal settlement is first to recognize Constitutional right of gay and lesbian students to be out at school and protected from harassment. *Lambda Legal*. Retrieved March 8, 2005, from http://www .lambdalegal.org/cgi-bin/iowa/news/press.html?record=1119

Day, E. (2003, September 17). Can I remember a time when Karl was not bullied? Only since we buried him. *telegraph.co.uk*. Retrieved September 17, 2003, from http:// www.telegraph.co.uk/news/main.jhtml?xml=/news/2003/06/08/nbully08.xml& secureRefresh=true&_requestid=63654

Deadly lessons. School shooters tell why. (2000, October 15–16). *Chicago Sun-Times Exclusive Report*, pp. 1–18.

Dedman, B. (2000, October 15). Bullying, tormenting often led to revenge in cases studied. *Chicago Sun-Times*. Retrieved July 22, 2003, from http://www.treas.gov/usss/ ntac/chicago_sun_20001016/case15.htm

Dedman, B. (2000, October 15). Examining the psyche of an adolescent killer. *Chicago Sun-Times*. Retrieved June 15, 2001, from http://www.suntimes.com/shoot/ shoot15.html

Demetriou, D. (2004, January 28). Boy committed suicide after suffering 12 years of bullying at school. *Independent.co.uk*. Retrieved February 2, 2004, from http:// news.independent.co.uk/uk/legal/story.jsp?story=485391

Di Novi, D. (Producer), & Lehman, M. (Director). (1994). *Heathers* [Motion picture]. Eatontown, NJ: United States: Starmaker Entertainment.

Draper, N. (2001, May 4). A 10-year-old taunted by bullies is living a nightmare, and can't keep quiet any longer. *Star Tribune* [Minneapolis, MN], pp. E1–E2.

Draper, N. (2001, May 23). Standing up to bullying. *Star Tribune* [Minneapolis, MN], pp. B1, B4.

Draper, N. (2002, May 16). Beyond the bullying. *Star Tribune* [Minneapolis, MN], pp. E1, E3.

Dubow, E. F., Huessman, L. R., & Eron, L. D. (1987). Mitigating aggression and promoting prosocial behavior in aggressive elementary schoolboys. *Behavior Research Therapies, 25*, 527–531.

Eisenberg, M. E., Neumark-Sztainer, D., & Story, M. (2003). Associations of weight-based teasing and emotional well-being among adolescents. *Archives of Pediatrics & Adolescent Medicine, 157*, 733–738. Abstract retrieved August 13, 2003, from JAMA & Archives database.

Elliott, S. N., & Gresham, F. M. (1991). *Social skills intervention guide: Practical strategies for social skills training*. Circle Pines, MN: American Guidance Service.

Eron, L. D., Gentry, J. H., & Schlegel, P. (Eds.). (1994). *Reason to hope: A psychosocial perspective on violence and youth*. Washington, DC: American Psychological Association.

Eron, L. D., Walder, L. O., & Lefkowitz, M. M. (1971). *Learning of aggression in children*. Boston: Little, Brown.

Eschbacher, K. (2004, January 8). Shocking cases of bullying abound in schools. *The Patriot Ledger.* Retrieved February 2, 2004, from http://ledger.southofboston.com/articles/2004/01/08/news/news04.txt

Espelage, D., Bosworth, K., Karageorge, K., & Daytner, G. (1996). *Family/Environment and bullying behaviors: Interrelationships and treatment implications.* Paper presented at 104th American Psychological Association Conference, Toronto, Canada.

Faceless cruelty. (2003, May 6). *ABCNEWS.com.* Retrieved September 9, 2003, from http://abcnews.go.com/sections/GMA/AmericanFamily/GMA030506Cyber_bullying.html

Fager, J. (Executive Producer). (2003, October). Suicide of a 12-year-old [Television series episode]. In *60 Minutes II.* New York: CBS Broadcasting, Inc.

Failed carjacking foiled alleged plot, police say. (2003, July 8). *Star Tribune* [Minneapolis, MN], p. A4.

FBI issues school violence guidelines. (2000, September 5). *CBSNEWS.com.* Retrieved February 1, 2003, from http://www.cbsnews.com/stories/2000/09/04/national/60II/printalble230493.shtml

Finkelhor, D., & Wolak, J. (n.d.). Nonsexual assaults to the genitals in the youth population. *Journal of the American Medical Association, 274,* 1692–1697. Abstract retrieved April 20, 2003, from JAMA & Archives database.

Foster, Herbert L. (1974). *Ribbin', jivin', and playin' the dozens: The unrecognized dilemma of inner-city schools.* Cambridge, MA: Ballinger.

Fox, J. A., Elliott, D. S., Kerlikowske, R. G., Newman, S. A., & Christeson, W. (2003). *Bullying prevention is crime prevention.* Washington, DC: Fight Crime: Invest in Kids. Available from www.fightcrime.org

Galley, M. (2002, December 11). Bullying policies slow to reach schools. *Education Week.* Retrieved December 11, 2002, from http://www.edweek.com/ew/ewstory.cfm?slug=15bully.h22

Garrity, C., & Baris, M. A. (1996). Bullies and victims: A guide for pediatricians. *Contemporary Pediatrics, 13,* 90–92, 97, 102–108, 111–114.

Garrity, C., Jens, K., Porter, W., Sager, N., & Short-Camilli, C. (1996, Fall). Bully-proofing your school: A comprehensive approach. *School Safety,* 20–23.

George, K. (2004, January 5). Court restores girl's harassment lawsuit against Bellevue School District. *seattlepi.com.* Retrieved January 11, 2004, from http://seattlepi.nwsource.com/local/155294_harass05.html

Gibbs, N. (2001, March 19). "It's only me." *Time, 157,* 22.

Gisier, P., & Eberts, M. (2001, February 19). Early warning signs can point to future academic problems. *Star Tribune* [Minneapolis, MN], p. E3.

Girl tormented by phone bullies. (2001, January 16). *BBC News.* Retrieved August 7, 2003, from http://news.bbc.co.uk/2/hi/uk_news/education/1120597.stm

Godfrey, G. (1998, November 12). Woodham apologizes. *ABCNEWS.com.* Retrieved February 1, 2003, from http://more.abcnews.go.com/sections/us/woodham1111_ptl

Gold, J. (2003, March 31). Preteens rarely accused of murder. *Newsday.com.* Retrieved April 2, 2003, from http://www.newsday.com/news/local/wire/ny-bc-nj—childkilled-rarit0331mar31,0,3112572.story?coll=ny-ap-regional-wire

Goodman, E. (2002, May 28). Suddenly, the media notice that girls can be mean, too. *Star Tribune* [Minneapolis, MN], p. A11.

Green, B. (1993a, April 29). "Why weren't you his friends?" father asks. *The Free Press* [Mankato, MN], p. 5.

Green, B. (1993b, May 11). Many people say they were a Curtis Taylor, too. *The Free Press* [Mankato, MN], p. 5.

Greene, B. (2001, March 11). When will there be zero tolerance for bullying? *Chicago Tribune*. Retrieved March 21, 2001, from http://chicagotribune.com/news/columnists/greene/0,1122,SAV-0103110221,00.html

Greene, B. (2001, March 18). The words echo: "Why weren't you his friends?" *Chicago Tribune*. Retrieved March 21, 2001, from http://chicagotribune.com/news/columnists/greene/0,1122,SAV-0103180213,00.html

Hahn, L. (2004, April 19). Some states enact laws against bullying. Retrieved April 20, 2004, from http://www.timeswrsw.com/N0119041.HTM

Hanna, F. J., Hanna, C. A., & Keys, S. G. (1999). Fifty strategies for counseling defiant, aggressive adolescents: Reaching, accepting, and relating. *Journal of Counseling & Development, 77*, 395–404.

Harassed gay student gets $451,000 in settlement with Reno school district. (2002, August 29). *Star Tribune* [Minneapolis, MN], p. A4.

Hastings hazings may spur charges against five teens. (2004, August 25). *Star Tribune* [Minneapolis, MN], p. B3.

Hazing common among high-school students, too, survey finds. (2000, August 29). *Star Tribune* [Minneapolis, MN], p. A9.

Hazler, R. J. (1996). *Breaking the cycle of violence: Intervention for bullying and victimization.* Washington, DC: Accelerated Development.

Hazler, R. J. (1996). Bystanders: An overlooked factor in peer on peer abuse. *Journal for the Professional Counselor, 11*, 11–21.

Hazler, R. J., Carney, J. V., Green, S., Powell, R., & Jolly, L. S. (1997). Areas of expert agreement on identification of school bullies and victims. *School Psychology International, 18*, 3–11.

Hingorani, J. (2003, November 18). Bullying linked to domestic violence. *News 8 Austin*. Retrieved November 18, 2003, from http://www.news8austin.com/content/your_news/default.asp?ArID=89768

Hoover, J. H., Oliver, R., & Hazler, R. J. (1992). Bullying: Perceptions of adolescent victims in the midwestern USA. *School Psychology International, 13*, 5–16.

Hostile hallways: Bullying, teasing, and sexual harassment in school. (2001). *American Journal of Health Education, 32*(5), 307–309.

Huesmann, L. R. (Eds.). (1994). *Aggressive behavior: Current perspectives.* New York: Plenum Press.

Huesmann, L. R., & Eron, L. D. (n.d.). Childhood TV violence viewing and adult aggression. *CDMH*. Retrieved May 23, 2003, from http://www.umich.edu/~edmh/longitudinal/huesmann2.html

Huesmann, L. R., Eron, L. D., Lefkowitz, M. M., & Walder, L. O. (1984). Stability of aggression over time and generations. *Developmental Psychology, 20*, 1120–1134.

Hunter, G. (2001, March 7). Teasing and taunting led girl to end her life. *The Detroit News*. Retrieved March 29, 2001, from http://www.detroitnews.com/2001/schools/0103/07/a01–196600.htm

Illinois Center for Violence Prevention. (n.d.). *Violence and television.* Retrieved May 23, 2003, from http://www.icvp.org/violenceAndTV.asp

Jhally, S. (Director). (1999). *Tough guise: Violence, media, and the crisis in masculinity* [Video]. Media Education Foundation.

Jhally, S. (Director/Writer), & Ridberg, R. (Producer). (2002). *Wrestling with manhood: Boys, bullying & battering* [Video]. Media Education Foundation.

Johnson, A. (2003, July 8). Father of teen accused of murder plot: Says scheme was just pretend. *7Online.com*. Retrieved July 8, 2003, from http://abclocal.go.com/wabc/news/wabc_070803_njteens.html

Juvonen, J., Graham, S., & Schuster, M. A. (2003). Bullying among young adolescents: The strong, the weak, and the troubled. *Pediatrics, 112*(6), 1231–1237.

Kauffman, H. (Reporter/Interviewer). (1999, September 2). *Untitled news clip* [Television broadcast]. CBS This Morning.

Katz, M. (2004, April 20). *Bullying takes toll on south Jersey schools: Students, parents: Officials must do more to fix problems.* Retrieved April 20, 2004, from http://www.courierpostonline.com/news/southjersey/m042004b.htm

Koules, O. (Producer), & Miller, T. (Director). (1994). *Dumb and dumberer: When Harry met Lloyd* [Motion picture]. United States: New Line Home Entertainment.

Labi, N. (2001, April 2). Let bullies beware. *Time, 157,* 46–47.

Lane, D. A. (1989). Bullying in school: The need for an integrated approach. *School Psychology International, 10,* 211–215.

Langan, P. (2003). *Bullying in schools: What you need to know.* West Berlin, NJ: Townsend Press.

Lefkowitz, M. M., Eron, L. D., Walder, L. O., & Huesmann, L. R. (1977). *Growing up violent: A longitudinal study of the development of aggression.* New York: Pergamon.

Letellier, P. (2003, September 25). Boy endures taunts at school: Father sues. *Gay.com News.* Retrieved September 26, 2003, from http://www.gay.com/news/article.html?2003/09/25/2

Linklater, R. (Producer/Director). (1993). *Dazed and confused* [Motion picture]. United States: Universal Studios.

Livingston, I., & Delfiner, R. (2003, July 8). Teen in "Matrix." *New York Post Online Edition.* Retrieved July 8, 2003, from http://www.nypost.com/news/regionalnews/2674.htm

Local school board member resigns to call attention to bullying: Woman said she resigned from board in defense of her son. (2004, April 14/23). *WRAL.com.* Retrieved May 10, 2004, from http://www.wral.com/family/3002914/detail.html

Local woman wants bullying issue to hit general assembly: Former school board member seeks better definition, enforcement of bullying. (2004, April 22). *WRAL.com.* Retrieved May 10, 2004, from http://www.wral.com/education/3032762/detail.html

Lochman, J. E., Coie, J. D., Underwood, M. K., & Terry, R. (1993). Effectiveness of a social relations intervention program for aggressive and nonaggressive, rejected children. *Journal of Consulting and Clinical Psychology, 61,* 1053–1058.

Lochman, J. E., & Curry, J. F. (1986). Effects of social problem-solving training and self-instruction training with aggressive boys. *Journal of Clinical Child Psychology, 15,* 159–164.

Marcotty, J. (2003, August 12). Teasing about weight takes toll on kids, "U" study finds. *Star Tribune* [Minneapolis, MN], pp. B1, B4.

Mason, C. (2003, November 18). Student kill list had 56 names. *Tribune Chronicle.* Retrieved November 18, 2003, from http://www.tribune-chronicle.com/news/story/11182003_new03student18.asp

Matrix murder plot teen "was picked on." (2003, July 8). *Ananova.* Retrieved July 8, 2003, from http://www.ananova.com/news/story/sm_797815.html

McClellan, A. (1997). *Bullying: The most underrated and enduring problem in schools today.* Teacher Ezine: Bullying. [Online]. Available from http://www.bctf.bc.ca/bctf/publications/ezine/archive/1997–05/support/bully.html

McDermott, J. (1983). Crime in the schools and in the community: Offenders, victims, and fearful youths. *Crime and Delinquency, 29,* 270–282.

McLain, W., & Lewis, E. (1994). Anger management and assertiveness skills: An instructional package for persons with developmental disabilities. In

M. J. Furlong & D. C. Smith (Eds.), *Anger, hostility, and aggression: Assessment, prevention, and intervention strategies for youth* (pp. 473–507). Brandon, VT: Clinical Psychology.

Meadows, S. (2003, November 3). Ghosts of Columbine. *Newsweek*, 54–57.

Meadows, S., & Johnson, D. (2003, May 19). Girl fight: Savagery in the Chicago suburbs. *Newsweek*, 37.

Media violence and children (1993–2000). [Fact sheet]. Media Awareness Network. Retrieved May 17, 2004, from http://www.media-awareness.ca/english/resources/research_documents/statistics/violence/media_violence_children.cfm

Michaels, L. (Producer), & Waters, M. (2004). *Mean girls* [Motion picture]. United States: Paramount Pictures.

Miller, P. (1982). Teasing: A case study in language socialization and verbal play. *The Quarterly Newsletter of the Laboratory of Comparative Human Cognition, 4*(2), 29–32.

Morrison, G. M., & Sandowicz, M. (1995). Importance of social skills in the prevention and intervention of anger and aggression. In M. J. Furlong & D. C. Smith (Eds.), *Anger, hostility, and aggression: Assessment, prevention, and intervention strategies for youth* (pp. 345–392). Brandon, VT: Clinical Psychology.

Mulvihill, G. (2003, July 8). Arrested New Jersey teen called disturbed. *The Mercury News.* Retrieved July 8, 2003, from http://www.bayarea.com/mld/mercurynews/6252993.htm

Nansel, T. R., Overpeck, M., Pilla, R. S., Ruan, W. J., Simons-Morton, B., & Scheidt, P. (2001). Bullying behaviors among US youth: Prevalence and association with psychological adjustment. *The Journal of the American Medical Association, 285,* 2094–2100. Abstract retrieved April 20, 2003, from JAMA & Archives database.

Neumark-Sztainer, D., Falkner, N., Story, M., Perry, C., Hannan, P. J., & Mulert, S. (2002). Weight-teasing among adolescents: Correlations with weight status and disordered eating behaviors. *International Journal of Obesity, 26*(1), 123–131. Retrieved August 11, 2003, from Nature Publishing Group database.

Nuttall, E. V., & Kalesnik, J. (1987). Personal violence in the schools: The role of the counselor. *Journal of Counseling and Development, 65,* 372–375.

Oliver, R., Oaks, I. N., & Hoover, J. H. (1994). Family issues and interventions in bully and victim relationships. *School Counselor, 41,* 199–202.

Oliver, R., Young, T., & LaSalle, S. (1994). Early lessons in bullying and victimization: The help and hindrance of children's literature. *School Counselor, 42,* 137–146.

Olweus, D. (1978). *Aggression in the schools: Bullies and whipping boys.* Washington, DC: Hemisphere.

Olweus, D. (1991). Bully/victim problems among schoolchildren: Basic facts and effects of a school based intervention program. In D. J. Pepler & K. H. Rubin (Eds.), *The development and treatment of childhood aggression* (pp. 411–448). Hillsdale, NJ: Lawrence Erlbaum.

Olweus, D. (1992). Bullying among school children: Intervention and prevention. In R. D. Peters, R. J. McMahon, & V. L. Quinsey (Eds.), *Aggression and violence throughout the life span* (pp. 100–125). Newbury Park, CA: Sage.

Olweus, D. (1993*). Bullying at school: What we know and what we can do.* Malden, MA: Blackwell.

O'Neill, H. (2004, January 18). Why did tragedy happen? Troubled boy committed suicide; those around him let him down. *Norwich Bulletin.* Retrieved February 2, 2004, from http://www.norwichbulletin.com/news/stories/20040118/localnews/247595.html

Oulton, S. (2000, December 2). Tales of bullying outlined. *DenverPost.com.* Retrieved July 29, 2003, from http://63.147.65.175/news/c011202.htm

Pankratz, H. (2000, October 3). Columbine bullying no myth, panel told. *DenverPost.com.* Retrieved from http://www.DenverPost.com

Parent hires attorney over alleged h.s. hazing. (2003, May 7). Retrieved May 7, 2003, from http://www.nbc5.com/news/2182593/detail.html

Parry, W. (2003, March 29). Child murder suspect had bad reputation. *Arizona Daily Star.* Retrieved April 2, 2003, from http://www.azstarnet.com/star/sat/30329 NchildKilled.html

Paulson, A. (2003, December 30). Internet bullying. *The Christian Science Monitor.* Retrieved January 11, 2004, from http://www.csmonitor.com/2003/1230/p11s01-legn .html

Pellegrini, A., & Bartini, M. (1999). *A longitudinal study of bullying, victimization and peer affiliation during the transition from primary school to middle school.* Paper presented at 107th American Psychological Association Conference, Boston, MA.

Pepler, D. J., & Sedighdellami, F. (1998). *Aggressive girls in Canada.* Applied Research Branch Strategic Policy, Human Resources Development Canada. [Online]. Available from http://www.hrdc-drhc.gc.ca/arb/publications/research/w-98–30e.shtml

Peterson, K. S. (2001, April 10). Net broadens reach of kids' rumors, insults. *USATO-DAY.com.* Retrieved August 7, 2003, from http://www.usatoday.com/news/ health/2001–04–10-bully-net.htm

Phillips-Hershey, E., & Kanagy, B. (1996). Teaching students how to manage personal anger constructively. *Elementary School Guidance & Counseling, 30,* 229–234.

Primary kids victims of text bullying. (2003, April 8). *BBC News.* Retrieved August 7, 2003, from http://news.bbc.co.uk/cbbcnews/hi/sci_tech/newsid_2926000/ 2926273.stm

Prowrestling: Lewd, crude, and on your tube. (1999). *National Institute on Media and the Family: Media Wise.* Available from http://www.mediafamily.org

Questions remain 2 years after boy's suicide. (2004, January 18). *New Haven Register.com.* Retrieved February 2, 2004, from http://www.newhavenregister.com/site/ news.cfm?BRD=1281&dept_id=31007&newsid=10828092&PAG=461&rfi=9

Reichgott, M. (2003, May 9). Parents probed in suburban Chicago hazing. Retrieved from Associated Press Newswire.

Ritter, M. (2003, March 10). TV violence tied to adult aggression. *Star Tribune* [Minneapolis, MN], p. A3.

Roberts, W. B., Jr. (2000, January). Why bullies belong in school! *School Safety Update,* 3–4.

Roberts, W. B., Jr., & Coursol, D. (1996). Strategies for intervention with childhood and adolescent victims of bullying, teasing, and intimidation. *Elementary School Guidance & Counseling, 30,* 204–212.

Roberts, W. B., Jr., & Morotti, A. (2000). The bully as victim: Understanding bully behaviors to increase the effectiveness of interventions in the bully-victim dyad. *Professional School Counseling, 4,* 148–155.

Roberts, W. B., Jr., & Morotti, A. (2002). *The schoolyard bully: Mean kid or victim, too?* Presentation at the 2002 American Counseling Association Convention, New Orleans, LA.

Robinson, B. (2003, September 9). "Bullycide" or neglect. *ABCNEWS.com.* Retrieved September 9, 2003, from http://abcnews.go.com/sections/us/GoodMorning America/scruggs030909.html

Ross, D. M. (1996). *Childhood bullying and teasing: What school personnel, other professionals, and parents can do.* Alexandria, VA: American Counseling Association.

Royce, G. (1999, September 24). Fit to watch? *Star Tribune* [Minneapolis, MN], pp. E1, E11.

Santora, M. (2003, October 29). Woman guilty in son's suicide says school bullying is to blame. *NYTimes.com*. Retrieved October 29, 2003, from http://www.nytimes.com/2003/10/29/nyregion/29MOM.html?ex=1068094800&en=7c912e31b6866df3&ei=5062&partner=GOOGLE

Scarponi, D. (2003, October 7). Connecticut woman convicted of playing role in son's suicide. *Star Tribune* [Minneapolis, MN], p. A4.

Scorecard of hatred. (2001, March 19). *Time, 157,* 30–31.

Secret service studies shootings. (2000, August 15). *CBSNEWS.com*. Retrieved February 1, 2003, from http://www.cbsnews.com/stories/2000/03/14/60II/printalble171898.shtml

Senate committee approves anti-bullying bill. (2004, January 14). *WishTV8*. Retrieved January 14, 2004, from http://www.wishtv.com/Global/story.asp?S=1601337&nav=0Ra7KCUB

Sexual harassment widespread in nation's schools, new AAUW report finds. (n.d.). *AAUW*. Retrieved July 1, 2001, from http://www.aauw.org/2000/hostile.html

Shapiro, J. P., Baumeister, R. F., & Kessler, J. W. (1991). A three-component model of child's teasing: Aggression, humor, and ambiguity. *Journal of Social and Clinical Psychology, 10*(4), 459–472.

Smith, B. (2003, May 7). Girls expected game to be rough, but not brutal. *Chicago Sun-Times*. Retrieved May 7, 2003, from http://www.suntimes.com/cgi-bin/print.cgi

Smith, J. P. (1990). *How to solve student adjustment problems: A step-by-step guide for teachers and counselors*. West Nyack, NY: Center for Applied Research in Education.

Smith, P. K., & Thompson, D. (1991). Dealing with bully/victim problems in the U.K. In P. K. Smith & D. Thompson (Eds.), *Practical approaches to bullying* (pp. 1–2). London: Fulton.

Smith, S. A. (2004, April 20). Five years after Columbine, bullying still a fact of life in Springfield schools. *News-Leader* [Springfield, MO]. Retrieved May 9, 2004, from http://www.news-leader.com/today/0420-Fiveyearsa-67313.html

Solholm, R. (2003, September 26). Bullying in Norwegian schools reduced by 50 pct. *The Norway Post*. Retrieved September 26, 2003, from http://www.norwaypost.no/content.asp?cluster_id=24583&folder_id=1

Some things you should know about media violence and media literacy. [Fact sheet]. (Undated). American Academy of Pediatrics. Retrieved May 17, 2004, from http://www.aap.org/advocacy/childhealthmonth/media.htm

Sprott, J. B., & Doob, A. N. (1998). *Who are the most violent ten and eleven year olds? An introduction to future delinquency*. Applied Research Branch of Strategic Policy, Human Resources Development Canada. [Online]. Available from http://www.hrdc-drhc.gc.ca/arb/publications/research/w-98–29e.shtml

Steffenhagen, J. (2003, December 1). Mother criticized in bullying case: School officials call a mother unreasonable after her daughter's drink was spiked by bullies. *Vancouver Sun*. Retrieved December 2, 2003, from http://www.canada.com/vancouver/vancouversun/story.asp?id=5FBC3C25–5B2C-44E6–8950–4908945212CE

Stein, B. D., Jaycox, L. H., Kataoka, S. H., Wong, M., Tu, W., Elliot, M. N., et al. (2003). A mental health intervention for schoolchildren exposed to violence. *Journal of the American Medical Association, 290,* 603–611. Retrieved August 5, 2003, from JAMA & Archives database.

Stephenson, P., & Smith, D. (1989). Bullying in the junior school. In D. P. Tatum & D. A. Lane (Eds.), *Bullying in schools* (pp. 45–57). Hanley, Stoke-on-Trent: Trentham Books.

Strauss, V. (2003, November 8). Anti-bullying programs compete for funding. *Detroit News*. Retrieved November 9, 2003, from http://www.detnews.com/2003/schools/0311/08/schools-319456.htm

Student roundtable on bullying. (2003, August 17). *Pensacola News Journal*. Retrieved August 25, 2003, from http://pensacolanewsjournal.com/news/081703/Local/ST013.shtml

Student claims he was bullied before stabbing, documents say. (2003, December 17). Retrieved January 1, 2004, from http://www.channeloklahoma.com/news/2710585/detail.html

Studer, J. (1996). Understanding and preventing aggressive responses in youth. *Elementary School Guidance & Counseling, 30*, 194–203.

Study: Bullies target victims early, often. (2004, April 13). Retrieved from Associated Press news release via *Kansas City Star* at http://kansascity.com/mld/kansascity/news/local/8422509.htm?1c

Study: Peer pressure influences bullying. (2003, January 22). *loca16.com*. Retrieved September 4, 2003, from http://www.loca16.com/health/1928542/detail.html

Study: TV violence begets violence. (2003, March 10). *CBSNews.com*. Retrieved May 23, 2003, from http://www.cbsnews.com/stories/2003/03/10/national/main543333.shtml

Talking with kids about tough issues: A national survey of parents and kids. *Nickelodeon*. Retrieved March 8, 2001, from http://www.nick.com/all_nick/everything_nick/kaiser/index.html

Tanner, L. (2003, April 14). Bullies, victims may carry weapons. *Yahoo!News*. Retrieved April 24, 2003, from http://story.news.yahoo.com/news?tmpl=story2&cid=519&ncid=519&e=39&u=/ap/20030414/ap_on_re_us/bullying_violence_2

Tanner, L. (2003, April 15). Bullies, targets called likely to be armed. *The Boston Globe*. Retrieved April 19, 2003, from http://www.boston.com/dailyglobe2/105/nation/Bullies_targets_called_likely_to_be_armed+.shtml

Teens arrested in taped bullying. (2003, November 9). *WPVI.com*. Retrieved November 9, 2003, from http://abclocal.go.com/wpvi/news/11092003_nw_njbullies.html

Teen troubles tied to the tube. (2002, March 28). *CBSNews.com*. Retrieved May 23, 2003, from http://www.cbsnews.com/stories/2002/03/28/health/main504880.shtml

Tench, M. (2003, January 21). Web tangle. *Yahoo! Groups*. Retrieved August 7, 2003, from http://groups.yahoo.com/group/worst_of_qmail/message/43

The terrible thing is that the news was no surprise. (2001, March 7). *Chicago Tribune*. Retrieved March 21, 2001, from http://web.filemaker.mnsu.edu/vehicles/online.htm

Tindall, J. (1989). *Peer counseling: An in-depth look at training peer helpers*. Muncie, IN: Accelerated Development.

Tollin, M. (Director). (2003). *Radio* [Motion picture]. United States: Columbia Pictures.

To stop a massacre. (2002, May 15). *CBSNEWS.com*. Retrieved February 1, 2003, from http://www.cbsnews.com/stories/2002/05/15/60II/printalble509196.shtml

Turnbull, L. (2004, April 10). Kent family files lawsuit over bullying at school. Retrieved May 9, 2004, from http://seattletimes.nwsource.com/html/localnews/2001892869_odea01m.html

Just shoot me—Episode guide. *tv tome*. Retrieved March 3, 2005, from http://www.tvtome.com/JustShootMe/guide.html

Violence in media entertainment. Retrieved from http://www.media-awareness.ca/english/issues/violence/violence_entertainment.cfm

Violent behavior seen in bullying victims. (2003, April 14). *loca16.com*. Retrieved September 4, 2003, from http://www.loca16.com/health/2112017/detail.html

Waters, M. J. (2003, November 4). Opposing views: Hard-working single mom, or neglectful parent. *Record-Journal.com*. Retrieved November 4, 2003, from http://www.record-journal.com/articles/2003/10/02/news/news03.txt

Wayne, I., & Rubel, R. J. (1982). Student fear in secondary schools. *The Urban Review, 14*(3), 197–237.

Wendland, M. (2003, November 17). Cyber-bullies make it tough for kids to leave playground. *Detroit Free Press*. Retrieved November 18, 2003, from http://www.freep.com/money/tech/mwend17_20031117.htm

Willis, M. T. (2001, November 28). Dark side of group identity. *ABCNEWS.com*. Retrieved July 29, 2003, from http://abcnews.go.com/sections/living/DailyNews/group_identity011128.html

Wolpert, S. (2003, December 9). Bullying in schools pervasive, UCLA study finds. *EurekAlert!* Retrieved January 26, 2004, from http://www.eurekalert.org/pub_releases/2003–12/uoc—bis120903.php

Wong, N. C. (On-line posting September 25, 2003). Father: District allowed anti-gay slurs against son. *San Jose* (CA) *Mercury News*. Retrieved March 3, 2005, from http://www.gsanetwork.org/news/october2003.html

Would-be bomber was bullying victim. (2004, March 19). Retrieved from United Press International news release via *Washington Times* at http://washingtontimes.com/upi-breaking/20040319–071123–4168rhtm

Wright, B. (2000, August 28). Hazing study suggests pervasive problem in U.S. high schools. *CNN.com*. Retrieved May 6, 2003, from http://www.cnn.com/2000/HEALTH/children/08/28/student.hazing/index.html

Yeon, P. (2004, January 28). Daughter edged out by friends: Recovering from bullying made her stronger. *Daily News Transcript*. Retrieved February 2, 2004, from http://www.dailynewstranscript.com/news/local_regional/bully01282004.htm

Zach, M. (2004, August 28). Six charged in Hastings hazing. *Star Tribune* [Minneapolis, MN], p. B2.

Zarnowski, T. (2003, December 23). Parents sue over bullying. *The Sentinel*. Retrieved February 2, 2004, from http://www.cumberlink.com/articles/2003/12/23/news/news03.txt

Index

**CORWIN
PRESS**

The Corwin Press logo—a raven striding across an open book—represents the union of courage and learning. Corwin Press is committed to improving education for all learners by publishing books and other professional development resources for those serving the field of PreK–12 education. By providing practical, hands-on materials, Corwin Press continues to carry out the promise of its motto: **"Helping Educators Do Their Work Better."**